# Still Standing

*Also by Chrissie Foster with Paul Kennedy*

Hell on the Way to Heaven

# Still Standing

A Mother's Fight to Bring the
Catholic Church to Justice

# CHRISSIE FOSTER

WITH PAUL KENNEDY

VIKING
*an imprint of*
PENGUIN BOOKS

VIKING

UK | USA | Canada | Ireland | Australia
India | New Zealand | South Africa | China

Viking is part of the Penguin Random House group of companies
whose addresses can be found at global.penguinrandomhouse.com.

Penguin
Random House
Australia

First published by Viking, 2023

Extract on p. 303 from *A Bigger Picture* (2020) by Malcolm Turnbull
appears by arrangement with Hardie Grant Books.

Cover design by Christa Moffitt, Christabella Designs © Penguin Random House Australia
Cover photography by Julian Kingma
Typeset in Adobe Garamond by Midland Typesetters, Australia

Printed and bound in Australia by Griffin Press an accredited
ISO AS/NZ 14001 Environmental Management Systems printer.

A catalogue record for this
book is available from the
NATIONAL
LIBRARY   National Library of Australia
OF AUSTRALIA

ISBN 978 1 76104 744 2

penguin.com.au

*We at Penguin Random House Australia acknowledge that Aboriginal and Torres Strait
Islander peoples are the first storytellers and Traditional Custodians of the land on which we
live and work. We honour Aboriginal and Torres Strait Islander peoples' continuous connection to
Country, waters, skies and communities. We celebrate Aboriginal and Torres Strait Islander stories,
traditions and living cultures; and we pay our respects to Elders past and present.*

*Dedicated to the beloved memory of Emma and Anthony,
and to my beloved Katie and Aimee, my extended
family and dear friends.*

*My thanks to Abi, for often encouraging me to write this book.*

This is what Jesus said about religious leaders 2000 years ago:

Woe to you . . . religious leaders! You are like beautiful mausoleums – full of dead men's bones, and of foulness and corruption. You try to look like saintly men, but underneath those pious robes of yours are hearts besmirched with every sort of hypocrisy and sin. Woe to you . . . religious leaders – hypocrites!

Matthew 23.27–29
The Living Bible
(Life Application Bible)

Sexual abuse by clerics has been a known reality in the Catholic Church since the first century. The earliest reference is found in a document known as the Didache or as it is known in English, The Teaching of the Twelve Apostles. Scholars have dated the document at around 98 AD [. . .] The Didache says quite simply that men shall not engage in sex with young boys and no-one shall engage in illicit sex [. . .] In 309 AD [a] gathering of bishops created eighty-one laws or canons for the Catholic communities in their area. Many dealt with sexual based offences and two are directly related to clergy abuse.

Father Tom Doyle, under oath in Sydney at the
Royal Commission into Institutional Responses
to Child Sexual Abuse, 7 February 2017

# Foreword

The sexual abuse of children by the priests, brothers and some nuns of the Roman Catholic Church caused great damage to many people. Struggling to understand what had occurred and often living with a sense of shame, but bound to silence by their abuser, the child's life could begin to unravel. They could come to distrust authority, distance themselves from friends and family and, at a young age, turn to alcohol and drugs and engage in a variety of risky behaviours.

Of course, some who are sexually abused as children manage to right their lives. Many do not. The abuse they suffered results in psychiatric problems, and destructive and criminal behaviour. Many commit suicide.

The Royal Commission into Institutionalised Responses to Child Sexual Abuse investigated the sexual abuse of children in many different institutions. Throughout its five years' duration the Commission conducted more than fifty public hearings. Given the constraints of time and resources, the Commission received complaints about abusers in many more institutions than could be publicly examined. The Commission conducted public hearings in proportion to the number of complaints it received about institutions. The greatest number of complaints came from people who, as children, were sexually abused by members of Roman Catholic institutions.

The Royal Commission was created in response to pressure from many people. Two of the most significant voices were those of Chrissie and Anthony Foster. A paedophile Catholic priest, Father O'Donnell, sexually abused their daughters Emma and Katie in their Catholic primary school. Emma committed suicide. Katie, who had taken to abusing alcohol, was hit by a motor vehicle and lives with the consequences of catastrophic injury.

Father O'Donnell's repeated crimes against Emma and Katie Foster had consequences far beyond their immediate family. Once the crimes were exposed, the failure of the Church to respond adequately caused Chrissie and Anthony to take upon themselves the task of agitating for a public inquiry. Others joined with them. They succeeded. The first inquiry was conducted by a Victorian Parliamentary Committee; the second was the Royal Commission.

No inquiry could ever reveal the full extent to which children have been sexually abused in Roman Catholic institutions. What we do know is that it is not a recent phenomenon. Canon law has contained injunctions against sex with young children for more than a thousand years. The Commission could only deal with the cases of survivors who were still alive. The number of those survivors tells us that unknown thousands of children must have been sexually abused in Catholic institutions in Australia and other countries.

When investigating the extent of the abuse in Australia, the Royal Commission also revealed the failure of those with managerial responsibilities within the Catholic Church to respond and deal effectively with allegations and abusers. Instead of reporting the abusers who had committed crimes against children to the authorities, the Church moved the abusers on, sometimes more than once, in the hope that scandal would not follow them. For many abusers this merely gave them access to more children.

The history of the sexual abuse of children within Catholic institutions is one of devastating criminal offending by individuals and catastrophic mismanagement by Church leadership. Cardinal George Pell, the most senior Australian Catholic of his generation and for some years the Director of the Aquinas Campus of the Institute of Catholic Education, and other senior clerics gave evidence to the Royal Commission to the effect that the Church did not understand that the rape of a child was a crime, seeing it as a 'moral failing'. I remain unable to comprehend how any person, much less one with qualifications in theology, could consider the rape of a child to be a mere moral failure and not a crime.

Chrissie Foster's book is a story of both betrayal and resilience. It is a compelling account of the multiple family tragedies that resulted from the criminal actions of a paedophile priest. But it is much more. It provides the reader with a detailed understanding of the failures by senior figures in the Church to respond to the family's needs and the needs of other families in similar circumstances. Chrissie describes how the Church repeatedly failed, seeking to protect itself and to evade responsibility for the crimes of its members.

Chrissie and Anthony gave evidence to the Royal Commission. They also accepted the obligation to bear witness by attending almost every public sitting of the Commission that examined the Catholic Church. This book gives Chrissie's account of those hearings and what she learnt from testimony and tendered documents. Her account is both comprehensive and accurate, and informed by her own unique insights and conclusions. By examining the issues that affected her own family, Chrissie has given the reader a compelling account of the Church's failures in leadership, responsibility, and ethics.

The history of sexual abuse by priests and brothers is a tragedy for the individual, but also for our entire society. It would undoubtedly have been better if the Church had itself responded effectively to stop the abuse and removed the abusers. If, rather than seeking to protect the Church's assets, it had accepted the responsibility to report abusers to the authorities and care for and provide compensation for those who had been abused, the infliction of further harm might have been avoided. Instead, by seeking to obfuscate and avoid responsibility, rather than the Church being protected, the institution has suffered what may be irreparable damage. It was not a case of just a 'few bad apples', but an institution that comprehensively failed to confront and deal responsibly with both the paedophiles in its ranks and those who were sexually abused as children by those paedophiles. These failures have done great harm and contributed to people's lack of confidence in many of society's fundamental institutions. Many will ask: 'If we can't trust the Church, who can we trust?'

I have come to know Chrissie Foster through the work of the Royal Commission. She carries my greatest admiration for her courage and perseverance in the face of multiple tragedies and her relentless pursuit of the truth about the sexual abuse of children in Catholic institutions. Anyone who seeks an authoritative account of that abuse in Australia, particularly Melbourne, and the Church's response should read this book.

The Hon Peter McClellan AM KC

# Prelude

A dry thunderstorm sparked fires close to my weekend place in the farming community of Tonimbuk, West Gippsland. It was the evening of the first day of autumn 2019. The blaze was causing carnage in the nearby Bunyip State Park, where firefighters could not extinguish the flames. I was due to go there on Saturday, the morning after the fire started. Lunch was booked at Jinks Creek Winery and Art Gallery, the popular and sole local haunt for a celebration of Tonimbuk friends, Roz and Lindsay, turning seventy. The fire only grew and by mid-morning the birthday get-together was called off. I waited in safety back home in Melbourne; others were in the neighbouring town of Bunyip anxious for news of our properties. Days passed. Heartbreakingly, I saw on the television news one evening that the much-loved Jinks Creek Winery was destroyed.

That Monday was Aimee's birthday. After brunch, I had to go to Sydney for the ABC's *Q+A* show. For days I was constantly studying the Fires Near Me app to see if my house was under siege, but there was no telling. At one stage the fire seemed to be burning at the edges of my property, then engulfing it. At the airport I found out a farmer had made it to his property and checked mine – it was safe.

When I was finally permitted to see my Tonimbuk home, I was stunned at how the fire had come out of the forest and burned towards the house on all sides. But then just stopped. It was amazing.

Everything below twenty metres was burnt black except the house, the surrounding garden and lawn, which stood out like a green oasis in an otherwise black and white photograph. I walked over to my large LPG gas tank. Given the devastation, I expected it to have exploded yet there it was untouched, dazzling white among all the black. The fire had scorched the earth around and below it but there had been no explosion. I shook my head.

I felt my late husband Anthony had protected his beloved farm at Tonimbuk from above.

Inside the tractor shed, structural girders had twisted owing to the intense heat radiating from the burning forest outside; a timber table had been charred; overhead lights had exploded, electrical fittings melted but amazingly a fire had not ignited inside the shed, thereby avoiding further damage.

I had been lucky; friends had lost their home and all their possessions.

I was later told by an expert that the fire was classified as cool, meaning the forest understorey was completely burnt out, but the upper storey less so. The tree trunks were burnt three-quarters of the way up, but the canopies survived and regained their lush green appearance weeks later. Still, many trees were lost. All that remained of large, mature gums were ash shadows, a powdery reminder of what once stood there.

I was overcome by a blend of feelings I knew so well. Heartbreak. Loss. Gratitude. I almost lost my bush paradise and spiritual refuge, but it – and I – was still standing.

Life would go on.

# Prologue

R age.
That is what it took. It was rage that sustained and compelled me to deal with the sex crimes committed against my children. I was overwhelmed from the moment I found out that our precious daughters Emma and then Katie were victims of our Catholic parish priest Father Kevin O'Donnell. The years of offending happened at their primary school, where I was not present. Soon I learned Fr O'Donnell had been grooming and assaulting children for almost fifty years with various Church leaders knowing of his crimes for decades. The rage built. It was not the sort of rage that makes you yell and throws things; rather it was one that empowers, giving you energy and clarity. A mother's rage.

I was forty when that fury started to burn inside me. I'm now sixty-six, and it still erupts and flares, it's always smouldering. How could it not? I have seen hypocrisy and injustice destroy victims, yet those awful realities only energised me to seek accountability and justice from the Catholic priesthood. I was lucky in that regard. The more I learned about the crimes against my family and others, the more I wanted to turn the fury back on the filthy-rich and cruel institution that pretended it cared about us.

I could not let the priesthood continue to get away with it. For years I felt a consuming urge driven by its duplicity, arrogance and wicked crimes. The urge took me beyond caring if I was called names

or given labels for actions I have taken – rage and defiance were necessary to bring about change.

Rage also helped dislodge from my eyes the scales placed there by
my Catholic education and upbringing, which had blinded me my
whole life, like generations before me. Once I was able to see the
clergy for what it was I pursued the truth for my daughters and all
the other survivors, although I did not know there would be so many.
My objective was to expose its history with a force powerful enough
to make brittle the church leaders' hiding place of holiness, to smash
its secrecy and codes of silence. It had to crumble, because how could
such evil exist in a church? The clergy had used its version of holiness
and its traditional social standing as protection when people like me
came along asking too many questions and demanding accountability. The power and influence it possessed were created in such a
way that nobody would dare believe the sex crimes these men had
been committing for centuries. Their reputations and status gave
them impunity and immunity. I was determined that, somehow,
society would understand what some so-called holy men and women
had done to children behind closed doors, and how each new generation of hierarchy had protected old and new offenders from civil law.
From the beginning, I held the belief that if society understood the
widespread practice of clergy sex crimes against children – the industrial scale of it! – there would be an almighty backlash. I couldn't wait
for that day.

The child sexual assault scandal we see in the priesthood and
communities of brothers and monks is not a problem of the Catholic
Church as much as it is a problem of the Catholic clergy: the brothers,
priests, deacons, monks, monsignors, abbots, bishops, archbishops,
cardinals and popes who make up the clergy. Ordinary parishioners, like myself, were unaware of the insidious crimes and criminal
cover-up the priesthood orchestrated behind our backs and enshrined
in secrecy. Instead, ordinary parishioners and their children were,
for centuries, the victim pool of clergy. Men – and they were almost
always men – created and worked within a void that purposely kept

their corrupt actions and clerical crimes hidden from us and the wider world. Countless innocent lives have fallen into their abyss.

So many of the hierarchy of the priesthood, especially, had knowledge of offenders through complaints they received. After bishops or heads of religious congregations received complaints, they, with utter contempt for human life and dignity, sided with offenders – not expelling them or reporting them to police, as would be expected, but instead hiding them among more children in different parishes or schools. In doing so, the hierarchy aided and abetted paedophile clergy to commit further crimes whenever they transferred these criminals – a systematic process that could persist for fifty years (the typical career span for a priest), meaning that *generations* of children suffered emotional and mental scarring, some of them taking their own lives. Owing to the hierarchy's chosen path of dealing with their criminal problem, the Catholic bureaucracy – the only people with knowledge and therefore the ability to intervene – has assisted paedophile priests, brothers and monks to get away with murder via their victims' suicides.

With every new piece of evidence, my rage galvanised me and gave me the tunnel vision required to stand up for myself and against the might of the Catholic Church. There was no point in being polite or ladylike. This criminal issue needed cauterising.

While fighting Church clergy, I was reminded many times that I was standing up to heartless men. In a way, it was a blast from the past. I first witnessed a criminal sexual offence at age eight. I was in Grade 3, walking home in my school uniform. There was a bus shelter and a man behind it. When I neared him, I saw he had opened his trousers. He was looking at me, touching his penis, showing me his erection, careful to hide from passing traffic. I felt a petrifying chill.

'What's wrong?' my mother asked when I arrived home.

I told her I had seen a dog run over by a car. This was true, too, but the dog was all right. I was the one in shock. Despite my recognition of malice in the man, I did not tell my mother. I never said a word.

Similar encounters followed my life, and – as we know from the outpouring of similar stories by countless women around the world owing to the #MeToo movement – follow women everywhere. As a sixteen-year-old travelling to work with a girlfriend, I saw a man on the other side of the train carriage exposing his penis to us. We froze. We hoped he would stop, but he didn't. I remember two other incidents at work. Once, when I was walking up a tight stairwell, a stranger off the street walked by me in the opposite direction, and, lifting his bulky jumper, flashed his penis at me. A couple of years later, I was going from one department to another when a man joined me. He engaged politely then started to prattle on. I responded by pretending I was listening. Eventually I did listen to his words. He was talking about masturbation. I looked at him, thinking how much I would like to hit him. Nothing else was said and he took off.

There were so many other times. Sexual harassment wasn't just a fleeting occurrence. I recall a male colleague repeatedly making a disgusting and degrading comment to the other female typist from an adjoining office as she exited the only female toilet – his workmates all laughing. I felt bad for her each time: I sensed her excruciating embarrassment. One day, the same man made the same comment to me. By this point, I was married so I went home and told Anthony, who came with me to make an official complaint to the staff manager. Anthony threatened he would take the matter further if I wasn't transferred. Days later, I was in a new city office.

Soon I was a mother of three young girls, walking home from the train station having attended a Girl Guide workshop for leaders. I was dressed in a dowdy blue tracksuit, one we all had to wear. Maybe I looked like a pushover or that I needed to be intimidated. I heard slow footsteps behind me. Another chill – I was being followed, stalked. I did not know such an instinct existed, but my body did. Nearing the end of the empty shopping-centre streets, I caught a glimpse of the man pursuing me. He was now on the other side of the street, looking directly at me. Because he had crossed the road, I thought perhaps I was mistaken, but minutes later he closed in, following me all the way to my street corner. I did not want him to know where I lived, so I stopped walking and leaned on a fence, turning back to stare at him as he approached. I felt the same rage I would later experience all too frequently. Suddenly he had lost his prey and therefore his purpose. Exposed in a different way, he had nowhere to go. As he neared me, I looked at him, arms folded in anger, and witnessed him turn to water as he walked past me, pretending he was suddenly lost; hesitating, stopping to read the street sign, studying it, stalling. It was a pathetic performance. I should've said something to him – followed him – asked him what was in his little back bag . . . But I didn't.

I never said anything to the men who sought to sexually intimidate me. Not a word. It is still a vexation to my spirit that I did not verbally defend myself. I wrestle with the long silences of my life. All of this became apparent to me in the past decades as I pondered my contribution to the uncovering of one of the world's most shocking scandals. I am satisfied that when it came to the sexual assaults of my own children by one of the most misogynistic institutions in the world, I found my voice to break the insidious silence that keeps sexual offending thriving.

Rage is what it took.

It has been a momentous journey with equivalent stresses. Since my first book *Hell on the Way to Heaven* was published in 2010, there have been standover tactics, groundbreaking commissions of inquiry, court cases, tears in parliament, trips to Rome, more cover-ups. The Church's men are still trying to get away with what they did. But I am not giving up. This book is a catalogue of their culpability and arrogance extensively exposed during Australian Government inquiries.


My soulmate Anthony died in 2017. Only then did I question whether I would be able to be whole again.

Two years later I went on my first solo holiday as a widow. It was a thirteen-day trip through the wonderful wilderness of the Northern Territory's Arnhem Land. Despite my trauma, nature's beauty has always felt like a gift to savour. I flew from Melbourne to Cairns, then on to Nhulunbuy in a smaller plane. In the tiny terminal I met a group of travellers, mostly women. We shared knowing smiles and it became obvious some of them recognised me from television and newspaper coverage over the years. I thought they were brave to come over and speak.

They offered me their condolences for Anthony. I thanked them. They asked me how I was going, and wondered how I had been able to survive these past decades – both very good questions that I hope I have answered in these pages. I started to think about how far I had come from those days as a run-off-my-feet young mother of three angelic daughters, packing their lunches for school, tucking them in each night, dreaming about what they might do with their futures. I was a long way from home, and this was my first lone step into the world of travel. I was still grieving, but the women's smiles, understanding and support made me feel at ease. It was going to be a good holiday. Memories of times with Anthony, Emma, Katie, Aimee and my new grandchildren would accompany me on my journey.

As much as I owe to anger, I owe more to love and truth. Truth is our weapon against clergy sex crimes. The truth saved lives. It saved me.

# 1

On an evening that fogged the breath and called for heavy coats, scarves and gloves, all the people I knew – and quite a few more than that – came by invitation to gather inside an old suburban hall with worn floorboards and framed photos from last century. There was no red carpet, but my family and friends were dressed up like a theatre crowd – it was a special event. There was sparkling wine, laughter, hugs, handshakes and nervousness. Most of the trepidation belonged to me because the event was a book launch, and it was for my book *Hell on the Way to Heaven*.

The venue was the Oakleigh-Carnegie RSL, two blocks from our home. I had imagined holding the launch elsewhere, somewhere closer to the city, but my co-author Paul Kennedy suggested we mark the occasion 'where it all happened' – in Oakleigh. That suggestion would change the course of history. The first domino was about to fall.

About two hundred copies of the book were stacked on a large table inside the entrance, ready to be signed.

An Australian mother's love.
The power of the Catholic Church.
A fight for justice over child sexual abuse.

Standing beside the book pile was a framed photograph of our daughters Emma, Katie and Aimee in petite nautical dresses. Three little faces, innocent and lovely, staring out at the excitable gathering.

Anthony and I made our way through the crowd, stopping every few feet to say hello and welcome friends. I was given kisses and a bunch of white flowers. I felt the love. When it was time for speeches, someone quietened the room. Anthony went first to the stage, dressed in a professorial white shirt/brown jacket combination, setting his jaw, peering out over the audience. Adding to his stateliness was the dark red velvet curtain backdrop. 'Good evening, everyone,' he said. 'Welcome to the launch of Chrissie and Paul's book.'

Anthony smiled, with no obvious nerves. My husband was a fine orator, a true master of ceremonies, commanding but friendly. He began reading, careful not to take his eyes off the audience for too long. First, he thanked guests, including child safety groups and Ann Barker, our local member of parliament. I had never met Ann and wondered where she was standing in the crowd. The only other politician in the room was Murray Thompson, Upper House member for Sandringham.

'Normally at an event like this, they would be the really important people and they are,' Anthony said of the dignitaries. 'But most importantly, I have to thank those who have travelled the terrible road of having been a victim of [Fr Kevin] O'Donnell and who have found the courage to be with us tonight. You are the brave people who exposed O'Donnell and brought him to justice in the courtroom. Without you, we may never have known what caused the destruction of our children's lives.'

Applause filled the room. Anthony paused until the enthusiastic sound faded, before adding, 'This is a book that we all wished had not been necessary. This is a book that bears witness to what happened to our family because of the failure of the Roman Catholic Church to ensure the safety of children in its care. But this is a book that is not just our story. It is a story that represents thousands of other stories and families in Melbourne, Victoria, and around the world.'

I was proud of Anthony, always proud. He constantly used the right words, caring and measured, to explain, inform and heal – especially for victims. (He had sterner words for churchmen.) That was where his heart was. At the beginning he didn't think I should write our story. But here he was at the launch, speaking with power and wisdom to support me. Months earlier, when the manuscript was done, he had written me a note: 'Congratulations on completing the book. I am so very proud of you and your achievement.' With the note was a copy of the book that he had printed out and bound with his own cover design as a surprise. I loved his special and thoughtful gift.

Anthony invited Paul to the stage to say a few words. I had known my co-author for fourteen years, although we had not had any contact for much of that time. Paul first reported on our family's story for the local newspaper, *Oakleigh Times*, in 1996, while he was a cadet. Twelve years later he returned to our home as a television reporter for Nine News to cover the death by suicide of our eldest daughter, Emma. Now, he was a thirty-five-year-old married father of two. Like Anthony, he saw the book as a call to arms.

'I hope one day it passes across the desk of a courageous politician who will pick it up, be moved by it, and take it into Parliament,' Paul said. 'And that there is an inquiry into how the Catholic Church has treated citizens in this country.'

I found myself nodding. It was the only way forward. This had to go to Parliament; there was no more powerful body in this country than our government to enforce change and hold the Church hierarchy to account. Researching clergy crimes had given us the knowledge we needed to demand answers from our elected leaders. We knew a lot more about this international cover-up than almost anyone in Australia. And one fact kept rising above all others: where justice was missing, politicians held the power to make it happen.

Anthony returned to the stage and introduced people who would read from the book. They were anti-child-abuse activist Cathy Kezelman, family friend Brigid, barrister Tim Seccull, and Barney, whose daughters had grown up with ours. Barney read a passage about our second daughter, Katie, being hit by a car as a teenager. Katie was at the launch with us. Hearing aloud the words that I had written about her brought all the horror and rage back to me. My thoughts bordered on murderous. Never in my life had I felt this towards anybody. I did now.

Finally, it was my turn to be introduced. Anthony became emotional. 'Chrissie's done a wonderful job writing this book,' he said. 'She's been one-tracked on it. It's been an amazing journey for her. It has given her a peace that only comes from getting the words out of your head and onto paper. Sometimes I wish I could do the same. My gorgeous wife, Christine Foster.'

An ovation followed me to the microphone. I made a joke about not being able to find my glasses, which caused laughter and broke my tension. '*Hell on the Way to Heaven* is a book I had to write because to say nothing, to remain silent, was too hard,' I began. 'I wanted to give voice to those children whose voices had been taken. I believe silence is the poison that keeps paedophiles safe – and speaking out is the antidote, the cure.'

I felt both honoured and empowered to be able to hold the book in my hands and speak about it as a mighty tool against child abuse. The writing process had been an exhilarating but exhausting experience, more up hill than down dale. People always ask authors how long it takes to write a book. Ours was unusually quick: a whirlwind six months. Eighteen months earlier, Anthony and I had spoken to a literary agent about the prospect of my memoir being published. I asked Paul to write it with me. We put together a brief pitch for publishers and sent it out. Most of the commissioning editors knew me from the previous year's Australian media coverage of the 2008 visit to Sydney by Pope Benedict XVI for World Youth Day. (Anthony and I had tried in vain to confront the Pope about clergy abuse only six months after Emma's death.)

While waiting to hear back, Katie, Anthony and I went to England to see Anthony's relatives, as it was his aunt's eightieth birthday. We were in countryside Buxton when I received an offer from Random

House, and I immediately started writing about the horrors of the past fifteen years. On the first night, I sat in bed typing into my laptop while Anthony and Katie slept. In the half-light of a 500-year old bedroom in historic Old Hall Hotel I began to write what happened. A second trip saw me write 30,000 words in the Arizona desert on a family holiday to the US. The following months were spent marshalling my thoughts. Such intensity caused my brain to be on permanent high alert. I started writing sentences on scraps of paper everywhere. It was necessary to do so as soon as they dropped into my consciousness, otherwise I was afraid they might become lost. Often in the shower I wrote the right words in the steam on the glass with my finger, then would later transcribe the near invisible imprints, sometimes fogging the glass with my breath to see them again. I was anxious that no words be excluded, I had to make sure nothing was left unsaid. Often the best expressions would come to me in the darkness and quiet peace of my bed. The blackness seemed to activate another part of my mind, revealing a world of inspiration, and I would jot down sentence after sentence.

Six months later, Paul and I had our manuscript. I dedicated it to my beautiful daughters – 'written in the hope other parents may see what we did not'. By then the book had become more than a memoir. It was an investigation of the Church's systematic crimes against children and how they tried to get away with it. I named names. The opening line was: 'My voice embarrassed me.'

Now, making my speech at the launch, this was no longer true. I was proud of my voice.

'Our daughters' voices were taken by the Catholic Church,' I said. 'I believe by telling our story, other parents will be able to see what we did not. Not seeing or not understanding child sexual assault only allows it to continue.' I expressed my deepest gratitude to all the special people in the room. 'This book is for Emma. This book is for Katie. It's for Aimee. It's for a better future for all children.'

Importantly, I gave thanks to the survivors of O'Donnell. 'Without their strength to speak to police in 1993, the guilty plea, a prison sentence and exposure would not have followed.'

This was a very important point I was always keen to make. By the time O'Donnell, a lifelong prolific sex offender, was caught, he was two years away from death. If not for the actions of twelve of his victims who gave evidence against him, he would have died without being punished. And the Church might have been able to lie about what he did, but his guilty plea to thirty-one years of offending erased that possibility. Fifteen months earlier, the Melbourne Archdiocese, O'Donnell's employer, had given the old rapist (they knew what he was) an honorific title of pastor emeritus. No doubt they hoped he would pass away without being exposed by the law. In the end the law was the only thing that stopped O'Donnell offending, when he was arrested on 16 February 1994.

The reality was that for fifty years so many of the Church hierarchy, various archbishops and bishops of Melbourne, enabled O'Donnell. That was the Catholic hierarchy's legacy. My book was an attempt to prevent the hierarchy from simply walking away as they always had.

The final speaker of the night was survivor John. With encouragement from leading advocacy group Broken Rites, John had been the first person to make a complaint to police about O'Donnell in November 1993. He used to think he was the priest's only victim. When I wrote about John's story in *Hell on the Way to Heaven*, I used a pseudonym – Bill Nelson – because he had never spoken publicly about his years of abuse as a child.

Displaying courage beyond measure, he walked onto the stage and talked to us about his past 'forty years of being chased by a dark, menacing demon'. He also educated the audience about his traumatic experience of going through the Catholic Church's own system to 'compensate' victims with small sums of money in exchange for their silence and future legal rights. The scheme, created by then Archbishop George Pell, was called Melbourne Response.

In John's case, the cruelty went further. When he tried to sue the Church in the late 1990s, he received a threatening letter from its lawyers, which listed the ways in which he (as an altar boy) had been negligent for: 'Failing to take care of his own safety; failing to make a complaint; failing to seek assistance; and failing to report any such alleged conduct'. John was already suffering severe trauma. This made his life even worse.

Yet now John turned to me and said, 'From the twelve-year-old boy inside of me, along with the innocent child within each and every survivor of O'Donnell, I say thank you.'

John called me back onto the stage and asked friends to present flowers on behalf of survivors and their families. Then, he declared, 'It gives me great honour to finally announce the book is officially launched.'

The rest of the night was a celebration. It might come as a surprise to some people to know that Anthony and I were able to have fun and enjoy the richness of special moments despite our grief, particularly of being surrounded by our closest friends. For me the overwhelming feeling was relief, the kind that comes when the job is done. When all the books were signed and the RSL lights were switching off, we went home with only enough energy to wonder what people might think of what I'd written.

A week passed.

It was early September. I was in Oakleigh shopping centre when I saw a woman I recognised. It was Ann Barker; she was on the other side of the road. Although I had not had a chance to talk to her at the book launch, I appreciated her interest.

Now Ann saw me and started crossing busy Atherton Road with obvious determination to talk to me. Her face was serious. It turned out she had stayed up reading my book until 2 am on launch night and finished it later that day.

'We have to do something about this,' she said, waving her finger at me.

Over the previous fourteen years I had written to a number of politicians asking for action, but to no avail. Here now was a politician whom I didn't need to ask – she was telling me that something had to be done. Ann Barker was ready to act. It was the spark, the moment, that I had longed for.

'Yes.' I smiled, realising the book was not an ending, but a new beginning. The next decade would prove to be the Church's true reckoning.

# 2

Survivors needed changes made to legislation to help them find justice. Among other reforms, Anthony and I also wanted the Melbourne Response to be dismantled by the state so that victims would then be able to seek fair damages in law courts. The Catholic Church would never willingly concede its criminal past, an attitude endorsed by the Vatican, nor would it hand over all its files without a fight. I sensed our campaign would be long and painful.

In the media coverage that followed the book launch, reporters would sometimes ask how I found the energy to keep going despite our family's grief. It was a good question. The answer is that I had to keep going, there was no choice. And it could only be all-out war with the hierarchy, a battle between us and them, because our views were millennia apart. We shared nothing. I liked it that way and it could only be that way because I chose to protect children and, centuries ago, they had chosen not to.

To fight so long and hard you need something else in your life. I had the love of my dear friends and family as a counterbalance to the Church's hostility. I also found peace and order in nature. The Australian bush provided the balance I needed; it was one of my sanctuaries. Not long after *Hell on the Way to Heaven* was published, Anthony and I bought our weekend house in an area called Tonimbuk, an hour's drive from our family home in suburban Oakleigh and a world away from city life. We planned to visit it as often as we could. There was no main street, no pub, no church and no post office – just Tonimbuk Hall. Almost every Australian animal and bird you can imagine lived in our front, side and backyards, as did the threat of bushfire. Memories of the deadly 2009 Black Saturday fires compelled Anthony to purchase a concrete fire bunker in case we ever got trapped in another catastrophe.

I adored the wisdom of the natural beauty at Tonimbuk; it provided me with a reprieve from trauma and heartache.

At first, I didn't enjoy interviews on television and radio. Anthony used to do all the media; I was reluctant, feeling nervous and unqualified to take on such an important task. I found speaking to media overwhelming. But in time, I saw it as an opportunity to keep pressure on the Church. Anthony came with me to most of my book interviews, sometimes waiting outside the interview room for me to finish and sometimes sitting beside me where I could see him getting fired up. Writing was my preferred way of expression, whereas Anthony was comfortable speaking from the heart. He was always eloquent and engaging in front of the cameras.

Our lives were given over to being advocates for survivors. Invitations came to me to speak at different events, including a forum for the National Association for Loss and Grief. At the same time, I was always looking to learn more about how the Church operated. Anthony and I were fortunate enough to be able to devote time and resources to this cause. In 1983 we had taken over the hydronic central heating business established by Anthony's parents in 1965. Anthony joined them at age twenty-one when his father, Ken, became ill, and he stayed on in the family business. We ran it for twenty-four years until we retired in December 2007.

Our fight for justice almost bankrupted us. In May 1999 it felt like we would lose everything. Anthony was expanding the business, having just purchased a new fleet of vans and employed more plumbers, when disaster engulfed our lives. That was the time Katie was hit by a car – she died at the scene but was resuscitated. The trauma meant we neglected the company for weeks, and in the aftermath of Katie's accident Anthony lost the drive to upgrade our operations, so we had to let the new plumbers go and sell many of the vans. It was a very hard emotional and financial time.

Days after speaking to the grief forum, Anthony and I flew to Sydney to attend the Australian launch of *The Case of the Pope: Vatican Accountability for Human Rights Abuse* by Australian human rights barrister, author and broadcaster Geoffrey Robertson. A couple of weeks earlier I had posted him a copy of my book, and now at the Sydney Opera House when it was our turn for him to sign our copy of his book, he was pleased to meet us. He said he had read my book on the plane from London. In reading Geoffrey's book, I learned a multitude of eye-opening facts regarding the Vatican. One still sticks in my mind. The papal nuncio is a diplomatic Vatican representative stationed in countries like Australia. Part of his job is to listen to all the Catholic politicians and make sure they do not speak out of alignment with Catholic Church tenets. The nuncio warns that the Vatican is watching. Robertson writes about the 'spiritual blackmail' of Catholic politicians around the world, explaining how this works in practice:[1]

> The role of its [papal] nuncio includes gathering information on such politicians and reporting back to Rome so that the Vatican can consider whether to threaten them with excommunication or a ban from mass.

Years after reading this passage I heard about a Catholic politician in my state of Victoria making a humane speech on abortion. He was speaking about it as a healthcare issue. Nonetheless, it was contrary to Church beliefs. When that politician went to his weekly mass the following Sunday, communion at the altar was denied to him by his local priest – a public embarrassment in front of the congregation. It has always seemed unfair to me that the Vatican should have such access to and potential control over politicians.

Robertson's book made headlines. Likewise, the media interest in my book remained strong for many months. At the end of an hour-long discussion on interstate radio, the broadcaster asked me if I would send a copy of my book to George Pell (by now Archbishop of Sydney and a cardinal, our nation's highest-ranking Catholic cleric).

'Well, I did think about that,' I responded. 'Then I thought, nah, he can buy his own copy.'

We both laughed.

I'm not sure if a representative of the Church bought a copy or borrowed it from the library, but *Hell on the Way to Heaven* was read by someone at the Sydney Archdiocese. I know this because Catholic Communications (the Sydney Archdiocese's public relations office) sent a letter to my publisher. It demanded they 'cease advertising the book' as a true story because it contained 'inaccuracies' and was in breach of section 52 of the *Trade Practices Act*. When it was forwarded to me, I was taken aback by the incorrect claim that my book was in any way untrue. I supposed the letter was meant to be intimidating. I was also worried my publisher might be suddenly afraid of the Church acting against it.

I hurriedly requested that the words 'true story' from the back cover be retained on the website: 'If you remove the words from your website, they can then demand you remove the words from the book cover, meaning a book recall, involving the removal of all copies of the book from every shelf in every bookstore in the country.'

I then turned my attention to dismantling the Catholic Communications 'inaccuracies' argument; while writing the book, Paul and I had already ensured everything could be proven. We never heard from them again. I found it strange that the letter to attack our book came from the public relations area of the Church and not from Cardinal Pell, who was in charge. I do not believe such a letter could have been sent without the consent or instructions of the big boss.

I later learned that Pell did send at least one personal letter to someone else (a professional in the field of child abuse prevention) who had written about my book in the *Weekend Australian*. This letter, signed by Pell, also suggested there were 'some inaccuracies' in *Hell on the Way to Heaven*. It contained nothing new to us, except the way he again tried to explain his decision to visit our daughter's rapist, Fr O'Donnell, in hospital not long before the convicted priest died: 'I visited O'Donnell to make sure that he realised the enormity of what he had done and realised that he would have to answer to God for it.' (The State of Victoria had already made sure O'Donnell understood the 'enormity' of child abuse by sending him to prison.)

To me, the George Pell letter was another hollow missive.

After another radio interview, the journalist followed up with a thank-you email. As an aside, she mentioned that she'd heard from the Catholic Church once our interview had gone to air. Her words made me stop and think. A second journalist hinted at something similar: negative feedback from the Church. Adding to the letter to our publisher, I wondered if something was going on behind the scenes. Was my book being targeted, undermined? I emailed several other journalists who'd interviewed me, asking of their experiences. One said she'd heard from the Church but described it as 'part of the job'. While it might have been part of their job, I wondered if reporters and broadcasters would contemplate a second interview after receiving letters or phone calls akin to warning shots fired over their heads.

Experienced journalists can hold their own. *Herald Sun* opinions editor Alan Howe wrote a scathing article entitled HELL – WHO'S JOINING ME? I didn't know Alan before reading his piece. Two days later, the *Herald Sun* published a response by Archbishop of Melbourne Denis Hart. In it, Hart stated: 'The damage caused to the Foster family by Kevin O'Donnell, followed by the heroin addiction and suicide of Emma and a tragic traffic accident involving Katherine, is a very sad example of human tragedy and suffering.'[2]

I was enraged. Many of the archbishop's words were attempts to muddy the waters. First, he had cunningly omitted Kevin O'Donnell's priestly title – Father. Fr O'Donnell remained a priest – an elevated and honoured one at that: pastor emeritus. As hard as we had tried to convince George Pell to laicise (defrock) O'Donnell, it was refused multiple times. Adding to insult, Archbishop Hart had dared to publicly depict Emma's suicide and Katie's debilitating injuries as 'a very sad example of human tragedy and suffering' as though fate had dealt us a dreadful blow, implying his beloved priesthood of paedophiles and complicit bishops and archbishops had nothing to do with its downfall. In fact, the archdiocese had begun managing complaints about Fr O'Donnell's offending in the 1940s. For decades they allowed him unfettered access to victims by moving him from parish to parish. Former archbishop Frank Little had respectfully retired Fr O'Donnell with honours in 1992. The assaults against children at Sacred Heart Primary School only stopped when the priest was no longer there.

Other words from Denis Hart grated. 'I would like to repeat the sincere and unreserved apology I first offered to the Foster family in July 2008, as I do to all victims of sexual abuse,' he wrote.

What apology? This was the first time I had heard of any apology from him to us. While I was still angry, I sat down to write my very first opinion piece for the *Herald Sun*. Six hours later, I sent through my response to counter the archbishop's jaundiced view, and three days later it was published under the headline THE CATHOLIC CHURCH MUST GIVE ALL VICTIMS A CHRISTIAN RESPONSE. I felt it was proper to correct the archbishop's authority and account of events. My contribution ended with a call for meaningful action: 'If you [Denis Hart] have nothing to hide and truly want to help victims, you must open all archdiocese files to the police and request the government conduct a full and open inquiry into all the facts of abuse by clergy in the Melbourne Archdiocese.'[3]

Hart offered no response to this. Perhaps he was used to having the last say and being obeyed, not publicly contradicted. The case against his Church was growing stronger. It was time we started using our laws against theirs.

# 3

In January 2011, I had the idea of donating copies of my book to the Victorian Parliamentary Library so every politician would have access to our story. While carrying a stack of copies on my way to Oakleigh train station, I dropped into Ann Barker's office to keep her updated. Ann had another plan. She had already thought of staging a book presentation ceremony in Parliament House's magnificent Queen's Hall before going into the Lower House to demand an inquiry. I took my books back home; Ann's idea was much better!

A date was set for an April presentation. Significantly, the master of ceremonies would be Victorian politician Ken Smith. He was a Liberal MP, whereas Ann was from the Labor opposition. But they had a shared view of child protection. He was, in fact, arguably the most educated anti-child-abuse official in Parliament. Seventeen years earlier he had chaired the parliamentary Crime Prevention Committee, which handed down the report 'Combating Child Sexual Assault'.

The committee's work was world-leading. Regarding Catholic clergy abuse, the report found, 'If the alleged offender was a priest or religious leader then the hierarchy of the church often conducted its own investigation, contaminating evidence and warning suspects.'

The 1995 report initially caused angst in Parliament. The Crime Prevention Committee wanted to charge the Vicar General of Melbourne, Monsignor Gerry Cudmore, with contempt of Parliament for lying in his sworn evidence about what he knew of paedophile priests in the Melbourne Archdiocese, but the government did not act. Soon after, Liberal premier Jeff Kennett allowed the Catholic Church to set up Melbourne Response, from which every victim in the Melbourne Archdiocese was ushered back into the hands of the offending institution to determine the level of compensation they were due.

Ken Smith felt let down and isolated within his own party after his pioneering report went nowhere. He believed it caused his career to stall. Now, in 2011, at our Queen's Hall book presentation to the Parliamentary Library, he shed tears. Eighty people watched him struggle with his emotions while making a speech. Our hearts were touched. We appreciated his care and support. At the end of the presentation Ann Barker walked into Parliament and demanded 'all members to join me in ensuring that these crimes against children are no longer subject to secrecy by the Catholic Church'. Ann wanted a state-led inquiry.

Action seemed to pick up pace after that day. My local newspaper, the Waverley *Leader*, and its reporter Tim Michell began a year-long awareness campaign calling for an inquiry, creating and promoting a public consciousness that kept pressure up. Tim wrote eight substantial articles. Two other local papers joined the push, and nationally, more and more stories were being told. Numerous journalistic investigations were underway. Meanwhile, courts prosecuted more priests. Victims' support groups spoke out. More victims came forward. Finally, they were being heard.

I was asked to sell my books at a clergy victim conference in Melbourne. I had a little table at the back of the hall. A gentleman approached me and asked to buy a copy. The man was sheepish before he spoke. 'I already have a copy,' he said. 'But I need another one.'

I was puzzled but didn't pry. Eventually, he explained his copy had been damaged because when he read it at home, it angered him so much he would hurl the book across the room in fury. Once he calmed down, he would retrieve the book and begin reading, only to repeat his actions. Now, after all the throwing, he needed a new book.

An hour or so later I saw prominent Melbourne Catholic priest Father Bob McGuire standing a few tables away. I walked over to introduce myself. 'Your book,' he said, 'it has thrown a grenade at them.'

Priceless.

A month later my book was sold to a large Italian publisher, Piemme, and translated under the title of *Così in terra*, meaning 'So it is on earth' (from the Lord's Prayer). Anthony and I arranged the necessary care for Katie and flew to Rome for its release.

Piemme's front cover was a photo of Emma and Katie aged six and four, taken in January 1988. The photos were both beautiful and heartbreaking because I now know that when they were taken Emma had already been sexually assaulted by O'Donnell and Katie would, within two years of that happy image, be a victim herself of the vile priest.

From that day, as we entered any bookstore in Italy – from Rome to Venice to Florence – Emma and Katie's smiles greeted us from the cover of *Così in terra*. Seeing their faces everywhere made it difficult for me to leave the books behind. I felt I should be taking them with me. One afternoon I stood on St Peter's Square at the heart of the Vatican holding the volume on my family's suffering, a silent but poignant protest. Anthony took a photo. Being in the heart of the Vatican was daunting. I felt the Church's enormity and our insignificance. Security guards wandering around looking at us, I felt we were about to be questioned, which added to my tension.

It felt right that our story was told overseas because this was a worldwide scandal. In July 2011, the Irish Government rose up against the Catholic Church and its systemic cover-ups. The Cloyne Report was Ireland's fourth such investigation. Headlines screamed PRIESTS WILL BE JAILED IF THEY DON'T REPORT ABUSE and THE GREAT

AND DELIBERATE DECEPTION. The Prime Minister of Ireland, Enda Kenny, tore shreds off the Church hierarchy, saying that the Cloyne Report 'excavates the dysfunction, disconnection, elitism, the narcissism that dominate the culture of the Vatican to this day'.[4] Of the child victims he stated, 'The rape and torture of children were downplayed or "managed" to uphold instead the primacy of the institution, its power, standing and "reputation".'[5]

Ann Barker travelled to Ireland for a two-week study tour where she learned how the Irish had carried out their groundbreaking inquiries so she could assist Australia in setting up the inquiry we wanted. She became the passionate expert our Parliament needed.

Then came another reminder of how desperately a local inquiry was needed, as our focus shifted to the Victorian town of Ballarat, where clergy sex crime was still taking an unthinkable toll. The Ballarat Courier's cover on 9 August 2011 was a black page with twenty-six white crosses. Its lead story concentrated on the damage caused by multiple paedophile clergy overrunning a boys-only Christian Brothers' school, St Alipius. The crosses represented 'twenty-six victims who had died by suicide'.

A surprising turning point in our fight for justice came a year later, during a harsh Melbourne winter. Anthony and I were invited to the city for a meeting in Exhibition Street, a block away from parliamentary quarters in Spring Street. It was bitterly cold and already getting dark under the shade of the high-rises when we arrived at four o'clock. Traffic was creeping. Pedestrians hustled. Everyone seemed to be heading somewhere else. We were the only ones standing still.

I love my home city of Melbourne. As a child, my mum used to bring my brothers and me into town as a treat during school holidays. We would go to a picture theatre to watch a movie, then get lunch at Coles cafeteria on Bourke Street, where we could choose anything we wanted to eat. As a teenager, I had my first job in the city and enjoyed wandering the streets, visiting shops during lunchtimes. Now, as an adult, I like to travel into the heart of the city every couple of months to experience the laneways and arcades. The Block Arcade and Royal Arcade were always my favourites.

On the footpath outside the large glass doors of the address we'd been given, we met Ann Barker, my co-author Paul Kennedy and our new friend Bryan Keon-Cohen, a Queen's Counsel we had met during the book tour. Once a lawyer on the Mabo case (and author of *A Mabo Memoir: Islan Kustom to Native Title*), he had been moved by my story to offer his services pro bono. This happened when he set up an action group called COIN (Commission of Inquiry Now). Bryan liked the acronym because it played on the image of money, which the Catholic Church hierarchy held dearest. We were most grateful for his professional legal opinions. The five of us were here to meet Attorney-General Robert Clark. It was the first (and last) big pitch we would make to the serving Liberal Government for a royal commission into the crimes and cover-ups of the Church.

Someone came from inside the building to show us up to Mr Clark's office. Not much was said as we passed through security. We caught the lift as a huddled group wondering whether the government was going to take us seriously, each of us with varying levels of hope and scepticism.

I had expectations of justice being exercised, believing we were on the cusp of a breakthrough. Anthony had spent the past two weeks preparing his ideal terms of reference for a royal commission, which was the inquiry he desired – one with powers to seize files and compel witnesses. How could the attorney-general be in opposition to us?

Politics would have to play a hand in deliberations. Geoffrey Robertson's revelations reminded me of that harsh fact, although maybe it was time for the needs of children to overrule any Vatican collar-wearing lobbyists. I didn't know enough about the finer points of politics to carry the burden of doubt. I believed in the system. If the truth came out then the law would take its course: that's all we needed for the law to work, wasn't it? And the affairs of the past year had been characterised by a bipartisan approach to child safety.

The meeting was shorter than I had imagined, but it seemed well-meaning. Mr Clark and his staff listened to what we had to say without giving any promises. Anthony led the discussion, quietly but sternly outlining what should happen next. Bryan chimed in with questions in a manner befitting his experience as a barrister. Ann spoke about 'proper process', something she deemed critical in the Irish experience. Paul sat quietly, taking notes.

I talked about what we wanted: an inquiry to open archdiocese files, removal of the cap on ex-gratis payments to victims from the Church's Melbourne Response, removal from the clergy of any priest who sexually assaulted children.

When it was over, we caught the lift back down to the street not really knowing whether the government had the gumption to do the right thing. It was late. The city was cold and dark. Few office buildings had lights on, but the fire inside me was flickering. Naive or otherwise, I thought we had been convincing. Turns out I was right.

# 4

Alongside the heated demands for justice and a royal commission, we attended a family gathering in February 2012. It was a day filled with love and joy.

We were in the St Kilda Botanical Gardens amid summer roses and a multitude of other beautiful blooms. It was a special place of natural beauty and peace smack-bang in the middle of a bustling suburb. We shared a wonderful day filled with celebration and happiness that ended late at night by the shores of Port Phillip Bay at the Stokehouse restaurant.

All the family was there, including our youngest daughter Aimee and her partner Luke. Aimee was now twenty-six. Until this point, her life had been difficult. She had witnessed the disintegration of her two older sisters' lives since the age of ten. This made her a secondary victim. It was a heartbreaking journey for our youngest girl, who could do nothing to ease the pain of Emma and Katie. Yet despite her grief, she excelled academically and blossomed into a kind, loving and sensitive person. I am always proud of her and the life she leads.

Anthony and I had a wonderful time. Love conquered fear and all the negative experiences we endured. It was love that allowed Anthony and me to still be with each other and enjoy life's best moments with friends and family, including our two daughters. No matter how harrowing some days were, there was always something positive to look forward to. Something to celebrate. Something or someone to love. The love of our family and friends has kept us from falling.

Happiness and heartbreak have both been present in my life. The heartbreak is there, and I never ignore it or run from it. It is reality and I cannot change any of our history. I accept it. How I wish things had been different, but I deal with what I have been dealt.

Katie was at the gathering too. Some years earlier, she had reached a plateau in her recovery, meaning her short-term memory loss and the inability to walk without assistance would remain. Nevertheless, she was in a happier place than she had been in previous years. After Katie's 1999 accident and following her year in hospital, we looked after her at home. We hoped that one day we could build her a house across the street so she could have her own place, albeit with 24-hour care. That day would come in November 2013.

By Autumn 2012, my frustration with the government was growing. It had been eight months since our high-rise meeting with Robert Clark. Why was he taking so long?

We weren't the only ones holding our breath.

The agitation of survivors and advocates in regional Ballarat was worsening. *The Age* had devoted another front page to the alarming suicide rate among students of the St Alipius school. The source was a policeman's report. Ballarat's history meant the city was becoming known as one of the world's most notorious for clergy paedophiles. Photos were published one day of young men who had died, including two brothers and a cousin from the one family. The following day, more pictures of child clergy victims who had died by suicide appeared. Their faces. Their families. Their heartbreak. An editorial called out to our premier, Ted Baillieu: 'Stop stalling, Mr Baillieu.'[6]

He was listening.

Four days later, Anthony and I were informed there would be a press conference at Parliament House. Premier Baillieu was to speak at 1.30 pm. We headed straight to the city and waited in a cafe at the top of Collins Street. Sitting there, feelings swaying between para-lysing tension and plain stress, we discussed what the announcement might be. Our best-case scenario was a royal commission, although I thought it was unlikely. The influence of the Church played its part in my cynicism. Maybe there would be an announcement that there would not be an inquiry at all.

When the time came we left the cafe and went straight to Parliament House, up the same steps where we'd held a rally months earlier. A staff member from the attorney-general's office was there to meet us. Anthony, always thinking, made conversation as he guided us along a hallway: 'I believe your office has had no contact with the Catholic hierarchy over the issue of a government inquiry.'

The staffer was surprised. 'Well, yes we have,' he said. 'We have been negotiating with the Catholic Church for twelve months.'

It was a rude awakening for two reasons. Firstly, the government should not have given the Church – the offending institution! – such a say over how it was to be investigated, especially since we, repre-senting victims, had been consulted only once. 'Negotiating' with the Church was like an accused criminal being consulted by a judge over how he might like his trial to be run. Secondly, Church staff had led us to believe that this was not the case. Only three weeks earlier Anthony and two other members of COIN had met with Church leaders, including the vicar general. (Archbishop Hart was supposed to attend but pulled out at the last minute.) At the meeting, a Church representative said that the Church had 'not put submissions to the government' over a potential inquiry. Now we were learning the opposite had happened. And it had been going on for a year. Attorney-General Robert Clark was later questioned about this in an ABC TV current affairs interview. 'We received representations from victims' groups, and we received representations from the Catholic Church,' he said.[7]

This was all happening so fast. I had to sideline my fears and anger while the staffer showed us to our seats. Mr Baillieu entered the room and made his announcement. No royal commission. Instead, a bipartisan parliamentary inquiry would be undertaken by the Family and Community Development Committee.

At last! Something was happening. Not entirely what we had hoped for, but it was *something*. It felt like an inspiring win. The people of Victoria had spoken, and the government had heard them. I was pleased the committee would be represented by both major parties (as well as the Nationals). After all, child sexual assault knows no political boundaries. Encouraged by Victoria's inquiry, Australians in other parts of the country were making their own investigations and demands – they were still demanding a royal commission. These people were very brave and very hard to silence. Victoria may have been placated, but a rumble was still echoing from over the borders. The dream of a much larger public inquiry was not over.

# 5

Debate raged as to the size, strength and suitability of the parliamentary inquiry.

VICTIMS WAIT FOR JUSTICE – SEX ABUSE INQUIRY GREETED WITH ANGER AND CONCERN[8] read one headline. CHURCH INQUIRY 'NOT ENOUGH'.[9] VICTORIAN GOVERNMENT UNDER FIRE OVER CHURCH INQUIRY.[10]

Many could sense another betrayal. Was it a government inquiry or a Church inquiry designed to let the hierarchy keep its paedophile secrets and shirk its responsibility once again? Did the inquiry have enough power? Media interest, as usual, brought forward more survivors' stories. It was reassuring to see the issue in the public spotlight.

The members of the Family and Community Development Committee would be Georgie Crozier, Liberal Party MP for Southern Metropolitan (Chair); Frank McGuire, Australian Labor Party MP for Broadmeadows; Andrea Coote, Liberal Party MP for Southern Metropolitan (Deputy Chair); Bronwyn Halfpenny, Australian Labor Party MP for Thomastown; David O'Brien, Nationals MP for Western Victoria; and Nick Wakeling, Liberal Party MP for Ferntree Gully.

Meanwhile, there was a lot happening interstate. New South Wales advocates, looking enviously at Victoria's latest action, were screaming for a royal commission. The town of Newcastle in the Hunter Valley was becoming notorious for its history of systemic abuse. Like Ballarat, Newcastle was both conservative and religious; it was home to generations of children who had suffered sexual crimes from Catholic clergy.

Journalist Joanne McCarthy was leading the charge at the Newcastle *Herald*. A veteran reporter with a decade of experience in exposing clergy crimes, her commitment to uncover the truth in her hometown began when a victim phoned her to ask why the conviction of a paedophile priest had not been reported in the paper. Joanne promised to investigate. She later found that indeed the conviction had not been reported, and, on further inspection, saw that other offenders – both Catholic and Anglican – had been accused or apprehended without significant public scrutiny. Joanne's professionalism and dedication to justice for victims led her to write over a thousand stories. Her articles and tireless effort contributed to a safer future for children.

Critically, Joanne's most recent story was about the death of John Pirona. Two days earlier John had gone missing, leaving behind a note that read: 'Too much pain'. His distraught family, friends, community and police searched for him. John was a much-loved member of his small town. He had been a child victim of the local Catholic priest.

I read about John's disappearance and hoped he would be found alive. But he died by suicide. Seeing his wife and their two little girls walking behind his hearse in a slow procession was heartbreaking.

The day of John's funeral was the same day our prime minister, Julia Gillard, visited Newcastle, including the Newcastle *Herald* newsroom. Joanne wasn't in the office (she was covering the funeral) but Ms Gillard heard all about her work. This experience was a pivotal moment in her understanding of the issue.

John Pirona's death was also the catalyst for Joanne and the *Herald* to begin a campaign – Shine the Light – for a royal commission.

Back home, our Victorian Parliamentary Inquiry called for statements from the public. I got to work on ours. On 6 August 2012, I submitted a twelve-page document outlining our story and my view on various aspects of Melbourne Response. It was amazing to have somebody to complain to about the treatment we received because, until now, there had been no such avenue available to anyone in my and Anthony's position.

Complaining to the clergy about the clergy had been a pointless and distressing dead end. There was nowhere to go other than back to the abusers and their bosses to criticise the unfair systems they forced upon us. Since 1996 the Church had held every card with arrogance and dominance. It was a crushing system endorsed by the state. Clergy answered to no-one.

I presented my submission in a folder. It contained my twelve-page document, my book, a compact disc I called 'Catholic Clergy Child Sexual Abuse Media Database', and twenty-two other documents attached as appendices. My love of order in archiving had emerged from my work as a teenager and young adult in the Department of Agriculture Library, where I was a trainee library technician. It was in this job that I learned archiving skills and the value of keeping infor-mation readily available, classified and in pristine condition. When dealing with the unusual men of the church, I had learned a long time ago that everything on this issue had to be 'proven'. Indeed, George Pell had driven home that point in a meeting back in 1997, when he responded to our concerns about some abusive clergy still working in suburban Melbourne parishes.

'It's all gossip until it's proven in court,' he said. 'AND I DON'T LISTEN TO GOSSIP.'

When then-Archbishop Pell said these words so forcefully I felt them like a physical blow. Emma's accusation had not been proven in court – so I felt he was saying Emma's words were gossip. Tragically, not many child sexual assault accusations get proven in court. I think Pell knew this and knew we had no proof, hence he silenced us.

Gossip. Pell often uses the word in a disparaging way, but gossip could otherwise be seen as simple communication between people. Conversations. I wondered why the priesthood had always condemned what it called gossip by making it sinful. Why did this oganisation choose to imply certain conversations were lies? Who decided which conversation was banned?

In my submission, the Catholic Clergy Child Sexual Abuse Media Database detailed every article on this issue I had collected. From the time Oakleigh MP Ann Barker first said she was going to request an inquiry, Anthony suggested I make a spreadsheet of my entire newspaper article collection to create a computerised database. It went back to the first day I stepped into this arena: 26 March 1996, when Emma disclosed her abuse. By 2012 my collection consisted of 3 115 newspaper articles in twenty-four volumes, with seventy-two pages in each volume. Of these articles, 2 334 related to child sexual assault by Roman Catholic Church clergy; of those, 2 220 related to Australia.

How could any organisation receive such long-term bad publicity about the rape and molestation of generations of children and still be in business? (Today, my volumes number fifty-one and the number of articles exceeds 6 000.)

I have great admiration for journalists who have covered stories of child sexual assaults by Catholic clergy over the past twenty-five years, not least the exceptional journalists doing it as far back as the 1980s. Dedicated reporters, through their articles in print media and television reporting, have been leading the in-depth analysis of a complex criminal issue for a generation, their stories vital to better public understanding. Their effort has given parents, grandparents and other relatives and carers an opportunity to protect the children in their lives. Media coverage has emboldened other victims to come forward, breaking the silence forced upon them as children by their abusers. In the past, people could not bear to talk about sexual crimes against children. This public reticence amounted to a knowledge-crippling silence, which, in turn, allowed paedophiles to offend in safety. Any Church acknowledgement of wrongdoing has only ever come about because of media pressure after reporting victims' stories.

The Shine the Light campaign was in full swing in Newcastle. On 15 September the Newcastle *Herald* published another three-page spread, SPECIAL REPORT: WHY WE NEED A ROYAL COMMISSION INTO CATHOLIC CLERGY ABUSE – 60 YEARS OF SHAME. On one page were photos or silhouettes of thirty-two priests and brothers from the Hunter Valley region who had either been charged with criminal offences against children or who were the subjects of Church payouts to victims.

A community forum followed. Hundreds of people attended, many parents spoke, some distraught, some angry – there were many tears. The outpouring of grief moved a local policeman, Detective Chief Inspector Peter Fox, to speak. Dressed in jeans and a T-shirt, he made his way to the front of the hall and to the microphone. He asked, 'Do we need a royal commission?' Then he answered, 'You bet we do.' He received a standing ovation.

The Victorian Parliamentary Inquiry was explosive, even before its first sitting.

Victoria Police had come out publicly to slam the 'Catholic Church for impeding investigations and moving abusers around the Church'.[11] We were stunned but heartened by the revelations put forward by Victoria Police and their long list of complaints against 'Catholic Church officials'. The Parliamentary Inquiry had not even started but it was consoling beyond words for victims to receive this unexpected voice of authority backing what they claimed was their experience of Church hierarchy. Media coverage erupted in Victoria. Abuse in the Church was called an 'epidemic'.[12] The coverage encouraged more victims to speak.

The following Friday, 19 October, Parliament House hosted its first sitting; the Inquiry into the Handling of Child Abuse by Religious and Other Non-Government Organisations run by the Family and Community Development Committee was underway. (This date was significant, as sixteen years earlier, on 19 October 1996, George Pell had announced his new Melbourne Response, with approval from Victoria Police and the State Government.)

We arrived early, not wanting to miss any of the hearing. The grand building was becoming familiar after my book presentation and Ann Barker's historic speech in the Lower House.

This time we walked in a different direction, down a corridor towards the Family and Community Development Committee's room where the hearings would be held. We were about to spend a lot of time in this room. The public gallery sat about eighty people snugly. Today it was full. There were seats for media and any member of the public who wished to attend. As time went on, a special task-force would be set up by Victoria Police to deal with any chargeable offences arising from the proceedings. The officers joined us and others as gallery regulars.

The first day's evidence damned the Catholic priesthood.[13] I had never heard or read such information. Law professor and child protection expert Patrick Parkinson told us that 'Catholic clergy commit six times as much abuse as those in the rest of the churches combined [. . .] the figures for the Catholic Church are strikingly out of proportion'. Victoria Police Deputy Commissioner Graham Ashton told the committee that 'police had statistics for sexual offences by clergy and church workers since January 1956, uncovering "shocking" figures – 2,110 offences against 519 victims – overwhelmingly perpetrated by Catholic priests and mostly against boys aged eleven or twelve. But in all that time the Church had not reported a single crime to police.' Professor Chris Goddard of Child Abuse Prevention Research Australia revealed that '$30 billion is the cost of child abuse to the economy'.[14]

The quality and quantity of submissions to the Parliamentary Inquiry banished any doubts over the committee's resolve and strength. With the exception of two half-days over the seven-month period and more than 160 hearings, Anthony and I attended every session of the statewide inquiry, travelling to Ballarat, Bendigo and Geelong.

After the first hearing and a weekend of media coverage, the barrage continued. RMIT professor Des Cahill told us, 'At least one in twenty Catholic priests in Melbourne was a child sex abuser, although the real figure was probably one in fifteen.' It was a shocking figure. Professor Cahill also told the Inquiry, 'The Catholic Church was incapable of reforming itself because of its internal culture.'[15]

*

Royal commission rumblings reverberated around the country.

Two weeks after that first Victorian hearing, on 7 November, the policeman from the Hunter Valley, Detective Chief Inspector Peter Fox, wrote an open letter to the Premier of New South Wales, Barry O'Farrell. Joanne McCarthy quoted the letter in the Newcastle *Herald*: 'Detective Chief Inspector Peter Fox has accused the Church of alerting offenders, destroying evidence and moving priests to protect its "good name", based on his experiences of thirty-five years. His comments mirrored Victoria Police submissions about the Catholic Church to a parliamentary inquiry.'[16]

The following evening Chief Inspector Fox appeared on the ABC's *Lateline* program interviewed by host Tony Jones. The interview was sensational and exposed further Church hierarchy obstruction of criminal child sexual assault cases in two major states – Victoria and New South Wales. Peter Fox would go on to write a book on his experiences, *Walking Towards Thunder*.

It was a case of same problem, different state, same clerical behaviour.

There was barely time to breathe. The following day a most abhorrent headline struck us: BROTHERS 'PACK RAPED' BOYS. It was a report on the Hospitaller St John of God religious order: 'A group of fifteen religious brothers led by an "alpha paedophile" are suspected of the unreported deaths of two boys and the sexual abuse of more than forty others.' The story said victims included wards of the state cared for by the brothers in homes for the 'mentally impaired'. At least seven had committed suicide.[17] Many of the boys had Down syndrome, some were non-verbal, others were orphans. These children without a voice made perfect victims and kept offenders safe. This paedophile situation reminded me of two years earlier when I had read an Italian report on a regional boarding school for deaf primary-aged children in Verona. Over two decades, 'twenty-four priests and lay brothers from the Company of Mary order'[18] sexually assaulted many of the deaf children who were isolated from their parents.

In Melbourne, the dreadful St John of God exposé encouraged others to speak up and give further information. Three days later a psychologist, Dr Michelle Mulvihill, previously employed by the order, called for George Pell to shut it down, stating, 'More than 70 per cent of the brothers in the St John of God order are suspected child abusers.'[19] Dr Mulvihill had reportedly 'met more than 120 of the child abuse victims during compensation negotiations between 1998 and 2007 [. . .] and alleged that the order had never properly supervised suspected paedophile brothers and hid documents in relation to the child abuse around its properties in Australia in places where police "would never find them".'

Despite all this cruelty and criminal behaviour against the young, helpless and friendless children whom the Order of Brothers enlisted to care for, the St John of God hospitals are flourishing today. Their name St John of God is proudly displayed in big letters, lit up at night, atop their hospital buildings for all to see.

More information in the news that day told us that 'A victims' group has uncovered the trail of eighteen paedophile priests moved around the Catholic Church in Victoria from parish to parish or further away, where they continued offending.'[20]

All of this news caused political waves. Prime Minister Gillard was facing growing calls for a royal commission.[21] I wondered how long she could resist.

For his part, Cardinal Pell questioned whether a royal commission 'would serve any purpose', suggesting victims had already been delivered justice.[22] His view was laughable. When Melbourne Response, which George Pell created, had a $50,000 cap on victim payouts, the average payment was less than half – $24,000. A scandalously pitiful amount to compensate for repeated sexual assaults and a ruined life.

The public disagreed with George Pell. *The Age* newspaper's poll revealed that 97 per cent of respondents supported the call for a royal commission, the highest support for an issue it had ever recorded.

A positive atmosphere was building. My natural optimism convinced me something good was about to happen. Then – it did! It was one of those moments in time you remember forever: everything you see and feel – a moment that marks the psyche.

# 6

Truth is indestructible yet gentle. It is right and honest. I guess that's why corrupt people want to hide it. It threatens their comfortable world of lies. Truth-seekers never feel like they've finished. That's the way I felt.

But the search for truth and its unveiling can be tiring work. Some days I needed to go somewhere to recharge my energy: to have a break from the harsh realities of child abuse. Often that place was Tonimbuk, our home away from home.

In November 2012 the house and its natural surrounds were still new to us. Anthony and I didn't just sit around and listen to the frogs and birds. We got to work in the gardens and on the house. I would lose myself exploring in the forest or working in what we called the English garden – an overgrown eighty-plus-year-old, non-indigenous garden that often reminded me of *The Secret Garden*, a book I had read as a child. Ours held the same magic and mystique from a bygone era; clearing the mass of weeds, we discovered its hidden pathways and robust plants. Anthony would take on the heavy jobs, often with his tractor. He had driven and loved tractors since his teenage years when he helped a family friend on his farm.

Working alongside Anthony was one of the joys of my life. We had worked together as marital partners, parents, business partners, clergy exposure partners and now as farming partners. In all these years of working together I could never get enough of Anthony's company, companionship and solidarity. I loved hearing what he had to say because he had a forensic mind, a wonderful ability to analyse any situation and come up with a solution. It was one of the many qualities I admired about him.

He'd always been that way. We met when I was twenty-four. Six weeks later, he proposed. We were so in love. The wedding was in July 1980. Emma came along in November 1981 and Katie was born in 1983, two years before Aimee.

Our lives were changed forever in 1995 when Fr Kevin O'Donnell was charged with his crimes. At first, we thought the girls were safe, since the first newspaper reports mentioned him targeting boys. When Anthony and I asked Emma if Fr O'Donnell had ever touched her, she forcefully said, 'No!', which perturbed us. By September that year Emma was in a teenage psychiatric unit with anorexia and had begun to self-harm. Katie, too, began to implode.

It was another twenty months before we found out about Katie also being assaulted. I found a suicide note she had written that said O'Donnell had sexually assaulted them both many times. The priest had taken Emma and Katie off the playground at lunch breaks. He was boss of the school so he could hire or fire teachers and the principal: he could do whatever he liked.

Nothing prepared us for the horrendous truth.

Anthony and I never argued. All our effort went into action. We stuck by each other, no matter what. The next decade was fought in and out of law courts. We eventually had a victory, settling our civil claim after mediation. Years later, Anthony said that was his only regret. If we had our time again, we would have rejected the Church offer and gone to trial, but at that time our settlement was the best we knew was possible (we were told it was a record sum). Yet it would never be enough, and although the overwhelming urge was to railroad the clergy into court to receive justice, the path to that was long and unpredictable, one which we had spent ten years travelling. I was tired of it all and by calling it quits and settling, we felt like we won out. Nevertheless, justice was not served, nor did the Church hierarchy face the public shame it deserved.

Initially, I felt a lot of guilt because I was the Catholic, Anthony an atheist. If I hadn't sent our girls to a Catholic school, this wouldn't have happened. But Anthony got upset when I talked that way. 'This happened and we are in it together,' he said. 'I don't want to lose you because that would be the end of everything.'

In my worst times, when I cried and couldn't stop, Anthony was the only other person who understood. He hurt as I did.

After my book came out, the 'Good Weekend' magazine of *The Age* newspaper featured Anthony and me in a regular column called 'Two of Us', a popular page about two people who were business, dance, sporting or life partners. The participants are interviewed separately about the other person and their shared experiences. You don't get to know what the other person said about you until you read it in the magazine.

Anthony called us soulmates in his interview. I read with fascination what he had to say about our family. 'There is a family photo in our front room taken not long before [O'Donnell] was convicted,' he said. 'I recall looking at it thinking *This is just perfect. What could go wrong?* But what could go wrong had already gone wrong.'[23]

He went on to talk about me.

Everything that has happened to Chrissie and me has always been underpinned by our amazing relationship. But there's never been a lot of time to just stand back and look at what has happened to us. At no point have we ever fallen into a heap. How could we? I don't know why none of the stresses we've experienced have affected our relationship, but I can say I have never doubted our bond. Chrissie is a natural person. There is no front. She is open, honest and warm, and is still the person I prefer to spend my time with. Our family has been destroyed, but our relationship is rock solid.

Anthony must've been asked to give an update on our lives. He called Aimee our shining light:

> But when we see her moving forward in life we think, *There should be two more*. It's a cruel twist of fate that Katie still remembers the abuse, but not something that happened three minutes ago, which means we are all stuck in this dark past. Our focus now is on trying to make the most of each day and to not get too down. We don't want to lose any more of our lives.

These are the things we would talk about as we worked overlooking Bunyip State Park, wondering about and discussing fate, fault and the future. How tall and beautiful the trees were standing on the verge of another summer; brave and majestic, they feared nothing.

We were hunched over the vegetable garden when Anthony's mobile phone pinged with a message. He looked at the screen and read the words out loud from our friend Lyn.

'Congratulations on the inquiry.'

We were puzzled. We assumed 'the inquiry' was the Victorian Parliamentary Inquiry. That was now months old. Anthony put the phone back in his pocket and we continued our weeding and beanstalk trellising. About ten seconds went by without comment. Then we both looked at each other in realisation that the message could have been about another inquiry. Dropping our tools, we ran out of the vegetable garden, down the path to the house. Inside, on the way to turn on the television, I grabbed my phone. There was a missed call from my co-author Paul Kennedy. This heightened the possibility of the breakthrough I was thinking about but dared not say. *No, it can't be, surely not a royal commission!* I didn't want to be disappointed. Ditching the phone, I grabbed the TV remote. It was already on the ABC and when the screen came to life our prime minister, Julia Gillard, was addressing the nation, describing child abuse as a 'hideous, shocking and vile crime'.

'I believe our nation needs to have this royal commission.'

It was barely believable. Anthony and I laughed. We jumped around. We hugged. It was amazing, an absolutely astounding turn of events. Suddenly we had all achieved the most powerful investigation our nation could hold. Finally, the truth could emerge on a scale the nation deserved. A champagne cork popped that afternoon and the sound echoed in the trees.

# 7

There was little time to celebrate the life-changing announcement. The state and national inquiries supercharged media coverage of clergy sex abuse and cover-ups. I resumed a role I'd been performing since the mid-1990s: chief chronicler. What became startlingly apparent to me in reading newspaper articles and speaking confidentially to people who came to us for advice was that almost every crime against a child came with a cover-up.

From parents and victims conned or forced into silent compliance, to teachers whose careers had been ruined after speaking out against criminal clergy at their parish school, the ability of the Church to conceal criminal behaviour knew no limits.

Prime Minister Gillard soon outlined the shape of our five-year $4.5 billion Royal Commission. It would be known as the Royal Commission into Institutional Responses to Child Sexual Abuse and would be the largest in Australian history. Legislation was altered to allow this commission to operate in a victim-friendly manner. Instead of the usual one commissioner we would have six. Private hearings would be scheduled so that victims could speak to a commissioner and staff without being exposed to the public glare. Public hearings in the form of case studies were to be established. Much care and consideration was being given to make our Royal Commission the best it could be. Chair of the commission was the Hon Justice

Peter McClellan AM. The other commissioners were the Hon Justice Jennifer Coate, Bob Atkinson AO APM, Robert Fitzgerald AM, Helen Milroy and Andrew Murray. The plan was initially to avoid holding hearings in Victoria owing to the ongoing Victorian Parliamentary Inquiry.

Cardinal George Pell was not pleased. He said the inquiry was 'unnecessary'. He blamed the media for a smear campaign. 'We are not interested in denying the extent of misdoing in the Catholic Church,' he told reporters. 'We object to it being exaggerated. We object to being described as the only cab on the rank [. . .] Because there is a persistent press campaign focused largely on us, that does not mean we are largely the principal culprits.'[24]

His predictable comments were at odds with the facts, and they were at odds with our family's experience.

'I wonder to what extent the victims are helped by this ongoing furore in the press,' Pell continued.

Someone asked the cardinal whether priests should be made by Australian law to report child sexual abuse after hearing about it in the confessional. 'The seal of confession is inviolable,' he replied.[25]

The Royal Commission would see about that. The views of Pell and other senior figures in the Church were finally going to be measured against evidence. Premier of New South Wales Barry O'Farrell didn't wait to give his opinion: 'I struggle to understand [. . .] that if a priest confesses to another priest [. . .] that that information should not be brought to police.'[26]

Jeff Kennett, the former premier of Victoria who let the Church run its awful Melbourne Response (subsequent Labor governments allowed it, too), was asked what he thought about scrutiny of the issue. For some reason, Mr Kennett talked about George Pell's predecessor as Archbishop of Melbourne, Frank Little. 'I don't think he could bring himself to believe that in his flock people had committed these deeds,' he told *The Age*.[27]

Nonsense. Frank Little knew precisely the capabilities of his criminal priests such as Fr Kevin O'Donnell. As with all the other comments made about the Royal Commission, I stored these words away and awaited the hearings.

As a counter to Pell's objections of 'exaggeration' by the media, newspapers ran a brief history of Catholic Church scandals in Australia, just as more scandals were uncovered.

In Victoria we were faced with a laughing David Rapson, former Salesian priest and vice principal at Rupertswood College in Sunbury. He seemed to think there was something funny about his being in court charged with child rape, abusing seven boys over a seventeen-year period. He blamed a higher power for making him do it. 'God made us this way and it is his fault,' he said.[28] The following year Rapson would be sentenced to thirteen years imprisonment.[29]

Rupertswood College had a shocking history of rampant sexual assault of students by at least nine of the Salesian Brothers and priests. As a response to the debate over a royal commission's value, I wrote an opinion piece. *The Age*'s headline read SO MUCH HEARTBREAK, SO MUCH PAIN – IT'S ABOUT TIME.[30] As time passed and public knowledge grew, people, especially journalists, sought the opinions of Anthony and me – we seemed to be at the spearhead of soundbites about clergy words and actions. Being quick to analyse Church announcements, Anthony would excel with his enlightening comebacks. The media seemed to go for neat, hard-hitting comments, and Anthony didn't waste words. We both saw our new public spokespeople role as critical to give the public understanding from a victim's or parent's point of view, given we knew how it felt to live such a horrendous experience. I was also aware that there were few people who *could* speak like this in the media glare. Often victims are unable to speak for themselves because of trauma and fear of public exposure. Being at the media coalface with Anthony was simultaneously uplifting and terrifying. I seemed to be better at writing than speaking, so that is where most of my effort went; in ten years I had fifteen opinion pieces published in major newspapers. There was something about placing words together to present the irrefutable truth. It also gave my soul some peace and solace in the whirlwind of hurt and chaos.

Our public role was a snowball compared to the avalanche of clergy sex abuse coverage in the national media, but I relished it, knowing that exposure and awareness were the antidote to secrecy. I had never dreamt that I would be a public figure. It was something I would shy away from, but the importance of the issue forced me to respond. Anthony and I were propelled by a force larger than us into the position to counter insidious crime. We knew how it had hurt people, our daughters. And it had to be exposed because nobody should suffer as we and others had – there was no choice but to fight it and that is what we did, two timid, ordinary people from the suburbs forced into a life beyond any nightmare. But we were good people who simply could not allow it to continue. So we acted. Sometimes speaking out against the richest and most powerful organisation in the world worried my mum, though our friends and family were always supportive and encouraging. Without that love and support it would have been a much harder road. The Catholic Church was enormous and we were nobodies. The imbalance was stifling. Nevertheless, we knew what we were doing was for the future good of children and therefore humanity.

In one week between 10 and 17 November 2012, I filled eighty-two pages of my scrapbook news collection on Catholic clergy child abuse. I was probably the only person in Australia collecting such information. I did it religiously. One day somebody asked me why I was preserving all the articles. I had to stop and think as I had been doing it blindly for years, then I realised that I was gathering proof, evidence of clergy crimes that the hierarchy downplayed and most people didn't believe. I found it a consoling task.

Headlines always shocked but never surprised me: CHURCH PAYS LEGAL COSTS OF PAEDOPHILE PRIESTS – REPEATEDLY;[31] ORDER [ST JOHN OF GOD] TRIED TO DISCREDIT VICTIM WITH FALSE CHARGES – CLAIMS.[32]

Another, even more intriguing investigation caught my eye. *The Age* and the *Sydney Morning Herald* were reporting on a body called Encompass Australasia, an Australian Catholic Church treatment centre for clergy offenders. I was shocked as I'd never heard of it – not even a whisper. I had only ever heard of St Luke Institute in Maryland and a second treatment facility called Servants of the Paraclete Center (which closed in 1994) in New Mexico, both in the USA, where Australian offending clergy were sent. Now, we were being informed that a similar place had existed here in Australia. And 'the Australian Catholic Church held thousands of pages of documents containing the psychosexual profiles of dozens of clergy'.[33] It was incredible news and showed the hierarchy had kept secret the extent of offending in this country while 'the profiles, often sent to bishops, were created as part of the Church's little-known 1997–2008 rehabilitation program' for those it described as 'sexual boundary violators'.

Unsurprisingly, it was found that 'none of the clergy treated under the multi-million-dollar Encompass Australasia program run from Wesley Private Hospital in Sydney was referred to police'.[34] There were claims senior church figures were aware of serious abuse allegations, even admissions, that led to clergy being sent for treatment, and their focus was resolutely on their own kind, not on the fate of the victims.

The establishment of this offender facility in Australia in 1997 was evidence of the size of the problem for the publicity-scared hierarchy. Despite public promises and assurances between 1997 and 2008 that they now had protocols and procedures in place to deal with their criminal element, they still did not protect young people by reporting clergy who sexually assaulted children. It showed they were still sorting it out themselves via in-house Church-sanctioned treatment and failing everyone in the process.

To my disappointment, I learned about the involvement of Bishop Geoffrey Robinson, who not only helped found the centre but 'led the Encompass Australasia board between 1997 and 2005'. In earlier media, I had seen Bishop Robinson portrayed as a priest supportive of victims.

Ironically, in that same week, Bishop Robinson had described George Pell as an 'embarrassment over his stance on child sexual abuse'.[35]

Then, when confronted about the treatment centre, Robinson went on to claim, as reported in the *Sydney Morning Herald*, that 'he was surprised to hear that any cleric accused of abuse had been relocated after treatment under the Encompass Australasia program'.[36]

Surprised? As head of the board of a treatment centre for paedophile priests and Brothers for eight years, and one of its creators, how or why did he not know where problematic clergy were going after treatment? He would have known if they were being laicised because it would have been Church news. He would have known if they were being handed over to the police because it would have been all over the media. There was none of that, so his centre must have been doing something else with offenders, something that didn't cause a ripple of bad publicity.

We soon found out. Instead of reporting offenders and their crimes, the hierarchy ensured criminals were 'quietly "transitioned" out of the Church, receiving generous payouts, accommodation and university education'.[37] One admitted offender was transferred to a job in 'Rome'. An unnamed insider said, 'Deals were cut [. . .] the whole operation was extremely confidential.' Meaning all of the offenders were free to reoffend.

By establishing the program, Bishop Robinson and others in authority presided over the 1 100 clergy and others who were treated at the sexual violators' facility. 'Dozens'[38] of clergy were treated for paedophilia, others for substance abuse and depression. Encompass Australasia produced a Church-favoured outcome that just happened to match other Church outcomes in relation to clergy child sexual assault both here and in other countries.

I first met Bishop Robinson at the launch of his book *Confronting Power and Sex in the Catholic Church*. The event was held in an Italian club on the other side of Melbourne from where I live. It was a huge gathering with a sit-down dinner. He made a speech. Afterwards, people like me could purchase a copy of his book, then have it signed. I was there because I had heard he was a decent clergyman on the side of victims, and he was a victim (of non-clergy abuse at sixteen years of age). So, I travelled the many kilometres to speak to him about my children and what they had suffered, hoping to add more fuel to his fire for understanding, empathy and action.

When it came to my turn to get my book signed, I mentioned that I had two daughters who had been sexually assaulted by our parish priest. Instead of starting a conversation, his demeanour hardened. The look in his eyes told me he didn't want to hear it. I looked at his resolute face and took the hint. No more words came from me. When I fell silent, he signed the book and said goodbye. I was devastated.

As I read news about Bishop Robinson being a leader in the Encompass Australasia program, I felt a better understanding of my first impression of him. With Encompass Australasia finally in the spotlight, other people found the strength to speak out.

Whistleblowers said the facility 'harboured known paedophiles and shielded them from police scrutiny'[39] and, astoundingly, they alleged 'paedophile clergy were diagnosed with a "mood disorder" to allow them to be treated at Sydney's Wesley Private Hospital by meeting private health insurance criteria'.[40] So not only was the hierarchy putting offenders back in circulation and protecting them from police investigation, the wealthy Church was misdiagnosing some of their paedophile priests and Brothers so they could cheat private health insurance companies, making others pay for the treatment of their dangerous men.

This situation reminded me of when I was dealing with Melbourne Response over Emma's medical bills. I believed the Church should pay for the damage it had caused (Fr O'Donnell should have been laicised in the 1940s when reports were first made of his sex crimes), and I was adamant the Church should foot the bill outright, not my private health cover nor Medicare. Taxpayers should never be made poorer by the Church's criminal activity.

I was being stubborn insisting they pay Emma's bills. Why should I save them money by using my private health cover? A year earlier, the Pastoral Response Office (the Church system before Melbourne

Response) had offered to pay my private cover premiums as a sweet-ener so I would comply with them. 'Isn't that illegal?' I asked.

So, months later, I objected to them again trying to use my private cover and Medicare and refused to make claims on months of Emma's psychiatrist, hospital and other medical bills. I sent the archdiocese the unpaid bills. Then-Vicar General Denis Hart wrote to me: 'They will be returned to you by Ms Sharkey [coordinator of Carelink, the 'care' component of Melbourne Response] for forwarding to HBA [my health insurance company]. If there is a gap between the HBA payment and the invoice, the invoice should be resubmitted to Carelink.'[41]

They were only prepared to pay the 'gap' if there was one!

Carelink was headed by Professor Richard Ball. It boasted coun-selling and professional support services for victims. According to a 1996 brochure, its services to victims were free of charge and staffed by a broad range of professionals.

When I received the pile of bills back, amounting to about $5 000, I posted them directly to Denis Hart with the message that I believed the Church should pay the bills for which they were responsible. The bills were posted back and forth three times.

Hart, as vicar general (akin to an archdiocese administra-tor), was trying to wear me down by returning the bills. Our home life with Emma was chaotic and heartbreaking, yet 'help' from the Church was truly a hindrance. Despite all this, I would not concede to paying those bills when it was their responsibility. Nine months passed and my guilt at not paying the providers became almost too much to carry around. Then, just when I was about to capitulate, I received a letter from Hart saying Carelink had paid all the bills and he now wanted me to claim on Medicare and then send the rebate money to Carelink.

This set-up was endorsed by an enclosed letter from the Health Insurance Commission, which just about made steam come out of my ears. Why was a government body supporting the Church like this? It was clear that the Church would only pay the gap.

'Complete the appropriate Medicare claim forms in respect of the invoices that Carelink has paid,' Hart wrote. 'When the Medicare rebate is received by you, it should be forwarded to Carelink.'[42]

Hell would freeze over first. That was in October 1997. They are still waiting for their 'rebate'.

It was a small win.

Bishop Robinson wasn't the only prominent clergyman on Encompass Australasia's board of directors. There was Archbishop Philip Wilson, who would become Archbishop of Adelaide in November 2000, and Father Brian Lucas, destined to be the general secretary of the Australian Catholic Bishops Conference. Both men would also be called to give evidence at the Royal Commission. I looked forward to that day.

Catholic Church Insurance (CCI), the Church's own insurance company, was also closely linked to Encompass Australasia.

A final word on this part of the Church's blueprint. A whistle-blower said publicly that a number of offending clergy 'did not have a mood disorder' but were 'cold and calculating criminals' who bragged about their exploits with children to others while at the hospital.[43] The person continued, 'Some of these people were not mentally ill, in my opinion. They were criminals who knew exactly what they had done and were proud of their achievements.' In conclusion, the whistle-blower said, 'People who should have been in Long Bay jail were still living in the community.' Another insider from the Encompass program added, 'One senior priest who received treatment was nick-named "Hannibal the Cannibal" because of the exuberant way he described his treatment of young boys.'[44]

# 8

During my years of campaigning for justice, I have realised there's a world of difference between silence and quietness. Silence, often imposed by others, comes with a weight that can crush you. Living without the ability to form words to tell your story is like being trapped under a bus. Quietness, on the other hand, is given as a gift and received as an honour. There is power in quietness, the kind that gives you the strength to fight on. In quietness the truth can be heard and understood, allowing change to be created.

I never felt amazing or impressive during these years of activism, and I still don't. It is difficult to contemplate that I failed to protect Emma and Katie as children from a paedophile, failed to save Emma and failed to avert Katie's accident. Thoughts like these are never far away. I stay on an even keel through acknowledging the truth. I endeavour and choose to keep going. Not letting the church win this battle was vital. So, try as we might, every breakthrough, every win was never enough. Each centimetre gained left kilometres still to go. I never lost sight of my insignificance in comparison to the powerful Church – we were forever striving, moving forward, trying to achieve progress. The fight was never-ending and I was willing to see it to the end. I guess that's what people saw in us: a single-mindedness.. We were saying what victims wanted to hear, needed to hear. Perhaps other parents who read about us or saw us on television wondered whether they would be like me if they were in my situation. Would they have the same healthy rage to pursue justice with a vengeance? I think they would. The goal, beyond holding the Church to account, was to warn other parents of the realities of paedophilia and how it can happen right under your nose (yet still remain invisible). I like to think of myself as intelligent and aware. I protected my little girls like a lioness yet fell into the paedophiles' trap – the *one* place I wasn't allowed to be with them is where I was deceived: the school. I didn't want other parents to suffer the same fate. My message was urgent, and children's lives depended on it, on me at least sending a message. I would articulate these beliefs to Anthony and he could only agree.

As for the Church, if some of their priests and Brothers think I am a monster, then I'm the monster they created.

Time came for the Victorian Parliamentary Inquiry to hear from victims and families. Anthony and I were invited to appear as witnesses. We decided Katie and Aimee should be with us at the evidence table.

It was the morning of Friday 23 November 2012. The room was packed with police, journalists, politicians and some people I didn't recognise. There was barely enough air in this cramped space for everyone to share. We sat in our seats, facing the members of the committee. I looked at them, knowing that we had brought our story to the right place.

Our family had never appeared in public like this before. I felt for Aimee and Katie. It was a battle Anthony and I had taken up; the girls agreed with our action but bringing them along to face the reality of such a public hearing was nerve-racking. I had spent hours putting together our submission evidence for the committee, as had Anthony, who had also considered the wider audience beyond the crowded room. It was an enormous responsibility accompanied by nail-biting, stomach-churning tension.

Committee chair Georgie Crozier gave us an introduction. 'Could you now all please ensure that your mobile phones are turned off while you are in the gallery,' she said. 'On behalf of the committee I welcome Mrs Chrissie Foster, Mr Anthony Foster, Ms Katie Foster and Ms Aimee Foster. Thank you for your willingness to appear before this hearing.'

Anthony was our spokesman on this very important occasion. 'Good morning,' he began. 'And thank you for the opportunity to present this oral submission, which is in addition to our written submission available on the committee's website. I am Anthony Foster. This is my wife, Chrissie, and our daughters Katie and Aimee. They survive Emma, who died nearly five years ago as a result of the trauma of her sexual assaults.

'We would like to thank all our supporters. Without the loving support of our friends and family over the past sixteen years we would not have been able to sustain our energy for justice all these years.'

Before Anthony went into details of our family's history, he spoke about the hierarchy. 'The late Archbishop Little's handling of paedophile priests was abominable and should be noted in any discussion about the Church hierarchy's cover-up.'

Then his voice softened. 'Our appearance before you today is, in a very personal sense, absolutely futile. We wish we did not have to be here, but we refuse to let the Catholic Church take any more children from us. Whatever we or you do will not restore Emma's life or heal Katie's injuries. But you can make a difference to the lives of thousands of other victims now and prevent the abuse of further children. What we are about to present to you is only a very small insight into the suffering our family has endured.

'We are the parents of three daughters, two of whom were raped repeatedly over years by our parish priest.'

In his stern-but-heartfelt way, Anthony told the hearing about the Church's knowledge of Father Kevin O'Donnell's sex crimes dating back to the 1940s. As evidence of Church inaction, he described a letter dated 31 October 1994, from a priest (Father A. P. Guelen, of St Mary's, Dandenong) to Monsignor Gerry Cudmore, Vicar General of the Archdiocese of Melbourne. In the letter, Fr Guelen admits to visiting a scoutmaster who had made a complaint against Fr O'Donnell in 1958. Guelen was the same priest who had been accused of once walking in on O'Donnell in bed with a child.

'Here are two glaring examples of crimes that should have been reported to the police and [got] O'Donnell removed from the ministry,' Anthony said. 'If they had been, Emma and Katie and scores of other victims would not have been assaulted by O'Donnell, and Emma would be alive today. It is that simple.'

He turned his attention to our engagement with the Church. 'We have attempted to positively engage with the Roman Catholic Church, right through from our local parish priest in 1996 to the Pope during his 2008 visit to Sydney for World Youth Day. In our interactions with the now Cardinal Archbishop Pell we experienced a sociopathic lack of empathy typifying the attitude and responses of the Church hierarchy.'

The 'sociopathic lack of empathy' description would be quoted in the media numerous times for years, but Anthony made another important point about George Pell, which related to our meeting with him in 1997. He told the hearing how we had shown the then archbishop two photographs of Emma: a picture of her receiving her confirmation certificate 'by none other than what was then Bishop George Pell himself', and a picture of her with cut and bleeding wrists. In an interview with *60 Minutes* in 2002, Pell had lied by saying he had not been shown the second photo.

I held this second photograph up for the committee to see. I did not show the public gallery. It was too awful. I always wondered why Pell had denied seeing the picture; it was shameful to us, because it amounted to an insinuation to the nation that we were liars.

I hoped the cardinal would be asked about it in his imminent appearance before the committee.

Anthony moved on to what he thought should happen now. 'This Victorian Inquiry still has a very important role to play, and indeed Victoria could lead the way for the rest of Australia by you recommending and the Parliament implementing the very necessary legislative changes to provide justice for past victims and protection for future children.'

He called for a truly independent review of Melbourne Response and a review of all its previous payments. And he called for a public education campaign to raise awareness of 'the danger, symptoms, causes and effects and the prevention of child sexual assaults'.

At the end of his submission, before taking questions from the committee members, Anthony surprised everyone in the room with this instruction: 'I would now like to observe a minute's silence for my daughter Emma.'

It was not a request.

The mood of the room changed, and I felt the deep love and sadness and grief and kindness of quietness. Emma was being honoured by an important gathering of dignitaries in a place built to take care of people, a special place where our politicians held the authority.

But there was more to this moment than a shifting of power. Quite simply, our eldest daughter was being remembered. Memories came of Emma as a very young child, an innocent, loving girl who displayed a deep empathy with others and who would tell me how she loved me, something she did right through all her traumas – she remained that loving and beautiful child. The loss of Emma was heartbreaking. Her presence and future had been stolen from us.

Aimee followed Anthony in addressing the committee. Her words, full of love, loss, meaning and emotion, brought so many tears to the Parliament and media that they made the evening news.

# 9

The work of the groundbreaking committee was gaining momentum, and its politician members were becoming experts in the topics of child sex abuse and cover-ups. That was critical. To become an expert on this issue is to understand, and never forget, the pain of victims who were abused by priests and abused all over again by the Church's systems.

Nevertheless, the Inquiry was emotionally draining. After almost seventeen years of fighting for justice, I was quite used to the feeling. Mostly it was frustration at the behaviour of the Church hierarchy. We would advance then be thwarted by their public comments, which worked to take away that advancement. The Church's representation of God gave the hierarchy a platform and authority from which to speak, something it had always possessed without being challenged. Victims had nothing.

When I felt myself succumbing to this energy-sapping despair, I turned to my secret weapon: my Oakleigh friends.

Most parents look for allies in the schoolyard in that first year of dropping off and picking up your little preppy. In 1987, when Emma started prep at Sacred Heart Primary School, I met other parents who would become lifelong friends. We bonded straightaway and created a parents' committee and worked together on various events, from Mother's Day stalls to schoolyard working bees. These occasions often ended with a barbecue bringing together parents and children to enjoy some relaxation. As time went on, we began dropping round to each other's houses for catch-ups, play dates, meals. One night we had a progressive dinner. Someone suggested we make it an annual get-together. Thirty-three years later, we're still doing it.

The company of my Oakleigh friends has been lifesaving. Cathie and Mick, Teresa and Gerard and others all live around the corner from us. Others were scattered throughout the neighbourhood. Most have stayed put in the same houses. We knew each other well and watched each other's children grow up. Emma's demise from 1995 was felt by all. Her abuse was an utter shock to us. It could have been any one of the kids.

Outrage gripped us all. Again, we formed a committee, this time not to work for the Church school but to work against an uncaring hierarchy. There was hell to pay.

We fought long and hard via meetings and a letter campaign to the hierarchy. Eventually, in February 1997, we achieved a visit by the newly appointed Melbourne archbishop, George Pell. Anthony and I saw him first in a private, disastrous meeting, in which we showed him the photos of Emma. Then forty-five parents met him for another disastrous meeting straight after. Without exception, every worried parent at that meeting left feeling defeated, trodden on and silenced by Pell.

When Katie was hit by a car in May 1999, our Oakleigh friends organised a roster and took turns to leave a meal on our doorstep for many weeks. We would spend all day at Katie's bedside in intensive care and then return home at night. The meals were of great comfort and told us we were in our friends' thoughts. We were loved.

During our worst times our Oakleigh friends, our family, my mum Dawn who lived the horror with us yet was a tower of strength, and other friends made our life easier through being with us and supporting us with their words, understanding and outrage at our circumstances.

*

Evidence of the Church's cover-up patterns was emerging so quickly it was hard to keep up.

A few days after we gave evidence to the Parliamentary Inquiry, we learned about Father David Paul Ryan. He was a sex offender priest who abused victims while he was receiving Church-sanctioned 'treatment' at Saint Luke Institute, Maryland, in the United States. Ryan went to the US seven times, once for fifteen months of so-called treatment. No matter his country of residence, he continued to assault children and the Church hierarchy continued to retain him as a priest, probably spending a small fortune on him. Ryan made his multiple across-the-world trips with the permission of his Australian Church bosses. Between periods overseas, he was shifted from parish to parish in Victoria. In 2006, he appeared in the Warrnambool Magistrates' Court charged with assaulting two altar boys. Survivors' advocacy group Broken Rites attended the hearing. 'It is impossible to estimate the number of boys who were targeted by Ryan in both Australia and the United States,' Broken Rites reported on its world-leading record-keeping website. Heartbreakingly, one of Ryan's Victorian victims, Peter, had died by 'suicide and was buried in an unmarked grave for six years before his body was identified'.[45] His distressed mother, Helen Watson, was looking for him all those years. Eventually, a diligent and caring police officer found her son. The Church covered up for Fr Ryan for many years but eventually he was jailed in Australia. (At the time of writing, he is facing legal action in the United States.)[46]

A week after Ryan's case was made public, the exposure continued. St John of God was involved this time, with the story coming from New Zealand. One of the order's clerics, Brother Bernard McGrath, claimed to a journalist that one of his superior brothers, Rodger Moloney, who was an Australian, had encouraged him to molest boys. Moloney had invited McGrath into his office at Marylands School for boys with learning disabilities in Christchurch. There in the office was 'some poor kid'. McGrath claimed he was asked to watch while Moloney – his scholastic master – assaulted the boy. Moloney then requested McGrath participate.[47] The following day we were to learn that the narrator of this terrible scene was himself a convicted paedophile 'wanted on more than 250 child sex charges'.[48] So, Br McGrath certainly did accept the invite to 'participate'. He didn't look back. Until he got caught by police.

Having given evidence, Anthony and I resumed our day-by-day place in the gallery of the Victorian Parliamentary Inquiry as it collected submissions, documents and answers to questions from committee members.

Our committee politicians quickly came to the fore in their questioning of victims and the Church hierarchy. Chair Liberal MP Georgie Crozier led the way. Labor's Frank McGuire MP was eager and persistent. Others followed and asked the questions that were bothering them. A new committee member had recently joined this cross-party group, Nationals MP and lawyer-by-trade David O'Brien, who knew a thing or two about questioning. Monsignors, bishops, archbishops and various other heads of religious orders had never been made to answer to civil authorities in this type of forum – on child rape or any other matter. It made for interesting viewing from the gallery. Often, Church leaders had no idea how aloof and pompous they sounded when the committee drilled down into their responses, while the politicians did themselves and their electorates proud.

Soon, the Inquiry was on the move. We headed to the beautiful but troubled town of Ballarat. The Ballarat hearing was a one-day affair from ten till four. Anthony and I drove the hour-and-a-half trip up to the Ballarat Mechanics' Institute on Sturt Street – just one majestic historic building in a street full of them.

In this genteel setting we heard about the destructive inaction of Catholic Church boss Ronald Mulkearns, Bishop of Ballarat from 1971 to 1997. The hearing was told that Mulkearns 'knowingly moved a paedophile priest around his diocese and overseas, where he constantly found new targets'.[49] Scandalously, Bishop Mulkearns was not unique in moving offenders around parishes after complaints.

Just before Christmas, the Catholic Church announced that Melbourne archbishop Denis Hart was going to set up a 'new commission'.[50] In fact, it wasn't going to be a 'commission' at all. It was to be a 'council'. But Hart, who was also president of the Australian Catholic Bishops Conference, was spruiking a 'new commission' anyway. Perhaps he was trying to upgrade his Church-run 'council' to compete with the Royal Commission. These word games irked me, although at least the newly appointed chairman of the Church group, Barry O'Keefe QC, called it a council.

The title of the initiative was the Truth, Justice and Healing Council. It sounded to me like a public relations measure. With Church leaders rapidly losing the confidence of parishioners, the Church's name and reputation were turning to mud and a facelift was needed.

Truth. Justice. Healing. The meanings of these honourable words were not to be associated with the Catholic Church hierarchy. The priesthood had provided no truth, no justice and no healing. The irony was galling. For me, there were many negatives about this 'council'. One of the statements made on its website read: 'The Council will approach its task with openness, courage and humility.' Anthony spoke out against the council; he called it 'a smokescreen'.[51]

When I read that the Church had put forward some parishioners to be on the council and its purpose was to act as a mouthpiece throughout the Royal Commission, I saw it as just another obstacle for victims, erected to protect the Church and its assets. My experience was the Church felt nothing for victims or children, hence the scandalous disaster it had created. As far as I could see, the Royal Commission – not a diehard faithful group appointed by clergy to speak for clergy – would provide the truth, justice and healing. Only eight months later we were to find out the council was 'controlled by bishops'.[52]

Nobody was surprised.

The extreme state of suffering among Ballarat survivors of clergy sex abuse was only rivalled by one other region of Australia: the Hunter Valley, another trauma hellscape in a lovely rural setting.

Anthony and I had made some shared-experience friends and acquaintances from the New South Wales region, but our bonds had not yet formed. That was about to change.

A day after the Truth, Justice and Healing Council announcement, we flew to Sydney for the book launch of *Holy Hell* by caring mother Patricia Feenan. Pat's son Daniel had been a fourteen-year-old altar boy when first sexually assaulted by their parish priest, Father James Patrick Fletcher, a name that made locals in the Newcastle-Maitland diocese shudder. Pat had bravely written of Daniel and her family's trauma over the years as tragic effects of the priest's sex crimes impacted on Daniel's young life and on the lives of his family and an entire community.

*Holy Hell* was launched in the New South Wales Parliament House on Friday 14 December 2012. It was here that Anthony and I met Detective Chief Inspector Peter Fox. Two months earlier, Greens MP David Shoebridge had introduced us to *Newcastle Herald* journalist Joanne McCarthy at his forum called 'The Need for a Royal Commission into Sexual Abuse' in Sydney.

It was an honour to meet these outstanding people – a leading policeman and groundbreaking journalist – who were calling for a royal commission. Joanne was a determined and friendly person. She was undoubtedly an authority on institutional cover-ups. Peter also cut a powerful figure: quietly spoken, friendly and a true gentleman. We admired him for his pursuit of truth – we all agreed that there had to be change. The doggedness of Peter and Joanne was obvious. They had staked their careers on it.

I felt a sense of relief in standing together. Sharing stories and comparing notes provided the comradeship I needed. We were in the company of like-minded people who went out of their way to protect children.

I felt certain Pat Feenan's book would be successful in reaching a significant audience because that is what had happened with *Hell on the Way to Heaven*. The issue of child sexual abuse is widespread, stretching beyond institutions and into homes around Australia and the world. People are seeking answers for a better way forward. Writing books is a good way to set the record straight. I was still signing my book many months after our 2010 launch. Some of the people I met at these sessions became friends, and some of them became allies.

One of the events I attended for my book was Writers at the Convent in February 2011 in the Melbourne suburb of Abbotsford. Paul Kennedy and I talked to a typically receptive and supportive audience and then sat down behind a table to sign books. We attracted a long line, and for about an hour signed books and spoke to people.

Towards the end a woman approached me. She was accompanied by her sister. Her name was Judy Courtin. Judy told me she was a lawyer but not yet practising as she was studying for her PhD. She was on her way to becoming a doctor of philosophy in law. Her intent was to represent clergy victims as people close to her had been affected by clergy sex crimes. Judy wore her passion and drive on her sleeve; her resolve is going to take her places, I thought to myself. We went on to become friends and stand together at protests on the steps of Parliament.

I had no doubt the Church was mustering all its forces (lawyers, money, political influence) for the fight of its life in Australia in the form of a royal commission, but so were we. It was us against them. One side was richer – the Church was backed by the Vatican, after all – but believe it or not, our coalition was more powerful. We had each other. We had the truth and now we had the commission.

# 10

The Royal Commission was going to take five years to complete its work. Anthony felt he needed to get away for a break before we started attending as many hearings as possible and he flew north to Darwin for a six-day wilderness fishing tour with his cousin-in-law Gary. He loved it. I smiled at the sight of him returning with a tan, his esky and spectacular photos of birds.

The day after Anthony came back to Melbourne, we attended the County Court in William Street for the history-making first sitting of the Child Abuse Royal Commission. It was the opening ceremony, 3 April 2013. At the courtroom entrance there was great excitement among attendees: many victim survivors, their families and supporters. We had all travelled a long and hard journey to arrive here. When it came time to enter, Anthony and I were the first to go in. Anthony told me to go before him. 'You can be the first person into the courtroom for our Royal Commission,' he said.

I smiled and walked ahead, uplifted by the moment. We sat in the centre of the front row; friends were beside us. When ten o'clock came, a chime sounded and the court assistant called us all to attention. 'Silence. All stand.'

We were to hear these words at every day's commencement, break, recommencement and ending at every public hearing we attended for the next five years. Anthony and I were happy to oblige and respected the court procedures. Now clergy crimes were to be under examination in the most powerful way. Even on the first day the courtroom felt like a sanctuary for victims. To be amid the protocols of the law's strict environment was empowering. Our confidence was monumental.

The County Court was the newest and most spacious building in the old legal precinct. I cast my eyes around the room to see how many people were with us. There were no empty seats.

Chief Royal Commissioner Peter McClellan, former judge of the New South Wales Court of Appeal, began by outlining the role of the Royal Commission: 'Although a painful process, if a community is to move forward, it must come to understand where wrongs have occurred and so far as possible, right those wrongs.'

Words of hope.

'It is already apparent from the work done by other inquiries and the cases which have been prosecuted in the courts that children have been sexually abused in a variety of institutions over many decades. The bearing of witness informs the public consciousness and prepares the community to take steps to prevent abuses from being repeated in the future.'[53]

Our long-awaited cries had been heard. We wanted to bring about justice, truth and a safer future for children. With Justice McClellan's words it felt like we were about to safeguard not only today's children but also the children of tomorrow.

Justice McClellan explained that the commission would hold private hearings before holding public hearings. He conceded the long process would be expensive. 'It seems likely that at least 5,000 people will want to talk to the Commission. The leaders of some of the groups representing survivors of abuse suggest that the number could, in fact, be much higher.'

Echoing in my mind at the opening ceremony was the quote from Prime Minister Julia Gillard about survivors, 'They have been heard and believed.' Her words were so important to me because of my history of being ignored and put down by the Church. From being cast as liars by the priesthood to having the PM of our country saying we had been 'heard and believed'. It was a new beginning. What we had been fighting for was here – salvation and retribution all rolled into one. It was time to rejoice. The opening ceremony alone felt like a triumph. The Australian Government and the commissioners had set the tone for the Royal Commission. I suspected the Commission's commitment would not diminish with the pressures of time.

Among our friends at the courtroom that day was John, who'd spoken at my book launch two-and-a-half years earlier. John had come a long way since bravely going to police with his statement about being repeatedly abused by Fr Kevin O'Donnell, from trying to hold the Church accountable through civil action, only to be met with legal intimidation and stonewalling. He had withstood the Church's meanness in order to be here today. He told me he was thinking about abused children all around Australia and how the power to take ownership of their stories would create a model for others around the world to demand justice in their own countries.

'The Commission welcomes the response from the Catholic Church,' Justice McClellan said, 'which has repeated on a number of occasions that it will fully cooperate with the Commission. We have had discussions with the chief executive of the Truth, Justice and Healing Council and we understand that the work of collecting and organising the documents held by the Catholic Church in its various manifestations has commenced. It is an enormous task.'

Documents. Previously sealed files? Secret archives? Our minds were going to hopeful places.

After Justice McClellan finished his address, the legal counsel assisting the commission, Gail Furness, took up the microphone. She outlined the Commission's procedures. It was her closing comments that made me emotional again: 'Your Honours and Commissioners, the next phase of the Commission's work will be to hear people's accounts and I anticipate that many of those will wish to do so in a private session. In conclusion, I repeat the invitation to everyone who wishes to tell of their experiences of child sexual abuse in an institution to contact the Royal Commission. Thank you.'

The eyes, ears and heart of our nation were finally open to children who had been left to suffer alone from nightmares inflicted upon them. On leaving the court I was wiping away tears that felt like the first drops of rain after a long and terrible drought.

# 11

The inquiries were now working back-to-back, if not side-by-side. Next day, Anthony and I resumed our regular places on the eastern side of the city, in Spring Street. The weather was turning, as it does every April around Anzac Day. Mornings became cold, with colourful sunrises fading to grey. Winter hid around the corner.

The Victorian Parliamentary Inquiry hearing was slowly climbing up the corporate ladder of Catholic clergy. After seven more hearings we came with heavy coats and umbrellas to hear from the bosses of St John of God Brothers and the Salesian Brothers, orders with multiple offenders and awful records of corruption.

This hearing was timely and topical. Two days earlier, a scandal had erupted over a Salesian priest, not just an ordinary priest but the Australian head of the second-biggest order in the world. Father Julian Fox had appeared at the Melbourne Magistrates' Court charged with three counts of buggery against a boy under the age of fourteen (among other charges). Fox had allegedly sexually assaulted multiple students in Melbourne schools over a ten-year period. Unsurprisingly, allegations had been made that the Salesians knowingly let Fox move to Rome after accusations were made against him to the Church.

I was familiar with the work of the Salesians. In 2004, the Australian chapter had been engulfed in global scandal after it was found local superiors had moved priests accused of sexual assaults across international and state borders.

With an offender like Fox at the head of the Salesian order, what could we expect to see anywhere he worked and presided? How could Fox, an offender himself, reprimand any one of his sex-offender underlings, protect children or see that justice be given to victims? Understanding what happens when an offender is in charge was reflected in his history.

He was one in a long list to offend at his school Rupertswood: Fr Michael Aulsebrook, Brother Gregory Coffey, Father Paul Evans, Father Frank Klep, Fr David Rapson, Brother Paul Van Ruth and Father Frank De Dood have all been convicted. An additional offender, Father John Ayres, also caused the Church to make a payout. That makes nine (that we know about). When Anthony learned of the Salesian offenders, he thought of a second Salesian Brothers College near our suburb of Oakleigh. Anthony was born in Oakleigh Hospital and had lived his whole life in Oakleigh. He thought back to when he was a boy in the Scouts. Not far from his home was the Don Bosco Boys Club building where his scout group met; it shared the same land, being at the back of the Salesian College in the suburb of Chadstone. Anthony loved his experience with the Boy Scouts. He was a member for many years, participating in activities and working his way up to becoming a prestigious Queen's Scout – the highest level a scout can achieve. This was in August 1969 when he was sixteen.

Being in the Scouts honed Anthony's talents as a boy and teenager and equipped him with lifelong skills, confidence, a love of the outdoors and good memories. He remembered one dark incident, though. When he was about ten, his scout group was going on a camp. Anthony was the senior scout and therefore should have led the camp with the Scoutmaster, but the Scoutmaster was a Salesian Brother. Instead of allowing Anthony to be camp leader, the Brother chose someone else – a young, quiet boy who did not have the skills to lead. Anthony did not understand why he was overlooked. It meant the other boy would sleep in the tent with the Salesian Scoutmaster.

Anthony was disappointed but didn't let it spoil his camp. However, the memory of it never faded. Now, with knowledge of paedophile priests and Brothers and how they manipulate, lie and deceive, he saw the situation differently. Anthony wondered whether the young, quiet boy was a victim of the Brother who manipulated the situation to gain time alone with him. They spent a whole night together alone.

And that's how it works, in plain sight, under everybody's noses.

Anthony considered it a lucky escape. But quite possibly he would not have been sexually assaulted by the Salesian Brother anyway for the simple reason that neither he nor his parents were Catholic. Having no Catholic religious brainwashing and no threats of hell from the age of five or earlier, Anthony was not in fear of the religious status of the Brother, nor was his family. As such, he posed a risk to any of the Salesian offenders. There was every possibility that Anthony would tell his parents if a sexual assault occurred, and his parents would believe their son. And they would ring the police: there would be no appealing to the offender's superior for justice – only the police. That would be a problem. My experience in researching paedophile clergy has taught me that longtime predators are always searching for a victim, not a problem. They need children who can be silenced – if not already frozen silent through shame, then through some form of threat. A child's silence leaves perpetrators free to reoffend. A child's disclosure can lead to prison.

The Salesian and St John of God leaders were questioned in the parliamentary hearing. St John of God admitted that one in four Brothers had been accused of abuse since the 1940s. Bishop Paul Bird, the current Bishop of Ballarat, was questioned in the afternoon, then Bishop Peter Connors, the previous Bishop of Ballarat, took the seat at the Inquiry table.

The testimony of the two Ballarat bishops was explosive and disgraceful. They admitted that the Ballarat Diocese had previously 'destroyed documents detailing accusations of paedophilia and moved offending priests to new parishes despite more than 100 cases of sexual abuse'.[54] In regard to one of Australia's worst paedophiles, Fr Gerald Ridsdale, stationed at Ballarat, Connors admitted 'the Church had effectively facilitated sexual offences against children by placing [. . .] Ridsdale in positions that enabled him to abuse'.[55]

Then Bishop Bird uttered words I will never forget. He stated that moving Ridsdale, the priest who raped children everywhere he went, was 'a tragic mistake'.[56]

Tragic mistake? No, it was *deliberate*. It was the international Catholic Church's trademark pattern of dealing with its offenders, their geographical solution. Tragic mistake! Only a Catholic clergyman could utter these despicable and misleading words. Claiming that deliberate actions were a 'tragic mistake' was a way of searching for cover from the bullets of criticism and compensation. For some measure of truth, we need to replace the word 'tragic' with 'despicable' and substitute 'mistake' for 'wilful criminal cover-up': a despicable, wilful criminal cover-up by clergy that led to more child sexual assaults. There was no mistake about it.

How they morally chose this deplorable path I do not know.

Thankfully the media was having none of the hierarchy's minimisation tactics at the Parliamentary Inquiry. News reports countered the bishops' weak excuses, noting the Church 'effectively facilitated' child sexual abuse. The Church was 'unChristlike'.[57]

Bishop Connors gave an unforgettable diversion from the truth. Referring to his predecessor Bishop Mulkearns, Connors said, 'He got bad advice and he very naively accepted that advice.'[58] Connors also said Mulkearns showed 'great naivety'.

Mulkearns was not naive. It was a ridiculous notion. He was a grown man, a bishop, a person in charge of a diocese for decades. He knew, like all of us, that raping or sexually assaulting a child was a crime, and that rape was a reportable offence to the police. Mulkearns 'was a canon lawyer with a doctorate in canon law; he was one of the founders of the Canon Law Society of Australia and New Zealand, and the first chairman of the Special Issues Committee set up by the Australian Catholic Bishops Conference'.[59]

A naive person would not have chaired the Special Issues Committee, which was created covertly to deal with its clergy child sex crime problems. To have been given such an important job, the Australian Catholic Bishops Conference could only have seen him as efficient in his handling of clergy sex crimes.

He knew exactly the significance of the crimes he was hearing about and how serious a charge they carried under Australian law. Why did he keep the rapes secret and not mention them publicly if there was nothing wrong with raping children? Because he knew, all along, that it was a wicked crime. Of course he did.

Bishop Mulkearns was moving offenders around, aiding and abetting them in further crimes for decades. It was proof of his obedience to Church rules, rules that the worldwide priesthood upholds for fear of excommunication if disobeyed. They all take oaths to obey canon law. Nothing to do with naivety.

And who gave Bishop Mulkearns the 'bad advice'? Fellow priests? Bishops? Archbishops? They don't obey non-clergy.

Perhaps it was the Pope, sitting up there in the Vatican.

# 12

We eagerly awaited the appearance of Cardinal George Pell, who was set to travel from Sydney for his grilling before the Victorian Parliamentary Inquiry. There were some questions I believed he would be unable to dodge. Unlike our disappointing meeting with him back in 1997, this would be a forum open to broad public scrutiny. It was only fair for it to happen this way.

Before Pell came to sit in the hot seat, others took their turn.

Unsurprisingly, after Bishop Bird's outrageous claim that Mulkearns made 'a tragic mistake', there was much disgruntled talk about the retired Mulkearns not giving evidence. Chair of the Parliamentary Inquiry Georgie Crozier asked why Mulkearns had not appeared before the committee. Bishop Bird said that Mulkearns' memory and focus had declined, and his 'best contribution was through the documents he had provided'.

Ms Crozier came out with a gem. She asked Bird whether the retired bishop was still regularly leading mass.[60] When Bird confirmed this was the case, Ms Crozier said the committee would require Mulkearns to come along and give evidence in person at a future date. Touché.

A lot of people in the gallery, including Anthony and me, were delighted at this requirement; we, Australia, needed to hear from Mulkearns. He had been given a free pass to conceal crimes since the early 1970s. We could all see through the Church hierarchy's attempt to prevent Mulkearns from testifying before the Inquiry with their attempts at evasion.

The greatly anticipated appearance 'at a future date' never happened. Church officials announced at a subsequent hearing that retired Bishop Mulkearns had been admitted to a nursing home. The public gallery groaned.

We would only need to wait another seven months to have our distrust in the hierarchy validated.

Next to front the Parliamentary Inquiry was Peter O'Callaghan QC, Independent Commission for Pell's Melbourne Response. It was 30 April. What stood out to me most in O'Callaghan's testimony that day was his statement, 'I must say, that having been here in this position for sixteen-odd years, I still have not worked out how paedophiles get gratification from fiddling with prepubescent children, and doing more than fiddling.'[61]

I will never know why O'Callaghan called the clergy sexual assault and rape of children 'fiddling'. As a man of law and therefore a master of legal language, surely this Queen's Counsel could use a more truthful word.

During his long period as Melbourne Response 'commissioner' O'Callaghan had listened to hundreds of people recount their heartbreaking stories of ruin. He had seen their tears and heard their pain. Yet he used 'fiddling' and 'more than fiddling' to describe their childhood sexual assaults. Fiddling means to play a tune on a fiddle, to fidget or to trifle, none of which comes close to describing the crimes at the centre of this Inquiry. Like his Church employer, in my view, O'Callaghan chose to minimise the crimes.

Taking the witness seat on the same day as O'Callaghan was Catholic Church Insurance's CEO Peter Rush. He brought information that was enlightening. Mr Rush said the Church hierarchy, knowing of the massive impending criminal liability problem that was coming, had taken out an insurance policy decades prior to protect assets against possible lawsuits – understanding the financial implications yet doing nothing to stem or stop the assaults. The insurer had paid out $30 million to 600 victims since 1990. Another revelation was that the Church insurer had an 'exclusion list' of priests they would not indemnify the Church against because they were known by the Church to be offenders. As an example, CCI had refused to cover any claims against Fr Ridsdale after 1975 because it had proof Mulkearns knew of the priest's 'propensity to offend'. The same prior knowledge test was applied to paedophile priest Michael Glennon.

This information landed close to home when the Inquiry heard CCI had not covered the Church's ($450,000) out-of-court settlement to our daughter Emma 'who took her own life in 2008'. Of course, the Church knew about Fr O'Donnell's sex crimes well before Emma was born, even before I was born.

Peter Rush then told everyone who was listening that paedophile priests were advised never to admit guilt as a way of limiting payouts to victims. 'Admit nothing,' the insurer advised.[62]

Three days later we were treated to the Christian Brothers telling us about their criminal members. They revealed that they had spent almost $1 million on the legal defence of convicted paedophile Br Robert Charles Best more than a decade after he was first convicted. Many of these offences would have taken place in Ballarat at their St Alipius Boys' School.

I sat in the gallery, listening to every word with astonishment, while Brother Brian Brandon from the Christian Brothers admitted his branch of the Catholic Church had spent $980,000 – 'including GST' – defending Best in 2010–11 when he was found guilty of abusing eleven young boys.

Brandon was the Executive Officer for Professional Standards when he shamelessly made the aside about GST. I wondered why his expression was anything but humble or ashamed. There was some audible contempt from the gallery at what they saw as flippancy. This witness oversaw a professional standards department of a highly touted religious order, yet his department tipped in close to a million dollars to assist one of the worst clergy offenders. I had to wonder why one particular paedophile was worth spending so much money on. Was he like another offender, Fr Searson, who, according to word-of-mouth by some of his parishioners, claimed to a non-clergy acquaintance about the hierarchy that 'they won't get rid of me because I know too much about them'?

Br Best was one of four Christian Brother offenders on staff at the same time at St Alipius Boys' School. Best, Ted Dowlan, Stephen Farrell and Gerald Fitzgerald were assaulting boys from Grades 3 to 6 – the only grades at the school. At that time, living in the presbytery next door was prolific paedophile Fr Gerald Ridsdale, the school chaplain.

A young Father George Pell also lived in the presbytery for one year during Ridsdale's residence. Cardinal Pell had since stated publicly that he never knew about Ridsdale's crimes in Ballarat (yet the Royal Commission's findings would later make it clear he knew more about Ridsdale's actions than he was prepared to admit[63]). In 1993, when Ridsdale was first charged with offences, it was Bishop Pell who walked by his side into the courtroom as a show of 'priestly solidarity'.[64] Pell reckoned he did not know the 'gravity' of the thirty indecent assault charges against Ridsdale.

Any child sex assault charge is grave.

Brother Julian McDonald, Deputy Province Leader of the Christian Brothers, took the witness seat. Br McDonald also riled listeners when he testified that the prolific abuse at St Alipius was 'certainly an accident of history'.[65] People in the gallery scoffed loudly.

The St Alipius Church–created catastrophe reminded me of Doveton in outer-suburban Melbourne, a working-class area with a large migrant population and Housing Commission homes. From the early 1960s, the parish of Doveton and Holy Family Primary School had five paedophile priests or assistant priests in a row. Doveton catered to many different languages and cultures and appeared to be a dumping ground for priests with complaints piling up against them. Perhaps the archdiocese bosses thought it best to hide their criminals in an impoverished area, assuming their offenders in collars would be absorbed into the residents' pre-existing problems.

Fr Searson was the fifth offender to arrive at Doveton. His history showed he was a gun-toting, army-fatigues-wearing, bird-stabbing, cat-killing, children's-toilets-loitering thief of $40,000 in school funds, with two parishes accusing him of sexually assaulting children. He was definitely out of control and needed hiding.

At his previous parish, Sunbury (the same suburb where Rupertswood Salesian College had at least nine offending Brother teachers), on the other side of Melbourne, local police had interviewed Searson in 1982 regarding one victim, but the parents did not want to press charges.[66] There were complaints from teachers and parents regarding Searson's sexual behaviour towards children, especially in the confessional. His conduct had been a problem to the extent that the Sunbury teachers made a rule: Fr Searson had to leave the confessional door open while children were in there with him. It was a demand that went against convention. Teachers would later pass their open-door advice to Fr Searson's next parish, Doveton.

Soon after Sunbury police interviewed Searson, he was gone, transferred to Doveton as parish priest. Out of sight, out of mind.

Only bishops or archbishops have the authority to make a relocation occur, often in consultation with the local curia or college of consultors. For religious orders it is the provincial head who can transfer members. In Searson's case it was Archbishop Little who arranged his transfer after the police showed up in Sunbury to question Searson about paedophilia complaints. Church procedure is to be followed for a priest's transfer, and that procedure took place with every paedophile priest who landed in Doveton – and every other parish in Australia.

Evidence at the Inquiry showed that Searson confidently quashed opposition to his disturbing behaviour by intimidating children, parents and any teacher or school principal who expressed concerns about him. Doveton school principal Graeme Sleeman lost his job after two years of trying to protect his pupils and complaining to the hierarchy about Searson – even a 1986 petition from sixty parents asking for Searson's removal fell on the deaf ears of then Vicar General

Bishop Hilton Deakin. Instead of siding with the principal, the hierarchy supported the predatory priest and Sleeman never worked in the Catholic education system again. The same fate befell a female teacher at Doveton, whose efforts to protect children saw her out of a teaching career.

Fr Searson's removal from active service in the priesthood came about through a surprising source: a ten-year-old child. An altar boy from Doveton complained that the priest had hit him. The priest said it didn't happen. Outraged at the priest's lie, the brave boy and his family pushed the matter all the way to criminal court, eventually securing a physical assault conviction. Finally, Fr Searson was gone. In typical fashion, the Church hierarchy had done nothing to take the dangerous priest away from children: it had been left to a young boy.

Searson's case is telling. Although prevented from publicly exercising his priesthood, he was not laicised. It was as though the hierarchy was afraid of him and of laicising him. Instead, it used the physical assault conviction to keep him out of Church activities – as per 'archdiocesan policy'.[67]

I would go on to discover fascinating information on an 'archdiocesan policy' in one of the 1.2 million documents acquired by the Royal Commission. It was the minutes of a Melbourne curia meeting on 8 January 1992. Under the heading 'Other Appointments', item number 22 related to Father Vincent Kiss, who had been charged with stealing $1.8 million. His friend Father E. Smith, perhaps trying to secure a new parish interstate for his thief colleague, was putting forward a job proposal:

22. REV. V. KISS: The Archbishop [Little] tabled a request from the Bishop of Wagga Wagga, which letter is a response to a proposal from Fr E. Smith of West St Kilda. The Bishop seeks the consideration of the Archbishop to the proposal concerning Fr V. Kiss of the Wagga Wagga Diocese. The Board advised and supported the Archbishop on the *policy prevailing* [my emphasis]

in the Archdiocese that a priest upon being charged with criminal offences, withdraw from the public exercise of his priesthood.[68]

I couldn't stop wondering whether this *prevailing policy* was part of the reason the archbishops and bishops protected paedophile priests from being reported to police. It made sense. If a priest was reported to police and was 'charged with criminal offences' he – all of them – would have to 'withdraw from the public exercise of their priesthood' according to the archdiocese's own prevailing policy. The hierarchy, on top of the shame of scandal, would bear the stress of being stuck with numerous paedophile priests who could not work.

Thankfully for the children at Doveton and the rest of Melbourne, Fr Searson was not seen again. The Church looked after him. When he died ten years later in June 2009, fifteen priests, including the then Vicar General of Melbourne, the Most Reverend Les Tomlinson, second to Archbishop Denis Hart, presided over the disgraced Searson's funeral at Sacred Heart Church, Carlton. It was a fine send-off for one of their own.

The damning evidence we heard from the heads of religious congregations at the Victorian Parliament caused stir after stir, but we were aware of another inquiry starting up in New South Wales. It was the Cunneen Inquiry, a special commission set up to investigate claims made by DCI Peter Fox. All I saw in Victoria were headlines: 'Police "mafia" hid church sex abuse'[69] and 'Police colluded with priests, says detective'.[70] Bombshell evidence accused New South Wales police of having a contingent of organised Catholic officers who 'colluded with church leaders to cover up sex abuse in the Maitland-Newcastle diocese'.[71]

I was constantly on the lookout for collusion or obfuscation in the Church's handling of the mess it created. Sometimes I came across seemingly small examples. Anthony was told that the Catholic hierarchy was delivering boxes of documents needed for Church-related hearings of the Parliamentary Inquiry at 5 pm on Friday afternoons. This left staff and committee members only the weekend to read copious amounts of files for the Monday morning start. When Church leaders publicly stated they would cooperate with the Parliamentary Inquiry, behind closed doors, this was the degree of cooperation they afforded. We weren't surprised.

By May 2013 the Victorian Parliamentary Inquiry had reached the top of the corporate ladder of the Catholic Church in Victoria. Archbishop Denis Hart appeared that day. Archbishop Hart admitted that the Church covered up child sexual abuse, was slow to act against abusing priests and placed its own interests ahead of victims. It was good to hear this admission at long last. He said the 'sexual abuse scandal' was one of the darkest periods in the Church's history. He conceded victims had committed suicide. Recognition of lives lost was also an admission that had to be made. Archbishop Hart then stated: 'The question of confidentiality of these matters was probably kept in one sense too much in that the Church was too keen to look after herself and her good name and not keen enough to address the terrible anguish of the victims.'[72]

I took great offence at this leading clergyman referring to the Church as a female. There is nothing feminine about the priesthood or the brotherhoods. They work very hard to keep females out of the clergy. It was the all-male clergy who carried out the crimes against children and then the all-male clergy who orchestrated the cover-ups and the all-male clergy who still fight victims in court over any form of justice and do their utmost to minimise compensation. Yet when it comes to laying blame, then, and only then, do they seek to feminise the Church by using the words 'herself' and 'her'. I considered their misogynistic attitude as seeking to blame the feminine as vain ('too keen to look after herself') and selfish (protecting 'her good name') for the crimes and cover-up of the sexually dysfunctional men of the priesthood.

Keep the *she* out of it.

Next, Archbishop Hart told the Inquiry that former archbishop Sir Frank Little covered up abuse reports by keeping 'all these things to himself and there were no records'. Pressed by the committee on whether there had been a cover-up, Archbishop Hart said he would have to agree with that.

It has been a pattern of the Church, when cornered by evidence, to blame the dead guy who is unable to speak for himself or explain his actions. With no proper explanation or confession, the blame stays hidden by the past.

During his gruelling three-hour testimony, Archbishop Hart was asked about the laicisation of paedophile priest Father Desmond Gannon. The Church had waited until 2011 to petition Rome for the laicisation of Gannon, who had committed offences between 1957 and 1979. Hart agreed his organisation had been slow to defrock the criminal. It seemed typical that it only thought to act when the scandalous delay was about to be made public.

'It took eighteen years for you to contact Rome?' Georgie Crozier asked.

Archbishop Hart replied, smirking, that it was 'better late than never'.

The gallery gasped at his attitude.

Bishops and heads of religious orders must have had a meeting to decide it would be a positive public relations exercise to read out a general apology before each of them gave their evidence at the Inquiry. It only took a couple of such apologies before the committee members wisely decided to disallow the apologetic words until after their evidence – after their questioning, after the examination, after getting to the truth. Still the hierarchy tried to read their apology speeches first, even when told not to. Perhaps they wanted to soften up the crowd by getting in first with their remorseful words or to make a good initial impression. I could only wonder. These apologies were not 'better late than never'. They were self-serving pieces of dramatic showmanship. I saw very little sorrow or genuine regret in them. Instead, I witnessed shallowness, ruthlessness. In the gallery of onlookers, we scoffed with bitter feelings at the false repentance.

After Archbishop Hart's testimony but before his syrupy apology speech, about ten of us stood up and made our way to the exit, interrupting the proceedings. We filed out of the room in protest, not wanting to hear his final, empty words.

# 13

Cardinal George Pell, Archbishop of Sydney, was next to give evidence to the Parliamentary Inquiry. Pell was an almighty figure in the Church, and he was well known to outsiders. We had our own history with the ultimate company man. Sixteen years after our first meeting with him, here he was and here we were. I was intrigued as to what he would say.

Among others, there was one line of questioning I was eager to hear, a potentially significant moment for Anthony and me. It had been a decade since the *60 Minutes* episode in which journalist Richard Carleton interviewed the Archbishop of Sydney about his response to the photo of Emma with cut wrists (the one we had shown him in 1997).

'I don't believe I've seen that,' Pell said. 'I have no recollection of that. I mean it's an awful . . . I don't believe I ever saw that.'

In uttering these words, the churchman painted us as liars.

Hundreds of thousands, if not millions, of viewers tuned into *60 Minutes* in those days; it was must-watch TV. Ratings were boosted for that particular episode because Pell had enquired two days earlier, on the Friday, about getting an injunction to stop it going to air on the Sunday. On the Saturday morning his enquiry to stop the show made the front page of the *Herald Sun*. Nothing shoots ratings through the roof like controversy.

Anthony and I had been interviewed for the program, but we were in disguise. We didn't want to go public with our identities because we were still trying to protect our daughters from any further fallout. Almost eleven years had passed. Now in 2013, at the Inquiry, all that was about to change.

Although he resided in the Harbour City, it was his experience in Victoria that made him a witness. As ex-Archbishop of Melbourne, his appearance would be the climax of the Victorian Parliamentary Inquiry (of the Catholic Church evidence, at least; the Inquiry did cover other institutions and we watched each day, every part of it with intense interest). Cardinal Pell had presided over Melbourne for five years between 1996 and 2001. He had also served as an auxiliary bishop in suburban Mentone for nine years from 1987 until 1996. He was a hardnosed sentinel. Up until now, the evidence of the hierarchy had been a letdown. Seeing them under pressure and being held responsible should have been pivotal moments, but I had been greatly disappointed. By the end of the sessions I usually had a headache.

On the day of Cardinal Pell's arrival, the parliamentary foyer was packed. A throng of people waited in the hope they could get a seat in the gallery. Those who did not make it in would be diverted into the overflow chamber to watch the proceedings via video link.

Anthony and I were waiting in the crowd. As we and everybody else stood patiently, I became aware of a man who was pushing past victims and their supporters, slowly making his way forward from the back to the front with an embarrassed-looking friend in tow.

The man carving his own path was a priest. When he drew level with me, I told him to stop pushing in. I said other people who had been waiting were just as important as him. I pointed out that we all had to wait. He did not appreciate my words, nor did he heed them. He wanted to support George Pell in the hearing room. The priest and his mate continued to pressure their way past those waiting. Everyone patiently tolerated his rudeness. In the end, he arrived at the very front of the crowd. Unfortunately for him he didn't make it inside as the room was already full. At that moment, a staff member came and signalled for Anthony and me to come forward past the barrier, past the priest.

There were two to three hundred people gathered in both the committee hearing room and the overflow room to witness the cardinal's evidence. 'On behalf of the committee I welcome Your Eminence Cardinal George Pell from the Catholic Archdiocese of Sydney and former Archbishop of Melbourne,' committee chair Georgie Crozier said. 'We have a large number of people interested in today's proceedings, and I welcome all of you.'

Pell had arrived with an entourage. They all sat down. While he was dressed in his usual black suit and white collar, the others looked as though they had just blown in from a country walk or off a farm. Ms Crozier asked the Cardinal to identify his supporters.

'Certainly,' he said. 'They are Danny Casey, the business manager from Sydney; Katrina Lee, in charge of our media; Jennifer Cook, the in-house lawyer for the archdiocese, a part-time position; and Michael Casey, my secretary. All of them are married people with children, keen to help us in the fight against this problem.'

The 'married people with children' part of his answer was a strange and unnecessary thing to say. The public gallery stirred with annoyance, exchanging looks. Did the hierarchy see married people as freaks but out of the goodness of their hearts employed them anyway? Or did he want us to think the Church's decision-making was informed by men and women who were married? In fact, it was tightly controlled by unmarried clergy.

Members of the committee wanted to ask questions of the cardinal immediately, although he wanted to make a statement. There was an exchange that revealed some tension between the cardinal and the politicians. Crozier asked Pell whether he agreed that most people saw him as the face of the Catholic Church in Australia.

'Thank you for the question,' Cardinal Pell said. 'I am happy to respond to it. I would like to say that I asked to make a brief opening statement of two or three minutes. That was denied to me, although I gather it had been extended to others.'

'Cardinal Pell, I will just stop you there,' Ms Crozier said. 'Yes, I did get that request. We have heard from many people, and it is true that victims, experts and other witnesses we have had before us have made a statement to us, but anyone who has dealt directly with children, including organisations, has made their statement at the end. So this is in terms of consistency. You will have an opportunity to make a statement at the end of the hearing.'

'My point is that if it is part of a consistent policy, I fully accept it,' Pell said. 'I would just like to say that I am happy to accept the invitation of the premier to say that I am fully apologetic and absolutely sorry, and that is the basis for everything that I will say now.'

'Thank you for that,' Ms Crozier said. 'Could I return you to my question in relation to your position within the Catholic Church and how you are perceived?'

I was so pleased that Ms Crozier did not give into Pell's persistence to get his apology in first and, in doing so, take control of the proceedings.

His answer attempted to diminish the perception of his power within the Church.

'I am not the Catholic prime minister of Australia,' he said. 'I am not the general manager of Australia. The Catholic Church is – and I will come back to this perhaps later – a very interesting example of a flat organisation. The bishops are answerable to the Pope via the congregations in Rome.'

Cardinal Pell was asked to give his opinion on a range of issues. He answers were predictably defensive.

'Why do you think there have been so many instances of abuse within the Catholic Church?' Ms Crozier asked.

In his response, Pell referred to media coverage of Catholic Church abuse as 'twenty-five years of intermittent hostility from the press'.

Ms Crozier asked why Cardinal Pell had infamously supported the sex offender Fr Ridsdale by walking into court with him in 1993.

'I knew there was a very significant number of offences,' Cardinal Pell said. 'I did not know the details of those offences. I knew that

Ridsdale was pleading guilty. His lawyer asked me to appear in court before him. I discussed this. I asked Archbishop Little and the curia about this, and they said it would be appropriate to do it. It would have been better if I had other advice, but I was the one who made the decision.'

Next to take up the questioning was committee member Frank McGuire.

'Do you agree that these heinous crimes blighted lives and led to suicides?' the politician asked.

Cardinal Pell: 'There is no doubt about it that lives have been blighted. There is no doubt about it that these crimes have contributed to too many suicides, and that is an ultimate tragedy.'

Mr McGuire asked Pell about our photograph of Emma. I felt great anticipation when this topic came up and hoped that the truth would be revealed.

'When Chrissie and Anthony Foster showed you a photograph after their daughter Emma had slashed her wrists, did you respond, and again I quote, "Mmm, she's changed, hasn't she?"'

'Probably,' Cardinal Pell said. 'But let us put this in context. We now know that was an attempted suicide. When you just look at a photo suddenly in front of you, how do you recognise just from the photo that this was an attempted suicide? When you say, "Well, there is blood on the arms" — sure. But you have got to understand that production of this photo was something sudden and I did not have a chance for a considered response. I fully understood the enormity of the suffering.'

And there it was. An admission that he had lied on *60 Minutes*.

Suddenly, eleven years later, Pell admitted he had seen the photo and – judging by his reply – remembered it very well. Yet, still now, there was no apology from the cardinal for making us look like liars for more than a decade. Instead, he preferred to speculate as to whether or not it was a suicide attempt. Cardinal Pell's response was a diversion to avoid answering for his inadequate response in 1997 when he hadn't needed a 'considered response'; we were showing him the effects of the abuse. Pell said he 'fully understood the enormity of the suffering'. I doubted that. I still don't think he understood anything about victims or their families.

Just before Pell finished his evidence, Anthony stood up and left as he had a live-cross interview booked on the front steps of Parliament. The cardinal's questioning had overrun because the committee was keen to continue. I stayed inside while Anthony quietly departed, but I later saw a replay of his interview on the news. According to Anthony it was the best interview he had ever done. The footage, shot in the gathering darkness of early evening, showed him walking down the fifty or so stairs from the lofty entrance of our Parliament House. Against a lingering twilight, Anthony had a beautiful backdrop of gas-lit street lamps surrounding the old building and its cascade of bluestone steps. With a smile and the power of truth and enlightenment on his side, he walked straight up to the camera and the waiting journalist. Anthony had a lot to say about what he had just witnessed in Parliament House.

Among other emotions, he was relieved that we no longer needed to live with Cardinal Pell's lie on our minds.

What's more, the Inquiry was winding down. Any doubt about the dedication of the parliamentary committee to seek out the truth of what happened to young children in churches and other organisations had evaporated over the months of hearings. The Inquiry had provided an education to the people of our state and beyond. We knew more now than ever before about the workings and attitudes of the priesthood. The Inquiry had dramatically dismantled the Church's status and mystique to reveal some heartless men who cared nothing for children, preferring to protect with corporate coldness their brand and membership like a ruthless group of thugs. Their aim was to retain their money, assets, power and control.

Cardinal Pell's four-hour hearing was reported in every media outlet the following day. I gathered all the newspapers and scoured the articles. One headline said the cardinal had admitted the Catholic Church had put paedophile priests above the law, covered up abuse and moved abusers. Other issues of focus were the Church having changed the date on a document making serial abuser Des Gannon a pastor emeritus, and paid almost $200,000 to another paedophile, Father Ron Pickering, who fled Australia to avoid police.

Committee member David O'Brien had questioned the cardinal about Father Gannon.

Mr O'Brien: 'It's utterly reprehensible, isn't it?'

Pell: 'It is.'

Mr O'Brien: 'It's un-Christlike.'[73]

Pell: 'I would have to agree.'

On Fr Pickering, Pell said under oath that he had been obliged to continue to pay the priest's stipend even after knowing he had fled the country to avoid being arrested over child sexual assault charges. Yet a week earlier, Archbishop Denis Hart had given sworn testimony that as soon as he became archbishop, he immediately stopped the payments to Pickering because he had left the country owing to abuse accusations.

If George Pell was obliged to pay Fr Pickering, why wasn't Hart?[74]

One of many news reports I added to my private archive said victims had a victory in the hearing when the cardinal said he would ask the Vatican to send all documents it held pertaining to Victorian sex abuse accusations. The 'victory for victims'[75] never eventuated because the files containing 'documents' on 'Victorian sex abuse accusations' of clergy never turned up for the Parliamentary Inquiry. Sending the files to the Vatican in the first place was the perfect cover-up. Once there, no-one could get their hands on the evidence within these files. Ever.[76]

In giving his evidence to the hearing, Cardinal Pell had ignited outrage and, if possible, more scrutiny from the press. Attention was drawn to Church indulgences, like Domus Australia, a building bought, restored and converted into hotel accommodation in Rome by George Pell. Thirty million dollars of Church money was spent while abuse victims were being offered pitifully low compensation payouts. Georgie Crozier said Domus Australia 'should be sold to fund compensation to abuse victims'.[77]

During the previous week, Pell's written submission to the Parliamentary Inquiry had been released to the public. In it he attempted to put a different slant on history that I felt needed countering. Unable to let it pass without comment, I wrote an opinion piece that was published in *The Age* on 6 June 2013. I wrote about bearing personal witness to experiences with both Archbishop Hart and Cardinal Pell that contradicted their limited vision of events. Nagging at me was my memory of our first meeting with Pell all those years earlier. In his submission, he stated, 'Although he [Fr O'Donnell] brought shame upon the priesthood and the Church he was buried with other priests in Melbourne. Had he been laicised before he died this would not have occurred.'

Seemingly the cardinal was lamenting that the career child rapist was not laicised before he died, so, sadly, a criminal priest was 'buried with other priests'. This sounded like a noble and reasonable lament for a pious and forthright cardinal.

Yet on 18 February 1997, I had sat alongside forty-four other distressed parents when we met with then Archbishop George Pell in Oakleigh. At this meeting we asked him that the imprisoned Father O'Donnell be laicised. Pell smiled condescendingly and said, 'We can't do that.' This time we were talking to the boss, so we persisted. We told Pell that his own canon law said it was possible. He replied that canon law was hard to interpret. We produced a copy of the 1 152-page book of canon law, reading aloud canon 1395.2. It clearly stated a priest could be laicised for the sexual abuse of a minor. Taken aback by the evidence of the book and its clear language, the archbishop back-pedalled by saying he would have to get back to us about it. He never did. Later that meeting we again asked for O'Donnell be laicised. Again, we were denied.

So, despite his 2013 public show of disappointment that O'Donnell was not laicised before he died, it was in fact George Pell, as Archbishop of Melbourne sixteen years earlier, who had refused to laicise O'Donnell. Pell had had from July 1996 until O'Donnell's death in March 1997 to laicise the imprisoned criminal 'before he died'. By this stage of his career, Pell had served seven years on the Church's specialist body, Congregation for the Doctrine of Faith, which laicises priests.

My focus then turned to Archbishop Hart's oral evidence to the Parliamentary Inquiry. He had stated that when victims decided not to accept the church offer of compensation, it had 'walked with them' through the court system to 'more generous payouts'. Later he had stated that 'no victim had made it to court'. So how could the Church have possibly walked with victims through the court system when it never happened? In addition to this, Anthony and I had personally sued Archbishop Hart (as then leader of the Melbourne Archdiocese) in our attempt to reach court. Denis Hart never contacted us. He did, however, send us a message. Instead of acting out his words of apparent compassion in 'walking with victims', he set his lawyers on us for years, engaging, directing and paying them to strenuously defend the Church to the point of refusing to admit Fr O'Donnell's guilt – even after the Church's 'independent commissioner' Peter O'Callaghan had found sexual abuse had taken place with both Emma and Katie. Astoundingly, their defence negated Archbishop Pell's earlier written apology to Emma.

I wrote in my opinion piece: 'Also Archbishop Hart, if you and the Church hierarchy are happy to "walk with victims" to achieve "higher payouts" as you say, why not simply remove the cap you hold in place to control and minimise payouts?'

Anthony wisely summed up the evidence of the Brothers, priests, bishops and archbishop we had listened to over the previous month: 'They are hollow men with hollow words.' I couldn't have agreed more.

# 14

I have cried an ocean of tears.

First there were tears of joy for the establishment of the Inquiry. Then there were tears at the heartbreaking stories we heard. Many a time I would sit in a hearing fighting back tears, trying not to cry at the depth of the witness's pain, the physical torture and soul destruction of the criminal acts. And now we would be back to tears of joy at the end of our Inquiry with the tabling of the committee's report. There was relief. It would be a proud day. The report's pages, we believed, would chart a path forward for victims, children in the future and our State of Victoria.

The tabling of the final report of the Inquiry into the Handling of Child Abuse by Religious and Other Non-Government Organisations took place on Wednesday 13 November 2013. Days before, the press had given us a taste of what we could expect. Recommendations were likely to include proposed legislation for mandatory child abuse reporting requirements for priests.

Those of us who had attended the hearings knew exactly why that change of law, among others, was needed. It felt good that our Parliament would agree and speak for us, make findings in favour of victims.

Anthony and I travelled into the city. Hundreds of us, from all walks of life, filed into Parliament House. After clearing security, we were ushered past Queen's Hall (where our book presentation had been two-and-a-half years earlier and Ann Barker promised to champion further investigations). All the dominoes had fallen, and we were now about to witness the presentation of the Inquiry's final report, *Betrayal of Trust*, to Parliament.

We were led upstairs to the elevated public gallery of the Upper House. Entering the beautiful chamber was like stepping back in time. For 157 years it had been a meeting place for decisions relevant to the population. Today was no different. It was a long-anticipated day, one that I hoped would change our lives and the future for children.

So many of us had put our hearts and souls into speaking publicly. None of us who gathered there wanted to see history repeated. The members of the Family and Community Development Committee had been amazing. As the months passed, and more details of abuse emerged, the committee appeared to upgrade its Inquiry presence. A retired judge, the highly respected Frank Vincent, began sitting in on the hearings as a legal adviser, and a new Victoria Police task force – SANO – emerged. It was SANO's job to look at criminal revelations during hearings and ascertain if prosecutions could be pursued. I was proud that our government was behind the Inquiry. We witnessed SANO build, asserting its authority and bringing previously untouchable men to account. These facts were not missed by victim survivors. I'm sure the process was also understood by those in powerful positions in the Catholic priesthood.

Anthony and I stood to one side of the chamber, looking down on our politicians gathered below. Never had victims been listened to by politicians with such intensity. Chair of the Parliamentary Committee Georgie Crozier stood and addressed the chamber. She said the Inquiry had referred 135 previously unreported claims of child sex abuse to the police.[78] She also accused Church leaders of trivialising the problem as a 'short-term embarrassment'.[79] Paramount too was the reference to the State Government recommending sweeping changes to laws behind which the Catholic Church had sheltered. They were thunderclap words. It was exactly what we wanted to hear.

The Church hierarchy had got away with too much. They had got away with raping our children.

Each committee member spoke in turn, and most of them cried. The enormity of children's suffering had affected them greatly. Ms Crozier had previously worked as a nurse and midwife; 'she had coped with cases of rape and incest. But nothing could have prepared her for the sheer horror or scale of what happened to thousands of young Victorians in orphanages, schools and church settings over decades.'[80]

David O'Brien delivered an unforgettable speech. As a Nationals MP, Mr O'Brien represented people from country Victoria where much abuse had taken place. Slowly and deliberately, he read out every town in his constituency that had been blighted by paedophile priests and Brothers assaulting innocent country kids.

'Apollo Bay,' he said, 'Ararat, Ballarat, Bannockburn, Camperdown, Colac, Edenhope, Geelong, Inglewood, Hamilton, Horsham, Kyneton, Maryborough, Mildura.'

They were all towns we knew. Towns we had visited, driven through or holidayed in.

'Mortlake, Ouyen, Penshurst, Portland, Port Fairy.'

Towns where the remorseless paedophile Fr Gerald Ridsdale and many other paedophile priests and Brothers had been sent by Ballarat cover-up merchant Bishop Mulkearns, causing a twenty-six-year trail of destruction to generations of children in each town.

'Sea Lake, Swan Hill, Tatyoon, Terang, Warrnambool, Wendouree, Werribee and Winchelsea.'

The ripples of these crimes will last centuries. I was reduced to tears at the summary of hurt at the hands of clergy, not just Catholic clergy but clergy from other religious organisations.

I thought of our family's overwhelming losses, so many irreversible losses, and thousands of other similar families around Australia. I thought how hard it was on children to be disbelieved. Isolated. Silenced. These were the images that had driven me to act. Now, to be in Parliament as it belatedly defused the time bomb of silence and cover-up – it was wonderful.

After the formalities, I was approached by a friend and survivor who broke down in my arms. The reality of it all had reached an emotional level that he was no longer able to contain. I held him.

There was a need to debrief but first we all received a copy of the two-volume, near-800-page *Betrayal of Trust* report containing fifteen key achievable and important recommendations.

The Victorian Government began the process of changing its laws to protect children. The Inquiry was over but the hope of its fifteen recommendations was not. In time, every single recommendation would be implemented no matter the objections from the Catholic hierarchy.

And that was just the beginning. The wheels were turning on the Royal Commission.

Anthony and I were ready to pack our travel bags and commit to bear witness again. We were prepared for more tears. I could never have imagined how many.

# 15

Reflecting on George Pell's evidence, Anthony and I took a deep breath. There seemed to be no triumph, yet the whole Inquiry was a kind of triumph. The satisfaction of a lasting victory would come with the pending law changes. Nothing is certain when politics is involved. History is full of breakthrough inquiry recommendations that sit on the shelf, leaving a void they were meant to fill.

Nevertheless, we had come a long way in a short time, and a modest recognition, if not celebration, was in order. My mother, Dawn, shared a bottle of champagne with Anthony, our friends and me. Mum had always been there, right from the beginning. At every turn of this monstrous affair, always supportive, always on our side.

Mum was my best friend when I was a child, teenager and young adult; she still is. But she had to share the title with Anthony soon after I met him. As a child, I used to love it when Mum was on tuckshop duty at primary school. I would run up with great excitement whenever she was there, and I could give her an extra hug and receive a big smile. Her presence was always a beautiful gift. One day, however, I missed seeing Mum at the tuckshop. At the start of school we had to stand in long rows after the bell rang, waiting until it was time to enter the classroom. This day, lined up with all the other kids, bored as anything, I looked down at my feet. Right beside my shoes was a white painted line marking out the netball court. I was seven, and in Grade 2.

I did a little sideways jump so that both feet were directly on the other side of the thin white line, very neatly, very tightly, barely noticeable. I did it a few times without looking up, enjoying the solo game within the confines of the moment. But my class teacher nun saw me.

I was sent to stand in the corner of our classroom. I stood there quietly with my face close to the wall among brooms and other equipment. I stood waiting, hoping to be allowed to go to my seat with the other kids. After a long time, the playtime bell rang, but I still had to stand in the corner. I thought about my mum wondering where I was and why I hadn't gone out to see her. I hoped the other kids didn't tell her I had been bad and was standing in the corner as punishment.

I was staring at the walls for hours. Just before lunch the nun told me I could sit down at my desk. When I finally sat, my vision went strange, perhaps because of the hours I'd spent looking close range at a white wall.

When the lunch bell rang, I went out to see my mum. She asked me where I'd been at playtime. I didn't tell her I was being punished even though I felt I hadn't done anything wrong. I well understand how powerless and silent children are to injustices against them. That nun was often nasty to me. I never said anything about my mistreatments. Mum probably would have had a piece of her if she'd known.

But the nun was not as bad as the teacher I had in Prep two years earlier at a different school. The whole class lived in fear of that teacher. She would ask individual five-year-olds to stand and read the words she had written on the blackboard. If they could not read one of them, she would march up, grab hold of their ear and shake their head until they said the word correctly. I lived in terror of her doing the same to me. Then one day it happened. There were two words: met and meet. I could not distinguish between the two. She marched me up to the blackboard and pointed to each word.

'Met, meet, met, meet.'

I didn't know the difference. I was only guessing and kept getting them wrong. I was terrified. The playtime bell rang and the other children were allowed to leave. I had to continue reciting the confusing words. She grabbed my ear and shook my head, saying the words and pointing back and forth. Crying didn't stop her violence. Eventually I must have got it right because she let me go. But the trauma lived with me for the rest of my childhood and well into my adulthood. I had trouble reading aloud at school and even at work, I would freeze up and read very slowly. It was only when I had children of my own, reading nursery rhymes to their non-judgemental joy of listening to a story, that I overcame my discomfort.

Even with the violent Prep teacher, I never uttered a word of her injustices, or rather assaults, for about forty years.

Mum was unlike the teachers: she was kind, encouraging and loving, forever there for me, and looked after my brothers and me so well. She was the heart of our home and life when we were growing up. She is now ninety-one, still plays golf and socialises with her 'golf girls' and other friends each week. Her strong allegiance to the Catholic Church goes back generations, but when clergy crimes were discovered in the youngest members of our family she joined me in going after the perpetrators. From 26 March 1996, the day Emma disclosed, I stopped attending mass. Mum did too, both of us risking eternal damnation, as dictated by Church clergy.

A month earlier Anthony and I had been told by Emma's psychiatrist that Emma was showing all the symptoms of someone who had been sexually assaulted. His words frightened us but they were not clear. That same day we relayed to our psychologist what Emma's psychiatrist had said. Our psychologist immediately said that the psychiatrist was saying he believed that Emma had been sexually assaulted. Our psychologist also believed Emma had been sexually assaulted and, from her behaviour, that it had happened repeatedly. We could not speak. The shock was profound. Our psychologist asked who in our lives could have done this. We floundered; we could think of nobody . . . I had taken such meticulous care of them . . . I thought back to old swimming lessons, old school holiday groups . . . nothing. Then Anthony flung back his head in realisation and groaned. Fr O'Donnell had recently been jailed.

The psychologist replied, 'That is who we would be looking for.'

I was gobsmacked. 'How could it be O'Donnell?' I asked. 'When? He never came to our house, Emma never went to the presbytery. When could it have happened?' I was the only one who could not be convinced. I needed to hear it from Emma. But of course, Fr O'Donnell had access to Emma five days a week at school. Over the next four weeks while Emma was still in the adolescent psychiatric unit in hospital, I vacillated between O'Donnell and someone else being the perpetrator. Mum, Anthony and I discussed the situation. I was still going to church, but with the possibility that O'Donnell had sexually assaulted Emma, the new priest's words all sounded like lies. I was stuck in between, since our guess as to who was responsible was only that – a guess. Four weeks later, Emma disclosed under distressing circumstances that Fr O'Donnell had sexually assaulted her in a room in the school hall.

After a lifetime and long family history – countless generations – of subservience and obedience to men of the cloth masquerading as conduits to God, Mum and I were free. The sexual assaults against our daughter and granddaughter broke the shackles. Emma, and later Katie, were more important than any priestly rule.

Still, Mum and I couldn't help but feel that our lives had been a farce, obeying these men through the fear of God and eternal damnation. They must have laughed at us behind our backs.

Mum had grown up with her parents telling her, 'Evil prevails when a good man keeps his mouth shut.' She had raised me with the same mantra. So when it came to priests verses the truism, family lore won out. We could not be part of their prevailing evil; instead, we used words to expose and expel their prevailing evil. We could see how the absence of dissenting words led to concealed crimes, then more crimes. Speaking out was the effective countermeasure, so we spoke.

Mum wrote a letter to Archbishop Pell on 5 August 1996. It was a plea from a broken heart and made clear her contempt, anger and disgust for Church leaders. She called herself a 'child of God' and then made a declaration that could in hindsight be seen as a prophecy: 'If your ways don't change you will completely destroy the Church on your own.'

Archbishop Pell sent a letter in reply. This is what he wrote on 29 August 1996.

At the outset, I must reject your suggestion that Archbishop Little took the side of a few errant priests who abused the trust placed in them. Archbishop Little and I, together with all Christians and all Australians, have nothing but disgust for the activities of these errant priests.

A few errant priests!

Pell finished the letter with: 'I can only trust that through this trial, you and your family might find new depths of faith within yourselves.'

These final words were an affront to us all. How could the multiple rapes of my eldest child by a priest and the heartbreaking and hellish aftermath help us to find new depths of faith? It had destroyed faith.

Nearly thirty years later, his words are still offensive.

Mum was my rock to cling to. Like Anthony and me, she suffered from the destruction of my children's lives, as well as the dismissive and minimising words the hierarchy continually issued to the media. She celebrated when we celebrated and cried when we cried. And her quiet words of love were worth more than a million of the priesthood's weak excuses.

# 16

Spot fires of scandal were not extinguished by the Victorian Inquiry and its recommendations. One of them involved Victoria Police. In July 2013 former Detective Denis Ryan published his riveting and heartbreaking book *Unholy Trinity*, co-authored with journalist Peter Hoysted. For years the *Herald Sun* had featured articles about Ryan's story of injustice between 1971 and 1972. What had happened to the young detective decades earlier needed addressing – fortunately Ryan, now in his eighties, would not go away.

*Unholy Trinity* tells the history of Ryan and his personal experience in Victoria Police when pitted against paedophile priest Father John Day in Mildura, my mother's birthplace. The young detective had moved his family to the Victorian border town for health reasons. In trying to carry out his duties and charge Fr Day with multiple child sex offences against sixteen children, Ryan lost his career and life as he knew it. The title refers to the forces against him: a Catholic bishop, a Catholic policeman and a Catholic magistrate. Ryan details how the police force in Victoria had a so-called 'Catholic mafia' working to protect the Church's good name.

At the time of the book's publication, the performance of the police force in New South Wales was being evaluated by Margaret Cunneen's Special Commission of Inquiry, which was looking into evidence regarding an unnamed boy abused by Father Denis

McAlinden. The victim, when seven years old, told his parish priest in Singleton about his sexual assaults during his first confession. 'This boy was given penance apparently for his sin in being abused by that priest,' counsel assisting the Cunneen Inquiry, Julia Lonergan, said. The boy was subsequently abused by another priest, Father James Fletcher, a name we would hear more often as the secrets of Maitland-Newcastle were finally uncovered. But when the Singleton parish priest took the actions he did in the confessional – giving the abused boy a penance – he was replicating the paedophile priest's silencing actions. In confirming the boy's supposed guilt (through the penance), he was making the paedophile's silencing of the child unquestionable and complete. The parish priest was aiding and abetting the paedophile priest in his crimes, future crimes and cover-ups.

Next day, the Cunneen Inquiry informed us that the Catholic Church had extensive knowledge dating back to the 1950s of child sex abuse by McAlinden. He was strikingly like our daughters' abuser, a career criminal allowed by high-ranking clergy to groom and assault victims.

Then there was the late Bishop Leo Clarke, who misled church leaders in Western Australia and Papua New Guinea by sending an abusive priest to their archdioceses. This was another clergy ploy – getting rid of their paedophile trash by sending them 'off to the missions' when their crimes became too much of a problem locally, burying them in remote places often among disadvantaged, seemingly powerless people.

It seemed to me forgetfulness was starting to become a feature of the Cunneen Inquiry. A former vicar general used the phrase 'I can't recall' (or something similar) more than fifty times in one morning. 'I can't recall' and 'I don't recall' were popular responses among most clergy when questioned about their knowledge of abuse. It would become almost a catchcry of the looming Royal Commission.

Another churchman with a 'complete lack of recall'[81] was Father Brian Lucas, whom I'd come to hear about over the years. When called to give evidence to the Cunneen Inquiry, his 'credibility was repeatedly called into question when he said he couldn't recall a crucial meeting with the disgraced serial child abuser Denis McAlinden in 1993'.[82]

'Father Brian Lucas approaches his work on behalf of the Catholic Church with the steady certainty that he is right, that proper procedures have been followed and that those in authority are untouchable,' journalist Richard Ackland wrote in the *Sydney Morning Herald*. 'The smiling smoothness, the unctuous tones, the baffling semantics. Essentially part of the church has been engaged in a large-scale cover-up of criminality.'[83]

Another New South Wales predator priest was Father John Denham, who had many victims, sixty of whom had been compensated by the Church at an estimated cost of $10 million. At least eleven of his victims had died by suicide.

Fr Denham was dubbed one of Australia's worst paedophile priests. He raped a boy with a cane at a Hunter Catholic school in 1979, and smiled as he said, 'This is for being a crybaby.'[84] Then he caned the sobbing boy's hands. Denham also raped a twelve-year-old boy across a school desk in 1977 and left him bleeding but silenced after threatening to tell the child's violent father. The sadistic Denham was the priest who had abused John Pirona, the man who left the 'too much pain' note before dying by suicide.

Where were the good churchmen who tried to stop clergy molesters and protect children? I know of two, both from New South Wales. One was Father Maurie Crocker of the Wollongong Diocese, who contacted his local newspaper, the *Illawarra Mercury*, in 1993 to oust two paedophile clergy, Father Peter Lewis Comensoli and paedophile Christian Brother Michael Evans. The second good priest to bravely make a report was Father Glen Walsh, who went to police in 2004 about Fr Fletcher.

Both Fr Crocker and Fr Walsh were ostracised from the Brotherhood for their actions. The Cunneen Inquiry heard Fr Walsh was told by his superior Bishop Michael Malone to 'Fuck off out of my diocese and don't come back.'[85]

After many years of rejection and bullying – five years of torment for Fr Crocker and seventeen years for Fr Walsh – both men died by suicide. Perhaps what they suffered was intended as a lesson to other priests, a message to toe the line and obey their superiors, that it wasn't worth betraying a fellow priest, even a criminal committing multiple atrocities.

With the NSW hearings over, we all had to wait for the findings and recommendations of the Cunneen Inquiry. Back in Melbourne, there was a post-Inquiry frenzy with new evidence emerging from ten submissions going public on the parliamentary committee's website. It was reported the Church put lives of victims in Victoria at risk, including telling one suicidal victim to ring back in four days.

A significant publication hitting the bookstores only a few weeks later was David Marr's *Quarterly Essay* entitled 'The Prince: Faith, Abuse and George Pell', a brave account of the highest-ranking Catholic cleric in Australia. Then hot on the heels of Marr's piece came scandalous news of a memorandum of understanding (MoU) that existed between the New South Wales Police and the Catholic Church. Police and the Church had quietly 'worked together for years under informal agreements that were in direct conflict with requirements to report child abuse'.[86]

I thought the MoUs were a disgraceful blight on Australian law, a kick in the guts for victims in their efforts to attain justice and a wanton display of corruption that apparently was fine so long as nobody knew. Appallingly, behind the scenes, justice was being bought and sold when it never should have been for sale. If we cannot rely on our police forces to protect innocence, especially our children, then what do we have? I was furious with the Church and with the NSW police, who had been persuaded by the hierarchy. It was a deeply disappointing betrayal of civil law and an outrage that such corruption could happen and then be maintained. I wanted the wrong acknowledged publicly.

Section 316 of the NSW *Crimes Act* says people must report a serious crime to police. Child sexual assault was and is a serious crime. The MoU sidestepped and overruled this obligation and permitted the Church not to report its offender priests by instead withholding the names of victims from police. This heinous system was known as blind-reporting.

When a senior New South Wales police officer advised the Church in August 2003 that 'an unsigned MoU appeared to be "in direct conflict" with legal requirement to report crime',[87] police did not investigate whether the Church had failed to report abuse cases.

It was astounding that while the MoU was unsigned by police and considered a conflict to reporting by the same police, the blind-reporting system continued to be used by the Church from the late 1990s. The MoU existed in a half-light, an unsigned and therefore unofficial agreement for police yet fully operational for two decades. This serious breach of public confidence was uncovered by longtime victim advocate and Greens senator David Shoebridge under freedom-of-information legislation. I was not surprised to read that he had sought out the scandalous MoU documents, as he was one of the first politicians to have pursued clergy child abuse issues.

One year later, on 3 October 2014, the ABC reported: 'The Police Integrity Commission in New South Wales will hold a public hearing as part of Operation Protea – an investigation into the relationship and agreements between police and the Catholic Church.'[88] In the wake of this announcement, the ABC's *Lateline* TV show interviewed Mr Shoebridge. 'There is a fundamental problem when you effectively coopt the police into your own internal inquiry,' David said. 'You can only speculate that the Church may well have set up this institution and the arrangement with the police, seeking to satisfy their reporting obligation under the Crimes Act and therefore avoid prosecution for failing to report to police.'

He was right. This MoU allowed the Church to fulfil its obligation for mandatory reporting of a crime to the police. However, if the Church withheld the names of victims, the police could not investigate the crime. A police officer attended all meetings but had to shred any written notes. Nothing was done to investigate. The crimes were all contained and killed within the 'unsigned' MoU.

The whole ploy was a success for the priesthood and Brotherhoods. Perhaps thousands of crimes against children in New South Wales fell into this abyss. Meanwhile, unaware parishioners were still being asked to make donations to the collection plate.

I wanted to see charges laid.

On 18 June 2015 the final report of Operation Protea was tabled in the New South Wales Parliament. Former New South Wales Director of Public Prosecutions Nick Cowdery accused the New South Wales police force of being 'party [. . .] to the Catholic Church conspiracy to thwart the criminal justice process'.[89]

I had wondered since I first heard about the MoUs how the setup had originated 'two decades' earlier. The final report stated that on 9 January 1997, at a meeting of the Professional Standards Resource Group, 'Father Brian Lucas, who had been nominated as a contact officer to liaise with the police' had 'informed the meeting that "agreements were being reached about a Memorandum of Understanding between the Catholic Church and the NSW Police"'.[90]

I should have known that the leading bishops had given their blessing and that the blessing was enough to make it happen.

Another year later, in 2016, the ABC would report that 'blind-reporting' [MoUs] of child sex abuse was continuing: 'New figures revealed NSW Police had received up to 1,500 blind reports during the previous eight years.'[91] Not only that: 'blind-reporting was still commonplace throughout the country'. It was still happening Australia-wide!

Unbelievably the Church had put through hundreds of blind reports since its exposure three years prior, perhaps to report cases before the loophole was closed.

# 17

Wondering was big in my life. Whenever you go up against a powerful organisation you are left to wonder, not in a good way. Those in charge have connections you don't even know about. They talk to each other. You wonder what is going on behind the scenes. All this wondering causes stresses you don't deserve. You wonder whether this anxious life that was caused by those in charge will ever go away.

I spent most of the 1990s and 2000s wondering whether I would ever see the action of meaningful child protection against the paedophiles who had been hiding in plain sight in the pulpits of our communities. I had dreamt about accountability. Then it happened. The Royal Commission began in earnest.

The case studies of the Royal Commission into Institutional Child Sexual Abuse were public hearings. There were fifty-seven case studies to be held over five years. The first was held in September 2013. They were open to the general public and presided over by one or more of the commissioners. The hearings were streamed on the commission's website. Counsel assisting the commission played an important role by examining evidence from witnesses through vigorous questioning. The lead counsel assisting the commission was Gail Furness. She was a gem.

Royal Commission evidence was given under oath or affirmation. When Ms Furness or one of her colleagues finished their questioning, witnesses would then be examined by persons with 'leave to appear' – a lawyer representing a witness or organisation. Formal protocols were in place. All six commissioners had to be addressed as 'Your honour'.

We were in the early stages of the Royal Commission, there was so much to unfold and I didn't want to miss any of it. This desire made easy the job of attending hearings, of making the effort and the financial commitment – such was our devotion to justice for all. After seventeen years of injustice, we wanted to witness corruption pulled apart. Our life fitted around Commission hearings but if there was a clash with family events, our private life received priority. With the Victorian Inquiry finished, Anthony and I were free to delve into the Royal Commission, not just read about it or watch highlights on TV. By December, the first Catholic Church case study was about to start. I had seen the notice outlining the content of Case Study 4: The Experiences of Four Survivors with the Towards Healing Process. The only problem was the hearing was in Sydney.

I suggested to Anthony that we go. He wasn't keen and had an appointment on the Monday anyway. Undeterred, I asked him to arrange a flight and accommodation for me, which he did happily.

The case study was held in the Royal Commission's headquarters on the seventeenth floor of Governor Macquarie Tower, a place that would become as familiar as my own home. Early Monday morning 9 December 2013 I was at Melbourne Airport awaiting my flight when I looked at a stack of newspapers and spotted a familiar face on the front page of the *Herald Sun*. It was Ronald Mulkearns, the dangerous and unrepentant retired Ballarat bishop. It gave me shivers. Mulkearns had a cold, evil heart. For twenty-six years he'd been at the top of the decision-making structure, and never stopped using his face-saving, Church-first protection policy. To uphold his cover-up, he had even destroyed documents that might one day be evidence. Children had suffered and died because of him.

I recalled the words of parliamentary committeeman Frank McGuire: 'Mulkearns kept few records and destroyed documents concerning crimes that used to be hanging offences. The Church suggested in evidence this was a coincidence. I have called in Parliament for further investigations to determine whether it was a conspiracy. Bishop Mulkearns may be the last keeper of the secrets.'[92]

I would go further to say Mulkearns was an ugly blight on the human race, protected, supported and honoured by the rest of the hierarchy.

In the newspaper photograph, the old man was out on a street. Only seven months earlier, after he had been asked to appear as a witness of the Victorian Inquiry, we had been told by clergy that Mulkearns was in a Catholic nursing home. Now, however, the disgraced retired bishop looked directly into the camera lens, mouth turned down knowing he had been captured by a photographer. Sprung! He was freely walking around the shops in a beachside country town. I read: 'The *Herald Sun* tracked down Father Mulkearns, who still conducts mass, and found a coherent, active man. Father Mulkearns was enjoying driving, doing his own grocery shopping, taking brisk walks and even carrying a slab of Cascade beer up a small set of steps to his home.'[93]

Perhaps Mulkearns had made a miraculous recovery after the parliamentary hearings. He was pictured on his own, collecting his mail, buying milk and holding car keys. Even more remarkable was the slab of beer he was pictured carrying to his car, then driving home to where he apparently lived independently. Bishop Bird had said at the Parliamentary Inquiry, 'His memory in general is not very good, and his ability to focus on things is not very good,'[94] but Mulkearns' multitasking, captured in the photograph, suggested a different story.

I started to wonder whether Mulkearns (now a mere priest) would be required to give evidence at the Royal Commission. Nobody doubted Ballarat would be a focal point. I hoped he would be forced to answer long-awaited and damning questions. I hoped he would live long enough to be charged by police. I hoped his final home would be a jail cell.

I boarded my flight and flew with a sense of foreboding, arriving an hour late for the hearing. I went through security and asked to leave my luggage. Remembering the protocol, I paused inside the hearing room and bowed my head to Justice Peter McClellan.

So, this was our Royal Commission.

The room was large and very much like a normal courtroom, with the front half dedicated to a raised sitting area for all five commissioners, a legal team and a multi-witness box. The public gallery sat about one hundred people.

The case study regarding the Towards Healing process was an examination of how victims were treated outside the Melbourne Archdiocese. Towards Healing was the scheme adopted by the Church in the 1990s. It shared similarities with Melbourne Response, both shepherding clergy sex abuse survivors back to the Church for meagre payouts, but it had no official cap.

Four survivors would be central to the case study. Two of them, Joan Isaacs and Jennifer, were unknown to each other. They had been through the church's Towards Healing process many years apart after suffering sexual assaults by their parish priests while teenage students at different Catholic schools in Queensland. Joan was fourteen and fifteen at the time; Jennifer was sixteen. The ongoing abuse had created suicidal thoughts in both women.

The commission drew attention to the different treatment the women received under the same Church system. While one was paid $30,000 and had to pay her own legal costs, the second was given $265,000 plus her legal costs.

Joan's evidence was that a Catholic priest ran a cult-like group sexually abusing young girls. One girl had Father Frank Derriman's baby. The priest told his victims that if they loved God, it was okay to have sex with him because he was God's representative. He also lied that he was terminally ill and wanted to have sex before he died. He told Joan if she didn't have sex with him then he would kill himself and it would be her fault.

Joan had been silenced for the past thirteen years because the Church ensured she signed a confidentiality agreement that 'prevented her from disclosing the terms of the settlement' and required her not to make 'disparaging remarks or comments' about the 'Church Authority'. Her shocking evidence and bravery drew gasps from the public gallery, and she left the witness box to loud applause. I applauded, too. I met this brave woman on the second day. We talked during one of the hearing breaks and haven't stopped talking since, remaining friends even though we live 1 600 kilometres apart.

Before I spoke to Joan, I observed her out in the commission foyer with her husband Ian and their two sons. I could see how protective and loving they all were towards her. Joan is much loved and is a kind and gentle soul. That their wife and mother had suffered so much at the hands of the Church distressed Ian and their sons greatly. Yet such treatment of people by the hierarchy after sexual assaults by their criminal colleagues was typical.

A shock announcement that day at the commission was that the Catholic Church admitted it had paid $43 million to silence victims, basically paying hush money to keep child sexual abuse away from public knowledge.

It was during Joan's case study that I first saw Gail Furness in action. She had been made a senior counsel in 2011 and was appointed counsel assisting the commission in January 2013. Her ability to question witnesses was outstanding. She did not let any detail slip.

One line of spectacular questioning is burnt into my memory.

An ageing, pompous and overweight senior Catholic priest took the stand and the oath on the Bible. Ontologically changed men are not used to being questioned, least of all by a woman. (The priesthood believes that when a man is ordained a priest, he changes into a being that is above other men, above the angels and just below God – he is ontologically changed, be becomes 'another Christ'.[95])

Ms Furness asked one question the priest seemed to resent. Instead of answering, he sat up on his high horse and with much verbal bluster went on a rant that lasted a minute or so. When he finished, Ms Furness calmly asked him the same question. Again, he broke into a lather of indignation. While he spoke, Ms Furness waited patiently for him to finish. When his words finally stopped tumbling out, the counsel assisting paused before training her gaze on him. In a clear and calm voice, she asked the question a third time, stating that this time he would answer.

And he did. What else could he do?

For someone like me, it was a beautiful moment to witness. At that time, I had known eighteen years of unaccountability and arrogance displayed by clergy who possessed no desire to answer anybody's questions. And now one of them had been tamed by a woman armed with the power of our laws (not canon law) and her intellect. Ms Furness' expertise and command made me smile – it still makes me smile. Her words, strength and authority before my adversaries make for a wonderful memory.

# 18

On day three of Joan Isaacs' case study, Brisbane's Archbishop Mark Coleridge took the stand. He spoke with what appeared to be compassion and understanding. He said things were different now, explaining that the Church had learned from the past. It was now treating victims better.

I was impressed by his words under oath. He was slightly younger than most of the other archbishops, and spoke easily, eloquently. 'I have learned many things, not only listening to the evidence but in preparing for the royal commission,' Archbishop Coleridge said. 'One is that in this case there was what I would take to be a drastic failure of oversight. I think the failure of oversight led them [previous hierarchy] to play a role which was most damaging [. . .] the buck stops with the archbishop.'[96]

As a matter of fact, I was so impressed by Archbishop Coleridge that when I saw him walking through the foyer at lunch time, I suddenly had an urge to meet him.

I was sitting alone when he appeared. Will I say something? My heart started beating a little faster. What would I say? I had a copy of my book in my hands. Perhaps I could ask him to read it. Maybe he could obtain more insight into the plight of victims. Will I or won't I? The moment and Archbishop Coleridge were passing by. He was directly in front of me, about to disappear, when I made my decision.

'Bishop,' I said.

He stopped dead in his tracks and turned only his head towards me. In an overly loud voice, he corrected me. 'Archbishop.'

I didn't think much of it except that I had made a mistake in calling him Bishop. I walked over to him with a copy of my book, my two dear little girls on the cover. 'Archbishop, I think you should read this book,' I said, showing it to him.

He took it from my hands. I told him what it was about, and I explained that this copy belonged to another person (I had already signed and dedicated it to a friend).

I was polite but perhaps Archbishop Coleridge took offence at not being allowed to keep the book, I don't know. He began to walk off with it, then basically discarded it with something halfway between a throw and a drop, like it was a piece of rubbish. I had to catch it. He continued to walk off. I stood in silent shock, watching his back.

Then, when he was about four paces away – without turning around – he said, 'God bless you.'

Once more, I glanced at my little girls' faces on the book, then at the archbishop as he strutted off with his nose in the air across the foyer, disappearing into a room for clergy and Church lawyers.

Anger overcame my shock. How dare he treat someone like that? He was rude and arrogant. What had I just heard him say under oath inside the commission? Words have meaning, and his sworn evidence now seemed hypocritical. What were we to make of the wonderful-sounding words of Church repentance? Were they always lies and public relations spin?

I felt stupid for being sucked in. I had just witnessed the natural reaction to a perceived victim from the hierarchy of the Catholic Church. Out of the commission spotlight, back to the usual treatment. But I was not a victim.

Still furious, I complained in no uncertain terms to the Royal Commission staff and Francis Sullivan, Church-appointed boss of the Truth, Justice and Healing Council. I described what had happened.

There must have been a discussion among the Church higher-ups because after the hearing Mr Sullivan brought Archbishop Coleridge to me to make an apology. The archbishop told me he would read my book, but I doubted he ever would, not with his attitude. Much easier to rattle off speeches and insincere apologies.

There was more insult for victims when we heard that the Brisbane Archdiocese had 'cash reserves of something like $30 million' but had spent a mere '$760,000' on victims.[97]

About the 'tsunami' of clergy child sex abuse, Archbishop Coleridge said, 'bishops and major supporters were like rabbits caught in a spotlight. They didn't know how to respond.'[98]

More nonsense. The bishops might be like rabbits, but they certainly did know how to respond, because they all acted as one in taking the same dysfunctional steps to protect clergy offenders. Their tactics had been lined up generations ago. A senior retired Catholic bishop, John Jerry, told the Royal Commission the Church could not be responsible for abuse because 'the Church, as I understand it, is not a juridic person, and action against the Church is very difficult to establish'.[99]

This was a big issue for victims seeking fair compensation. The hierarchy had long claimed there was no such legal entity as the Catholic Church and therefore it could not be sued. I'd heard for myself Pell describe the organisation as flat, meaning there was no overseeing office, no real headquarters – not even the Vatican.

How I wished their claim of the Church's non-existence were true, but it certainly did exist. Joan Isaacs, like me, took Archbishop Coleridge at his sworn word before the Royal Commission when he said, 'In the case of sexual abuse, given what a crucial issue it is, I would certainly be willing to authorise payment from funds such as this.' The archbishop was talking about the Archdiocesan Development Fund, worth $22 million the previous year. He also said he 'supported the establishment of a national compensation fund which has already been flagged by the country's archbishops, to which people like Mrs Isaacs would be able to return to seek further compensation'.[100]

After the hearing, Joan applied for a more just monetary outcome than her $30,000. Yet it dragged out over time and Joan was again traumatised by her treatment in the Church process. She went on to write a courageous book about her experience, *To Prey and To Silence: One survivor's story of child sexual abuse and her fight for justice.*

The evening after Archbishop Coleridge had taken the stand, Anthony flew into Sydney, deciding he wanted to be with me in attendance for the case study. It was lovely to see him, as always. Sometimes phone calls just don't do it.

The following day we went together to the hearing and had the honour of meeting Justice Peter McClellan, who was a gentle man, softly spoken. I was overwhelmed. It was hard to know what to say or how to say it. He was so important to Anthony and me, as well as everyone else who had experienced this crime. Here was a man who was powerful and intelligent, gracious and wise. More than ever, Anthony and I believed the Royal Commission was in good hands.

The first week of the hearing finished the following day, Friday 13 December. It was time to fly home back to Katie and our lives in Melbourne. That day was our friend and neighbour Cathie's birthday. We knew there would be a celebration happening, as with every birthday, even if we were a little late arriving. There was time to share our experience in Sydney at the first Catholic hearing, to toast a birthday and enjoy this warm get-together.

At such milestone celebrations with friends, we didn't avoid talking about our situation. Often, we discussed priestly crimes and betrayal, which were constantly in the media. The conversation was always robust with strong opinions, healthy attitudes and much damnation. It helped to vent to loved ones, who vented back. We relentlessly spoke of the deception we had all suffered and lifelong repression after growing up under a Church regime of hellfire, punishment and guilt. There was a lot to get over. Good company helped counter what was taken from us.

Joan Isaacs' experiences were picked up by the Melbourne press. A story surfaced about Joan's abuser, Fr Frank Derriman, who was living in Victoria, working as a social worker! The *Herald Sun* tracked him down. He was photographed in a large white cap, looking unhappy in the glare of the lens. The newspaper reported Derriman was still a Catholic priest despite serving four months behind bars for indecent assault in 1998 (Joan's case). The Church had done nothing about having him laicised when he was convicted. Archbishop Mark Coleridge had conceded at the commission that this was an 'oversight' and revealed that it is extremely difficult to remove a priest who has abandoned the ministry if he doesn't consent, even if the priest has criminal convictions and has married, as in Derriman's case.

This was news to me. I believed the Church didn't necessarily defrock its criminals, but I was under the impression that once a priest married a woman, he was immediately laicised. Apparently not. Doesn't that mean all priests, if they wanted to, could get married and their bishops and archbishops could do nothing to remove them?

Some good news came before Christmas. The Victorian Napthine Government was introducing the Crimes Amendment (Grooming) Bill 2013. The bill altered the *Crimes Act* 1958 by inserting a new offence of grooming for sexual conduct with a child under the age of sixteen years. It was one of the recommendations from our Victorian Parliamentary Inquiry and the first of many Victorian law changes to come. I felt the legal changes as a breath of fresh air.

# 19

On New Year's Day 2014, serial child rapist Michael Glennon, one of Australia's most notorious paedophile priests, died at Hopkins Correctional Centre in the Victorian town of Ararat. It's a special facility that houses sex offenders separately from mainstream prisons to provide protection from other prisoners who might attack them for sexually assaulting children. Glennon had been convicted five times since 1978 and was unremorseful to the end.

Derryn Hinch, ex-broadcaster and later Justice Party politician, had brought the Glennon case to public attention in the 1980s before society understood that many priests were paedophiles. Glennon's first criminal conviction came in 1978. He was forced to resign from the priesthood by the Catholic hierarchy in 1984, but thereafter was left unchecked in the community to commit more crimes. With his freedom, Glennon established the Peaceful Hand Foundation, a youth group that took participants to karate camps on his rural property, where he sexually assaulted them. One victim testified during a 1986 committal that Glennon told him he had lost count of how many people he had raped.[101]

Hinch believed that Glennon's story was one of neglect by the Catholic hierarchy.[102] He asked why this convicted offender was running a youth foundation and camps. In November 1985 Hinch had publicly named Glennon on air as a convicted paedophile, but as another case was pending against Glennon, Hinch's announcement was ruled to be prejudicial to potential jurors, and he was charged with contempt of court and imprisoned for twelve days.

The issue of laicisation (or defrocking) never seemed to go away.

The Vatican captured headlines about this time when it was revealed retired Pope Benedict had 'defrocked child-molesting priests at a rate of more than one every two days during his last years in office'.[103] The estimated figure was 400 priests in two years, more than double the previous rate.

This was pleasing to hear but also very surprising, because the same man – Cardinal Joseph Ratzinger, before he was made Pope Benedict XVI – came very close to being sued by US lawyers in Texas for protecting offender priests instead of children. For twenty-three years, from November 1981 until April 2005, Cardinal Ratzinger was the Prefect of the Congregation for the Doctrine of the Faith (CDF), previously known as the Inquisition. Ten of those years (1990–2000), saw then bishop and later archbishop George Pell serve on the same body with Ratzinger. The CDF dealt with complaints about paedophile priests – worldwide – and possessed the power to laicise priests for such crimes.

As head of the CDF, Ratzinger sent a letter on 18 May 2001 to every bishop in the world, co-signed by his secretary Cardinal Tarcisio Bertone (who would become the Vatican Secretary of State), reminding them of the strict penalties facing those who revealed confidential details concerning enquiries into allegations against priests of certain grave ecclesiastical crimes, including sexual abuse of children. Ratzinger's letter included a reference to *Crimen sollicitationis* (the crime of solicitation), a Latin document of instruction written in 1962, itself an update of an earlier 1922 version. Both documents had emanated from the Holy Office, stating all cases of child sexual assault were to be handed over to the CDF.

Also contained in Ratzinger's letter was the warning that all proceedings of cases and all those involved came under the 'pontifical secret', meaning clergy or victims who broke their silence to outside authorities could suffer excommunication.

These Church hierarchy measures made the child sexual assault issue a watertight secret for clergy and victims alike, leaving societies around the world ignorant of the clergy's crimes.

In 2010 US attorney Daniel Shea gave a legal opinion of this Vatican set-up, saying Ratzinger's actions 'constituted an international conspiracy to obstruct justice' and '*Crimen sollicitationis* [. . .] contains written orders from the Vatican laying bare a system for protecting child molesters'.[104]

For Shea, *Crimen sollicitationis* was more than a smoking gun, it was 'a nuclear bomb' and 'the letter ordered everyone involved in these cases to keep the evidence confidential for ten years after the victims reached adulthood'. This time delay meant that in many jurisdictions the statute of limitations for a victim to report such a crime to local police would expire before the victim heard back from the Vatican about their case. The whole mechanism allowed the offending priests to be free of the possibility of civil law being actioned against them, and free to reoffend.

Mr Shea was acting for a victim in Texas when he took a verbal flamethrower to Church rules. In the lawsuit, he cited the 18 May 2001 letter from Ratzinger: 'Ratzinger's involvement arises out of this letter, which demonstrates the clear intent to conceal the crimes involved.'

Just to make it clear, pontifical secret is the code of confidentiality that, in accordance with the canon law of the Roman Catholic Church, applies in matters that require greater than ordinary confidentiality. For clergy or any other churchpersons, the threat of excommunication is frightening because separation from the Church means separation from God and heaven.

The case against Ratzinger escalated until he was elected Pope in April 2005. I remember watching coverage of the papal selection process. When the grey smoke finally emerged from the old chimneypot and an announcement was made, BBC commentators were shocked at who had been elected. One of them said it was a surprising selection because Cardinal Ratzinger was a theologian, not a people person.

At least one interested onlooker was not surprised. Daniel Shea believed that Ratzinger's election as Pope was to give him diplomatic immunity from the papers Shea had served on him for his role, as head of CDF, in moving alleged offender priest Patino-Arango to where he had abused Shea's client.

Unsurprising, only weeks after Ratzinger was made Pope Benedict, on 20 May 2005, the Vatican sent a diplomatic memo to the US State Department requesting that the US Government grant the new Pope Benedict immunity from being sued by US lawyers because he was now the head of state at the Vatican. The US responded that the Pope automatically received diplomatic immunity. The Texas test case failed. This immunity protected not only Pope Benedict but the whole system within the priesthood and the Vatican.

In light of this, on that January 2014 morning, I was surprised to read that as Pope, Ratzinger had taken steps to laicise at least one child sex offender priest every second day in the last two years of his reign.

Perhaps he had finally understood the damage he had caused in not taking a stance against clergy criminals from as far back as 1981 when he had received complaints and possessed the power and author- ity to make a difference for children, and was making up for lost time and ruined lives.

Two weeks later the United Nations attacked the Vatican over its child sexual abuse problem. It blasted its 'code of silence' and told Church leaders to 'hand over abusers'.[105] In an unprecedented inter- vention the UN demanded the Vatican 'immediately remove all clergy who are known or suspected child abusers and turn them over to authorities'. The UN's Committee on the Rights of the Child said Catholic Church officials had imposed a code of silence on clerics to prevent them reporting attacks to police, and moved abusers from parish to parish 'in an attempt to cover up such crimes'.[106]

Barbara Blaine, founder and ex-president of US-based group Survivors Network of Those Abused by Priests (SNAP), said she was pleasantly surprised by the UN report. 'This is what we, as victims, have been saying for decades,' she said. Barbara then made mention of Australia. 'The brave survivors in Australia who have spoken up, this acknowledges what they have been saying and I believe it also affirms the necessity for the royal commission that is taking place.'[107]

It was gratifying to read Barbara's words on the necessity of our Royal Commission and have it recognised by the head of SNAP, the largest victim support group in the US.

But did the Vatican take the Committee on the Rights of the Child advice to hand over the secret archives containing criminal evidence and hold to account those clergy who concealed crimes? It hasn't yet.

# 20

My years of following the Royal Commission – with its highs and lows, breakthroughs and breakdowns – began in earnest. We felt obliged yet proud to attend. It became our job, but it was a pleasure and honour.

When the Royal Commission was announced Anthony and I felt (much like we had with the Victorian Parliamentary Inquiry) that it was our very own, that we had asked for it and by some stroke of history we were granted the most powerful inquiry in Australia. Our home life was such that Katie received 24-hour care from carers in her own home, and Aimee, a young adult by now, was no longer living with us, so we had the time to devote to this forum. Attending hearings was an education I valued. I never tired of the commute, the hours listening, the pain, because it revealed what I had been pushing to expose and stop: clergy child sexual assault. The Royal Commission proved we were right. Each day would reveal more of the priesthood's corrupt workings and perverse attitudes, providing me with more building blocks of knowledge, having spent almost twenty years studying and researching to satisfy my hunger for justice. We would attend our Royal Commission gladly.

It was a heavy burden to even begin this journey, but it was a necessary journey to take. I didn't want to miss any of the evidentiary twists and turns. And, in a way, Anthony and I were the lucky ones in the gallery. We had each other – one to pick the other one up when it all became too much.

Impressed by the first Royal Commission case study on the Catholic Church, I eagerly anticipated watching the second, Case Study 6. This was an examination of the Catholic Education Office (CEO) of the Toowoomba Diocese, Queensland. Unfortunately I couldn't get there, so I watched every minute on my computer screen at home. It began on 17 February 2014 and was set to run for two weeks.

I only knew the background in general terms. In 2010, former Catholic primary schoolteacher Gerard Vincent Byrnes was jailed for ten years after pleading guilty to forty-four child sexual abuse offences against thirteen girls aged between eight and ten. Under the commission's microscope were the actions of the principal, school staff and Church-appointed education managers at the CEO of Toowoomba Diocese.

What I learned from the case study was that a school investigation began when one of the girls abused by Byrnes told her father what had happened. He rang the school principal to complain and, I imagine, demand an explanation. The principal, the father and the daughter had a meeting. Among other things, the girl said that Byrnes 'put his hand up our skirts'.

During the meeting, the mother of another child rang the school and spoke to the assistant principal. The mother said the previous day her daughter had overheard a conversation between two other students in after-school care. One girl said that her teacher Byrnes had put his 'hands down [her] pants'. This complaint went nowhere.

Only the first complaint was passed up the chain to the local CEO, where there was apparently some confusion over whether it should be a written or oral complaint. The story went back and forth between the primary school and the CEO staff. The commission heard that the school principal did not comply with procedures in that 'he failed to report some allegations of sexual abuse to the police'. The principal tried to avoid responsibility for reporting to the police by maintaining it wasn't his job, rather 'the responsibility to do so was that of the Toowoomba CEO'.[108]

Also hindering the complaints process was the fact that CEO staff had a motto of shielding the big boss from scandal. 'Protect the Bishop' was said repeatedly during the commission hearing. It seemed like an unwritten mantra, and was seemingly so effective that the Bishop of Toowoomba, Bishop William Morris, never heard anything about the complaint.

During the hearing, the principal received the full brunt of a media backlash.

Most galling was the fact the principal and the CEO dithered for over a year. This took place between September 2007 and November 2008 when the Church hierarchy, schools and the CEO claimed to have clear protocols in place for action on child protection. Yet their handling of the abuse case was poor, even though it was within the jurisdiction they presided over and where they were bound to protect children. Byrnes continued to teach the children until another girl told her mother that he 'had put his hand down her pants and touched her chest'. The mother rang the police the next day and the teacher was immediately removed, then charged.

On the day of his arrest, Byrnes was working at the school as a relief teacher. So, after fourteen months of procrastination and denial, it was really that easy to sort out – just ring the police. In the meantime, the principal, assistant principal and CEO all prolonged the danger.

The school's 'student protection officer' testified she did not understand why the victims 'did not have the courage to come forward'.[109] Perhaps it was because the children who *had* come forward were disbelieved for fourteen months. Regardless, it was a classic case of attempting, even in 2014, to blame the child victims and not the grossly inadequate behaviour of the adults.

The case study highlighted what can go wrong in the Catholic system after we are assured by Church hierarchy that our children are safe. Unless protocols are implemented and enforced in schools, they are merely words on paper.

An important factor in this case was the deference paid to a bishop by those who were not clergy. There was great effort from these ordinary Catholics to 'protect' their employer, the bishop. (The commission said Bishop Morris later did the right thing by creating an investigation, appointing an independent mediator to assess reparations and setting up a Child Abuse Response Team for better child protection.) The godly status placed on priests and bishops also hinders best practice. It reinforces a pecking order where few people want to rock the boat. This, in turn, can cause the children – at the bottom of that pecking order – to be left vulnerable. Such an environment is a disaster for children.

The details of Case Study 6 sent shockwaves across the country. Media went over it with a fine-tooth comb. It was perfect to study, providing strong lessons. It was also an opportunity for the general population to see how the Catholic system could still fail.

Bishop Morris appeared as a witness at the Toowoomba hearing. He struck me as an open and honest man, as he had back in May 2011 when he was singled out by the Vatican, in particular Pope Benedict, and was dismissed as Toowoomba's man in charge. I had followed his demise as it unfolded because it was an unusual occurrence. Bill Morris, as he was known, was very popular among parishioners. He had been an advocate for married priests and the ordination of women. When he was sacked, people wanted to know why. The Royal Commission found it was because of his 'pastoral initiatives'.[110] But I wondered.

I had followed the articles about Bishop Morris. I read of the Temple Police, staunch parishioners who reported priests to the Vatican if they spoke out of turn regarding doctrine. They denied it was them. When the axe came, there seemed to be no official reason for his dismissal, although his progressive teachings were mentioned. It didn't sit right with me. Why wait five years to punish a rebel bishop? Then it occurred to me that his kind actions were a threat to the Church's assets.[111]

His first sin of compassion was to admit the Church's liability in the Toowoomba case. This saved victims, thirteen little girls and their families, from a potentially torturous campaign for justice through lawsuits. Bishop Morris' actions resulted in thirteen families receiving payouts of about $500,000 (the maximum was more than $1,000,000). Even compared to today's payouts, the sums went beyond any Church compensation set-up, given their limits to payouts. The bishop even sidestepped the Church's claim that it did not exist legally, which had been blocking all cases attempting to attain fair compensation through lawsuits. I believe Bill Morris lost his position because he did the right thing.

The Church lost more money on this case than it would have done had it used the legal stonewalling it employed against my family and many others. Morris had committed the unforgivable in the Vatican's eyes: he had admitted liability and given away the hierarchy's money without a fight. The kind-hearted bishop's sacking would serve as a warning to all others contemplating a similar Christian response.

# 21

Abuse survivor and lawyer John Ellis asked Anthony and me to sit with him during his Royal Commission Case Study 8 in Sydney, so we flew back there for what would become an emotionally draining and famous chapter in Australia's long history of clergy sexual abuse. The examination would put under the microscope John's treatment by Towards Healing. Towards Healing? It was more like Towards Hell.

In March 2014 we returned to Governor Macquarie Tower and took our places in the hearing room beside John and his partner Nicky. Waiting for the hearing to start, he looked his typically placid self. There was a lot at stake. It was to be a groundbreaking intrusion into the inner working of the Church's own unregulated, self-serving system that no government body had ever bothered to scrutinise. There was a time in my life when this type of examination was unthinkable. As a child, I behaved like other Catholics and tried to respect the Church. Bit by bit, my attitude changed. I was confused by changes to mass during Vatican II. I witnessed the Church's disregard for women, although I put up with it for a long time. Then came the betrayal. Nothing could be the same again. All I wanted was for another powerful body to drill down into the Church's deceptions, strip bare its pretence of Christianity. I had a high expectation that everything was about to change because a royal commission was on the verge of seeing what I could see.

And there were higher stakes. The Church had been using the so-called (John) Ellis Defence against victims who attempted to avoid Towards Healing to seek compensation through the courts. It was a decision handed down by the New South Wales Court of Appeal in 2007, which stated that the Catholic Church Property Trust – the keeper of the money and property of the Church – was not responsible for the child sexual abuse by priests and therefore victims could not sue the Catholic Property Trust. The Ellis Defence was about to be held up to the light.

I remembered back to when I first met John. It was in Sydney in July 2008. World Youth Day was being held in the city. We had been holidaying in Scotland when my co-author Paul Kennedy contacted us about a scandal to do with then Archbishop of Sydney Cardinal George Pell and two victims of the same priest. Pell had sent letters to both victims of the priest on the same day: to one victim he apologised for the abuse and to the other he claimed the alleged offender was the suspect of no other complaints. The contradiction was untimely for the Church, given the Pope was about to visit.

From London, Anthony was interviewed by Tony Jones on ABC TV's *Lateline* program. Anthony finished by saying we were cutting short our time away and returning immediately to Sydney to confront the Pope. While we were flying home, Bishop Anthony Fisher, who oversaw World Youth Day, said at a press conference in response to a question about 'the Foster family' and our challenge, that we were 'dwelling crankily [. . .] on old wounds'. Emma had only died six months earlier and Katie's injuries were permanent. None of our wounds were old. Never would be.

We arrived in Sydney not knowing what to expect, but a crowd of about thirty journalists greeted us at the arrivals hall – it was astounding.

Next day, among mayhem and exhaustion, we met John Ellis. We already knew about the notorious Ellis Defence. Victims had already learned that they could not sue the Catholic Church because the priesthood claimed there was no such legal entity as the Catholic

Church. Similar restrictions applied to suing bishops or archbishops. The hierarchy was well known for claiming they did not control or employ priests (a claim refuted by at least one high-ranking Melbourne official as far back as the 1990s). One remaining option was for victims to sue their perpetrators, but rarely did any of them have sufficient money for a lawyer. It was all a stitch-up to protect the Church's assets. Protection was afforded when the churches were given their own Property Trust Acts by each state government around Australia, many dating back to the 1930s. The Ellis Defence ruling set a precedent and basically cemented the Church's invisibility to our legal process across Australia. The ruling would stand forever or until another legal challenge proved successful, an outcome that was nowhere in sight. So, victims were left with a case of take-whatever-pittance-they-throw-you in Towards Healing, Melbourne Response or nothing at all.

On the day we met John, he was quiet. It seemed to me he'd been ravaged by what life had dealt him. He sat down in a lounge chair in the hotel lobby, the leather almost swallowing him up. He looked ghost-like, haunted by his abuse and lost court cases, as well as the final insult: a threat from the Church that it could take his home to pay the legal bill he owed them. Calling in the debt was in the hands of Pell. I saw it as intimidation, silencing and control – even sadism.

Anthony and I both had great concern for the fragile man. John didn't stay long that day, but we kept in contact and with time he grew from strength to strength. At some stage, we were relieved to learn that the Sydney Archdiocese had forgiven John his financial debt, so he kept his home. John established his own law firm and put his heart and soul into his clients, who were mostly fellow clergy abuse survivors. His hard work took him from one success to another. He met and married Nicky and they ran the law firm together.

Now it was his turn to give evidence to the Royal Commission. Other witnesses in the case study were Pell, bosses of the Church's 'professional standards' department, a former vicar general, lawyers, a private secretary and the diocesan business manager.

John's testimony was heard on day one. All the other witnesses testified regarding the roles they played for the Catholic Church. The first week of the three-week hearing was an eye-opener. Witnesses talked about oaths of secrecy that priests in various offices had to take, and needing permission from the papal nuncio in Canberra to speak the truth before the commission. It was also revealed a Church solicitor had sent an email to Church barristers promising they would be 'greeted with open arms at the Pearly Gates' for their work against John Ellis' legal claim.

It was a disgraceful spectacle.

I found it fascinating to learn about the Church's oath of secrecy.[112] In short, clerics believed they could ignore the oath to tell the truth required by civil court. Not only were clergy bound by the religious oath, but office staff were also confined by the Church's promise of secrecy.

Dr Michael Casey, private secretary to Cardinal Pell, testified that he had gained permission from the cardinal to speak freely to the Royal Commission. Reverend Monsignor John Usher had also obtained permission from Pell to speak the truth. Without knowing who had taken the oath of secrecy, how could we tell if they were lying when they were answering the simple question of permission to speak the truth? It made a mockery of the swearing-in (on the Bible!) procedure.

With this knowledge, Justice McClellan asked all clergy during this case study if they had obtained permission to tell the truth. I thought, given the deception, it should have been asked of every priest, Brother, bishop and archbishop and their employees who took the stand in every Royal Commission hearing, for all the good it would do. Have you obtained permission to tell the truth under oath?

The sleight of mind had the capacity to run very deep. We would never know if they were telling the truth. Of course they would not want to expose details of what they had always kept hidden, especially when retaining their assets depended on it.

When Friday came, we were all exhausted by the evidence presented at the Towards Healing case study. We felt sorry for John but not pity. He had handled himself superbly under a day and a half of intense questioning. Thankfully, we discovered Fridays were often a day off for the commission.

On Friday 14 March, Anthony and I had our Royal Commission private session. We felt fortunate that it was being handled by commission chair Justice Peter McClellan. This time we went to Governor Macquarie Tower's sixteenth floor, which accommodated the commission's office staff and 100 lawyers who worked tirelessly.

When we walked into Justice McClellan's office he was seated at his desk and welcomed us in. We sat opposite him and his assistant. I handed him my submission, including a copy of my book. (My submission was basically a replica of my submission to the Victorian Parliamentary Inquiry – there is only one truth, so there was no variation, just an updated version.)

It was a very relaxed meeting. Justice McClellan put us at ease and the conversation flowed. He asked if I would be prepared to be a witness if the commission ran a case study on Melbourne Response. I felt excited and scared at the same time. I had hoped our story would be part of a forensic pull-apart of Church procedures, but I had also imagined that Anthony would be the witness as he was our spokesperson for good reason. He had an analytical and intelligent mind. Anthony was brilliant at furthering an argument and explaining an issue. But that is not what was being asked. I had never appeared as a witness in court before.

'Yes,' I said. I would just have to be brave.

The second week of the Ellis hearing exposed some events the priesthood would otherwise have preferred to conceal under its oath of secrecy.

At the commencement of their Royal Commission testimony, members of Pell's office staff made statements that covered the several years of John's attempt to obtain justice from the Church. All stated that they had initiated the cruel legal steps taken against John and that it was not Cardinal Pell who had acted in the inhumane way. However, under Gail Furness' skilled questioning, the truth emerged.

Pell was always in charge of such important decisions.

The hearing was going to run for twelve full days. Anthony and I would fly to Sydney on Sunday afternoon or Monday morning, stay in a hotel near the commission, then return to Melbourne Thursday afternoon. On one of our trips back home, we were waiting in the packed departure lounge at Sydney Airport when I noticed a monk sitting with a young man. A novice of the monastery? I didn't think much of it but hoped I wouldn't be sitting near the monk on the plane.

Anthony and I were supposed to sit together, only that didn't happen. It was one of those large planes with two aisles and seven seats across. I had a centre aisle seat; Anthony sat on the other side of the aisle and one row ahead. There was nobody sitting in the other two seats beside mine, so I placed my handbag on the empty seat next to mine while I stowed my luggage in the overhead compartment. I sat down, did up my seatbelt, and went to grab my bag when a jumper landed beside my hand. I looked up at the source of the projectile to see the eyes of the monk. He looked annoyed, perhaps because my bag was near his seat. I thought how rude he was. He was nowhere near needing to sit down, standing in the other aisle waiting to place his overhead luggage.

Soon the monk made his way along the seats and sat next to me. I could not believe it. How unlucky could I be? The plane was huge – there must have been hundreds of other seats. Do I win TattsLotto? No. Do I get to sit next to the monk? Of course I do.

I was incredulous. Anthony thought it was hilarious; he couldn't stop laughing. He said it was something about the look on my face. At one stage he turned around with camera in hand and took a photo of me sitting next to the monk. He wasn't helping. He didn't even offer to swap seats with me because he was enjoying it too much.

Some background is important to understand my being irate. Not so long ago, at a Victorian parliamentary hearing in Geelong, I had listened to the heartbreaking story of an illiterate 72-year-old man who had been sexually assaulted as a child by a monk in a boys' home.

The offending monk had used his hood to hide his identity. He would walk into the dormitory at night with his hood already pulled over his head, covering his face, then turn off the lights before silently sexually assaulting this boy and others. Later in life, a group of the traumatised boys tried to obtain compensation from the order of monks but were offered a meagre $5 000 each because none of them could name their attacker. So, the current monks, more than sixty years later, were using the same lack of identity to now evade their responsibilities and offer $5 000 to each man for living with the horror and disadvantage that can accompany the life of a victim.

A symbol of that crime, one of those hoods and its cloak, was rubbing on my arm. Every time the monk moved, the loose material flapped and rubbed my bare arm. His bulk filled his seat, so the material of his cloak spilled over into my seat. After putting up with the rubbing for some time, I eventually turned sideways in my seat towards him and without saying anything gathered up the excess material of his cloak and tucked it behind the cushion of his seat before going back to reading.

On our return to Sydney the following week, additional evidence emerged from a reliable source – Pell's own solicitor, Paul McCann – as to who had been in charge of taking the harsh legal steps against John Ellis.[113] This was reliable evidence coming from a Church-employed solicitor. What solicitor acts on their own? Lawyers are engaged by the client, in this case the cardinal, and follow that client's instructions.

With such damning evidence now on the record, I felt confident that Pell would agree he had instructed his solicitors to act in the way they did. Not quite. When it came to his turn to take the stand, in a wave of bluster he criticised senior Catholic Church clerics, staff and lawyers over their roles in the Ellis case. He called one church employee 'a muddler'. He went on to say that his former chancellor was 'a good person' who found his job 'completely beyond him'. And he said his private secretary had previously given evidence to the commission that was in part 'inaccurate'.[114]

The question was: Why did Cardinal Pell deny he had taken specific legal actions against John Ellis?

It was incredible that the cardinal could take that stance, so much so that I thought his relationships with his staff would be in tatters. But then I saw footage on the news that evening showing a group of about five of them making their way down a ramp into the underground car park of the commission building with Pell. The boss had seemingly just thrown some of them under the bus in court, yet there they were, united.

The show went on. Towards the end of his evidence, Pell was asked what he would like to say about the disastrous Ellis Defence, the effects of which had caused John enormous suffering, including the loss of his job as a lawyer in 2005 due to his trauma and a world of other torment from the case. We had learned that behind the scenes and unknown to John, Towards Healing had made an assessment in his favour, finding that abuse had taken place. Regardless, Cardinal Pell's office had continued to fight him.

In questioning, Gail Furness asked the cardinal, 'Do you understand now, from your learnings in the area of the effects and impacts of child sexual abuse, the impact it had on John Ellis to have the very church that he had gone back to in Towards Healing dispute that he had ever been abused?'

'I do,' Pell said.

'And what do you have to say about that?' Ms Furness asked.

'I regret that,' Pell said.

It was poor but telling testimony, a pathetically inadequate three-word reply. At the end of his examination, Cardinal Pell made an apology to John Ellis. The two men were sitting on either side of an open aisle. Cardinal Pell read out his prepared apology to John without even looking at him, as if John wasn't even there. When Pell got up from the stand, he walked along the aisle that separated them. Now they were only centimetres apart. I watched the cardinal closely in the hope of some form of recognition or a sympathetic response, but he simply walked past John without so much as a glance in his direction.

We would have to wait quite a while for the Royal Commission to evaluate the evidence and reach conclusions on the merits and future of Towards Healing. But another interested party had already brought his gavel down on the scheme. It was sacked Toowoomba bishop William Morris, former head of the Church's National Committee for Professional Standards. Before he gave evidence at the Royal Commission, he told a newspaper reporter Towards Healing had often hurt victims and damaged the prospects of a thorough investigation. 'It was a dreadful thing that happened, it should never have happened,' Bishop Morris said.[115]

# 22

In bearing witness at the Royal Commission we saw the predictable and unpredictable, inside and outside the courtroom. Some moments came out of nowhere to set our hearts racing.

On that last day of John's case study, at the lunch break, Anthony had asked Truth, Justice and Healing Council CEO Francis Sullivan if we could speak to George Pell. For the past eighteen years, Anthony had endeavoured to have Melbourne Response go back and look at victim payouts and recompensate victims fairly. We knew of many who had been forced to accept less than $20,000, one as low as $2 600, for lifetimes of damage resulting from clergy sex assaults. Some victims could not read or write. One victim in about 1997 was asked by the Melbourne Response Compensation Panel how much he owed his solicitor for his unsuccessful case against the Church. He answered $17,000. Weeks later he received an offer in the mail of $19,000, leaving him with $2 000 after settling the legal bill. It was a matter of take it or leave it. There was no other course of action. It was a disgraceful situation that the priesthood was happy with, as we had all witnessed in the case against John Ellis.

Our request to meet with Pell was denied. A Church representative said that we were 'welcome to use the transcript' for anything we wanted. The pompous response was taken as the insult it was meant to be. We simply returned to the hearing after lunch and thought nothing more about it. We were aware Pell had been trying to leave Australia for his new posting as head of finances at the Vatican. The hearing had delayed his departure by a couple of days. I supposed he was anxious to leave.

On the hearing's conclusion, we shuffled out with everyone else and mingled in the foyer. I began talking to journalist and author David Marr. Behind him, I could see Francis Sullivan motioning to Anthony. It was obvious something was happening. There were urgent whisperings. I excused myself and went over to join them. Francis was saying George Pell wanted to speak to us.

I did not want to meet Cardinal Pell again. The last time we had met privately with him was in February 1997 in a cramped room full of disused furniture at the Oakleigh presbytery (the same presbytery in which our daughters' abuser, Fr O'Donnell, had lived and committed crimes for seventeen years against countless victims). It was very unpleasant. Back then, Pell had been rude and angry. I remember standing on the front lawn immediately afterwards, fuming at our treatment. The Archbishop of Melbourne had slowly closed the door on us, and I had loudly called him a derogatory name. Before that night I had never called anybody that. Neither had I used swear words. This was the effect Pell and his priesthood was having on a devout and gentle Christian woman.

I knew he'd heard what I said because I was watching as he slowly shut the presbytery door; at my words, the door paused, before continuing to close.

Now we were about to meet his eminence for a second time, seventeen years and one month later. Francis Sullivan took us into a side room usually reserved for lawyers and their clients. Inside were George Pell and Hon Barry O'Keefe, chair of the Truth, Healing and Justice Council.

We all shook hands and sat down. For me shaking hands with Cardinal Pell was unpleasant: it felt like a compromise. You honour and show respect by shaking a person's hand – but my feelings were a long way from that. Anthony spoke first. He requested that

Melbourne Response's payment cap be removed, all past Melbourne Response cases be reassessed, and all cases that had been processed by Melbourne Response be recompensated at Australian civil law levels.

In response, Pell said that the Truth, Justice and Healing Council was looking at a national response. Anthony pointed out that that was for future cases. Again, the cardinal suggested that a national approach was coming. Again, Anthony stated that for the sake of past victims and their wellbeing, reassessment and recompensation was fair and necessary; he said he understood this would cost the Catholic Church in Australia hundreds of millions of dollars.

Pell nodded. The cardinal said he would phone Denis Hart, Archbishop of Melbourne, to discuss what we had asked of him. He added that Francis Sullivan would also be involved in future conversations. As the meeting neared its end, Pell said it was good to talk with us. He acknowledged we had suffered. Anthony said he did not want to talk about that. Pell then began praising his Melbourne Response. Anthony responded that part of it was good, but the cap needed removing. Anthony was keeping it simple and did not want to go into all that was wrong. We had a long list and not much time to talk.

To Anthony's answer Pell said enthusiastically, 'And it was independent.'

'Well, there were some problems,' Anthony said. 'But I don't want to talk about that now.'

'Now what do you want?' Pell asked. He seemed to want Anthony to repeat his request.

Anthony obliged. No cap. Reassessment of settled cases. Compensate to civil law levels.

Pell had already agreed to the fairness of this amount of compensation under oath, conceding Church payments should mirror Australian (not US) civil law payouts.[116]

Anthony was being careful and deliberate to ensure there would be no misunderstandings. I was watching this conversation with some anxiety. It was stressful but I wholeheartedly agreed with Anthony. I only relaxed a little when he seemed to be getting through to the cardinal.

Anthony's three requests – given for the second time – prompted Pell to count them on his fingers. One, two, three. It felt like confirmation he was agreeing to the changes – getting the facts straight to pass on down the line.

'I know it's only your personal opinion [the civil law levels of payment],' Anthony said, 'but you have the power and influence to change the set-up within Melbourne Response, especially through your friend Archbishop Hart.'

Goodbyes followed this exchange. Hands were shaken again. Always the gentleman, Anthony wished Pell luck in Rome. I said nothing except goodbye.

Outside, the foyer was all but empty. Anthony was excited because he felt he had obtained Pell's oral assurance that Melbourne Response would be changed. For eighteen years, Anthony had been pushing for this type of reform. Now, my husband thought that moment had arrived.

We got into the lift and Anthony burst into tears of joy that victims would get justice after all this time and effort. I smiled and put my arm around him but found it hard to share in his heartfelt relief. I couldn't shake my bitterness. We had fought these churchmen with hearts of stone for a long time. I would need proof before I celebrated them finding their humanity. Once out of the lift, we walked through the cavernous marble reception area of Governor Macquarie Tower to the taxi rank outside for a taxi to the airport. Again, in the taxi, Anthony began to cry. As we pulled away from the kerb, I decided I had to document the meeting. I always carried a pen and notebook. I made a record of what had been said while it was still fresh in my mind. I looked at my watch. It was 5.08 pm. Either way, this was going to be a milestone moment: a groundbreaking change or another priestly betrayal of clergy childhood victims. As ever, when dealing with the men of the priesthood, things needed to be proven.

Anthony's emotional reaction to the conversation lasted quite a while. As I thought about it, I found it harder to believe that anything would change. I smiled with my husband but believed that these men, who didn't appear to bat an eyelid at revelations of child abuse, would not suddenly be so conciliatory and generous. It was possible the cardinal was contrite after being battered and exposed in the commission hearing, but I didn't think so. Money was still the bottom line in all of this.

I needed proof through actions from the hierarchy before I would believe.

Back in Melbourne, we waited almost a week for the promised call from Archbishop Denis Hart's office. No call came. Anthony rang Francis Sullivan, who had witnessed Pell's promise to speak to Hart, saying we had not heard from the archbishop. This prompted an appointment with Archbishop Hart.

We arrived for that meeting at Cathedral Place, which we were told was in the presbytery of St Patrick's Cathedral. Not knowing exactly where to go, we entered the cathedral's front courtyard and went looking for the presbytery. A man dressed in blue denim overalls stopped us and asked where we were going. He had several pens in the top pocket of his overalls and a business shirt and tie underneath. He looked odd, a contradiction. We were asked for our names. The man then produced a hand-held radio which he spoke into. I concluded the odd-looking handyman was a security guard.

The archbishop's assistant greeted us at the door. We met Denis Hart. There wasn't much to say except to repeat the points of change to Melbourne Response we had outlined to Cardinal Pell. That same day, 4 April 2014, after our meeting Hart released a media statement saying he would revisit the compensation arrangements. 'Today I asked Anthony and Chrissie Foster to participate in the process,' he said.

The archbishop said consultation would be held by the end of April. But none of it happened. It was just a public relations exercise to achieve accolades. And to placate us. Annoying too was the fact that he had used our names to legitimise his empty plan.

Instead, we went on the following journey:

- 29 April: Melbourne Archdiocese Business Manager Francis Moore rang Anthony to say Archbishop Hart had written to the Royal Commission regarding the issues paper on redress (avoiding the promised April consultation).
- 23 May: Anthony rang Francis Moore, but he was in Sydney and couldn't talk.
- 28 May: Anthony rang Mr Moore again but had to leave a message with his secretary.
- 29 May: Mr Moore rang Anthony to say that Archbishop Hart had had a reply from the Royal Commission but had not read it and would ring tomorrow. But he did not call the following day, and we did not hear from him again.

However, on 3 July we did get a second-hand message that the hierarchy would only speak to us after the Royal Commission hearing. All our hope and anticipation amounted to nothing. We now had to wait until late August and the end of our case study into Melbourne Response. The men with the power and authority to change things chose not to do it. Even with the Royal Commission in full swing, to me they acted uncaring and aloof.

As it turned out, Denis Hart would have nothing to present to the Royal Commission as promised because there was no 'reaching out to victims to seek their input'. I noted a pattern developing. The Church would put out a statement, win praise and the faithful's approval, then do nothing, leaving the faithful to believe the problem had been fixed.

The months between meeting Pell in Sydney and our August case study in Melbourne passed slowly, with the newspapers still telling victims' stories. The Royal Commission travelled to Perth at the end of April 2014. Under the microscope was the Christian Brothers' order at a school called Bindoon. Many unaccompanied child migrants had been sent from England to remote Bindoon where they were used as child labour to construct buildings for the Christian Brothers while being brutalised and sexually assaulted.[117] Hours from Perth, the children had no escape.

Victorian premier Denis Napthine continued to introduce new measures in our state by announcing that every minister of religion who had any contact with children needed to have a 'Working with Children Check'. This new law was a result of the Victorian Parliamentary Inquiry's *Betrayal of Trust* report. Importantly, the premier also announced new changes to the statute of limitations in cases of child sexual abuse. The Napthine Government would rewrite the archaic and restrictive civil law provisions that had enabled lawyers to limit or even block compensation claims.[118] Civil leaders were acting where religious leaders would not.

Victims had some wins with the Royal Commission but there were disappointments, too. As if to rub salt into our wounds, it was discovered in July that the Vatican had declined a request to hand over every document it held relating to child sexual abuse committed by Catholic priests in Australia. A letter from the Vatican to Justice McClellan stated that it 'respectfully suggests that requests for all information regarding every case – which includes requests for documents reflecting internal "deliberations" – are not appropriate'.[119]

With that, the request and the evidence it would have provided were simply wiped away.

Given the Royal Commission was delving into all Australian paedophile clergy, it sounded like the Australian hierarchy had sent all paedophile files – not just the Victorian ones – to the Vatican, which made sense because it would have been the safest place to send such documents for concealment. Examining these Church papers would have revealed the true depth of the hierarchy's knowledge, action and inaction. No records meant no proof, no legal responsibilities, no punishments, no costly payouts.

I believed the hiding of the documents could only be seen as evidence of guilt. These Church documents on paedophile clergy have a name. They are known universally as Secret Archives.

# 23

Perhaps the title Secret Archives originated at a time when the priests' arrogance was so great that they believed non-clerical eyes were incapable of ever beholding them. That nobody would dare or be able to desecrate their sacred realm. Who knows, but the title alone should have set off curiosity alarm bells for anyone.

I first heard about the Secret Archives in 2010. An opinion piece by Barbara Blaine (of US support group SNAP) referred to the mysterious filing system in the case of a priest named Father Gerald Robinson, from Toledo, Ohio. At the time I highlighted the following with yellow marker pen:

> When the detective asked the chancellor for Robinson's person-nel file, he was given just three pages. Puzzled, the detective, who is also an attorney, began researching canon law. He learned that each bishop is required to keep a secret archive, and to not ever disclose its existence. Armed with this knowledge, the police secured a search warrant.[120]

The detective later got his hands on 'a two-inches thick' file on Fr Robinson. The fact that there were files on priests was nothing astonishing. Most employers hold personnel files on people who work for them. And we knew from 1996 that Fr Kevin O'Donnell had a file because the Church hierarchy had referred to it.

However, the 2010 Barbara Blaine article referring to Secret Archives felt, to me, to be potentially something quite major.

The next time the Secret Archives popped up was the following year, in *Rolling Stone* magazine. A six-page feature covered clergy sex abuse and cover-ups in Pennsylvania. The Philadelphia case referred to one former priest, three current priests and a Catholic teacher, three of whom had raped the same ten-year-old boy. The article said a monsignor who reported to the cardinal was the custodian of a trove of documents known as the Secret Archives files. 'The files prove what many have long suspected,' *Rolling Stone* reported. 'That officials in the upper echelons of the Church not only tolerated the widespread sexual abuse of children by priests but conspired to hide the crimes and silence victims.'[121]

A former priest was quoted as saying it was 'cult behavior'. 'If you have a monopoly on God, you can get away with anything.'

It was both fascinating and chilling to read these insider words, but most of all it was angering to learn what lay behind the sexual assault of our children, Australia's children, the world's children. The mechanisms were put in place by the priesthood of the Catholic Church to enable protected and repeated attacks on the bodies of our most vulnerable people.

At the announcement of the Victorian Parliamentary Inquiry in 2012, Anthony and I had talked publicly about the rumoured vault of incriminating papers. Although we still did not know the full extent of them, their name or their relation to canon law, we understood they existed. We began calling for access to them for the Inquiry. Anthony told reporters the Inquiry needed to have 'real bite' to ensure all records were handed over by the Catholic Church.[122]

Not long after this I saw for the first time, in a newspaper report, a reference to a Secret Archives canon 489. I immediately looked it up:

canon 489

1. There is also to be a secret archive in the diocesan curia or at least a safe or file in the ordinary archive, completely closed

and locked which cannot be removed from the place, and in which documents to be kept secret are to be protected most securely.

2. Every year documents of criminal cases are to be destroyed in matters of morals in which the criminal has died or in which ten years have passed since the condemnatory sentence; but a brief summary of the case with the text of the definitive sentence is to be retained.[123]

At last, I could see the enormity of what the existence of the Secret Archives entailed. Being a canon law, a church law, meant that every bishop and archbishop in the world was bound to keep and maintain a secret archive for 'criminal cases' in relation to his diocese's priests. Every bishop of a diocese and every archbishop of an archdiocese in the world therefore managed a Secret Archive. This, in turn, meant that every diocesan bishop and archbishop in the world had the potential to be a part of a conspiracy to keep under lock and key any and every complaint of child sexual assault that came their way.

As stated in canon 490.1, 'Only the bishop may have the key to the secret archive.' Therefore, the sexual assaults and rapes of children could be kept under wraps from parents, parishioners and police. Church bosses worldwide have all participated – and still do – in upholding canon law in its entirety as nothing has been repealed. Offender priests should have been thrown out of the priesthood at the first sexual assault but that did not happen. Nefariously, members of the hierarchy preferred to keep child rapists and sexual assaulters in its organisation, unpunished, unrepentant and unexposed.

Canon law Secret Archives dictate and reveal that the highest-ranking bishops – the cardinals and popes – earlier in their careers, in their local dioceses, all inherited files.

Canon 489 and the other laws supporting it must be eliminated.

# 24

A foreboding chill pressed against the windows of our suburban home. It reflected how I felt. It was Monday 18 August 2014. I had marked the date on my calendar at the beginning of the Royal Commission. Today I would take the witness box. My evidence was to be broadcast to the world.

Anthony grabbed his keys and we made our way to the car. Locking the front door behind us seemed definitive. There was no turning back. Angst engulfed me as we left the comfort of our house – only confrontation lay ahead. What was to come was all-consuming; no thought beyond this day.

We drove out of our quiet avenue. Fleeting thoughts and emotions came and went as we reached the Monash Freeway. The four-lane traffic was crawling, same as it always was at this time. The slow pace only added another tier of concern – would we be late? Thankfully, we kept moving as the city buildings came into view on the horizon.

On top of my stress, I was exhausted. Sleep had been almost impossible the night before. I had never 'appeared' in court before. Now I was to do so under immense emotional strain, on a most personal level – sex crimes committed against my children by a priest.

We arrived in the bluestone William Street legal district and parked near the County Court. We then walked hand in hand through the waiting media. Though the cool morning air calmed my nerves, something to lighten the mood would have gone down well. I needed one of Anthony's jokes, but this was serious business. There was no way to break the tension.

A glance at the *Age* newspaper showed my own face, with a write-up of our case. It was accompanied by yet another front-page clergy scandal: NEW CASE ROCKS CHURCH.'

My heart pounded faster for the weight of history I was carrying into court, as if the voices of my past were whispering to me. I was testifying against what I had been brought up to believe was a holy institution blessed by almighty God. I was supposed to revere and bow down to the Catholic Church and its priests. Not anymore.

Anthony and I said hello to the security guards as we queued alongside lawyers and journalists to pass through the metal detectors.

So began the first day of our public hearing: Case Study 16 The Melbourne Response. I knew the history of this scheme as well as anyone. I had been there when it was announced by then Archbishop Pell on 19 October 1996. At the time, the number of clergy sex abusers was growing and could not be ignored any longer. Pell had decided to speak publicly at a gathering of victims and families called Melbourne Forum. I called it Pell's Forum.

It took place seven months after we had learned of Emma's abuse, and thirteen months before we learned of Katie's. We were shocked, angry and, most of all, heartbroken that such a terrible crime had befallen our eldest child, causing her to suffer from anorexia, medication overdoses, self-harm and depression. Life had been a nightmare – courtesy of the Catholic priesthood.

We did not know it at the time, but the Roman Catholic Church was in damage control. Stories were starting to appear in the media about clergy sex abuse. The Australian branch of the Church had been trying to come up with an uncapped process of 'compensation' (it was not technically compensation, rather ex-gratia payments). This ended up being Towards Healing. But the ambitious Pell had wanted to go it alone in Melbourne; he wanted to cap payments made to raped and abused children. The archbishop's process, given the green light by

Victorian premier Jeff Kennett and Victoria Police, dealt only with Melbourne's Archdiocesan priests, meaning other assaults committed by Catholic Brothers, monks and nuns in the city were not included. Among other things, I imagined it kept the Church's assault statistic in Melbourne down, and left knowledge and control of Melbourne's offending priests and their victims in Pell's hands.

They could define it however they liked. I knew it was unfair. I knew it in 1996 when it was announced and again in 1997, when we had our dealings with it. And I knew it on this momentous day in 2014, as I entered the County Court to give my evidence to the Royal Commission.

I had to appear brave even though I didn't feel it.

Inside the court, we walked to our reserved seats in the front row. I noticed Peter O'Callaghan QC sitting a few rows back. He looked a dreadful shade of yellow. This lawyer had been hired by Pell to manage Melbourne Response from the beginning. It was supposed to be a six-month secondment. As it turned out, he would be in the job for decades. The courtroom was full, with many of our friends and relatives in support. Apart from a few murmurs, there was no sound at all as we awaited the arrival of the commissioners.

I was listed as the first witness for the day. Along with the stress came pride. When I had received my summons to appear, I framed it and hung it on my office wall. I had waited a long time for this day in court.

Our barrister Tim Seccull QC was sitting with Dr Viv Waller, our solicitor, and other members of our legal team. I received reassuring smiles.

Months earlier, after I had been asked to be a witness by Justice Peter McClellan during our private hearing, Anthony and I had contacted Tim (who had recently been made a QC) to request he represent us. He had done a fine job during our civil proceedings against the Church (after we decided Melbourne Response was never going to provide a just outcome for Emma and Katie). We had first met him in 1996. He'd become a kind and trusted friend whom we wanted on our side during this time.

Waiting there in the courtroom I thought of the many hours Viv, Anthony and I had spent searching through subpoenaed documents, covering nearly two decades of Church records. With their help, I had put together a witness statement. The plan was to read it aloud and then face cross-examination from the Church's lawyers. My statement would reveal the treatment Anthony and I had received from the institution responsible in every way for our children's assaults. I now held that statement in my hand, all twenty-three pages of it. Knowing that addressing an audience was never my forte, Anthony had kindly offered to share the daunting task of reading it with me. We would read five pages each until the statement was finished.

'All rise.'

His Honour Peter McClellan stood before us, bowed, then sat. The entire gallery returned his gesture.

'All be seated.'

The counsel assisting the commission, Gail Furness, read a summary of the witnesses. There would be three cases used to examine the failings of Melbourne Response. Ms Furness summarised each of them.

Anthony and I walked to the witness box. I tried to calm my breathing. The room was silent. I sat inside the witness box, with Anthony outside. It was strange sitting in this part of the courtroom. Many times, for hundreds of hours, I had attended hearings but always from the public gallery. Now I was sitting sideways to the gallery with the judge on my left. On my right were five legal teams representing the various groups. It was quite a row of stern faces.

I was sworn in, choosing to take an oath to tell the truth, instead of swearing on the Bible. I was through with religion. The age of deference to clergy was over.

One last deep breath. I read my first five pages. I had worried that my voice would give out, but it didn't. Anthony then read the next five pages. We alternated in this way, expressing our distress and heartbreak over our daughters, and our disgust at the priesthood. We talked about how unfair it was for victims to go through Melbourne

Response. We mentioned how we had decided to bow to their process. We talked about how the ordeal had hurt our children, and how it had damaged our lives.

My statement recounted our horror at discovering that Fr O'Donnell had spiked cans of Coca-Cola and given them to Emma when she was a small child in primary school. Back then, she had cheerily told other children, 'Coke makes me drunk.' Years later, we learned the truth of what those words meant.

We had encountered this terrible reality only after years of subtle, and seemingly unrelated, oddities. Details had fallen into place piece by piece, like a menacing puzzle. This part I read breathlessly.

'I asked Emma, "What sort of 'drunk' did the Coke make you feel?" Emma considered her answer and replied, "Very drunk and dizzy and it made a loud noise in my ears." She told me this after her disclosure and that it happened in the "school hall".'

Soon after, Anthony had telephoned a police liaison officer familiar with the case against Fr O'Donnell, and said, 'My wife thinks O'Donnell might have got Emma drunk before he sexually assaulted her.' The police officer corrected, 'No, not alcohol – O'Donnell used to drug kids.' It was a gut-wrenching horror to imagine as reality.

'It was part of his MO,' the officer told Anthony.

There were more mysteries along the way, which I did not read out in court. While in the junior primary school grades of Prep to Grade 2, one of Emma's teachers had said to me that in the afternoons Emma was often 'off with the birds'. I was stunned and confused when I heard these words: it somehow seemed my responsibility coming from the teacher. I thought, *What am I doing wrong? Should Emma go to bed earlier? Am I not giving her enough lunch?* Not in my wildest nightmare would I have imagined that the answer to the mystery was that during lunchtimes the priest was taking Emma off the playground, into the school hall, drugging then sexually assaulting her.

She experienced what I called anger headaches. Because of these I took Emma to have her eyes checked, thinking maybe that was the problem. The optometrist said that she had a slight vision problem but didn't need glasses. Months later when there was no end to the explosions of anger, tears, then headaches, I insisted he make Emma glasses, but they made no difference.

When I finished reading my statement, I looked up. There was a cavernous silence. No-one was moving. It was as if people were preserving the fragile air. Many were crying.

Justice McClellan asked the legal teams: 'Does anyone have any questions of Mrs Foster?'

This was the time for the dreaded cross-examination. The Church's three legal groupings could now challenge me on any point. This was their big chance. For almost twenty years they had opposed our family. If they found anything I had said to be mistaken or misleading, they could now pounce.

With the judge's question hanging in the air, I awaited the onslaught. My expression was a patient one. I was ready to answer anything these men in suits could throw at me.

One by one, a lawyer from each Church group stood to reply to the judge.

'No, your honour,' said Mr Ruskin, appearing for Richard Leder, partner at Corrs Chambers Westgarth, solicitors for the Archdiocese of Melbourne.

'No, your honour,' said Mr Andrew Woods, appearing for Mr Gleeson and Mr O'Callaghan, both independent commissioners for Melbourne Response.

'No, your honour,' said Mr Peter Gray, appearing for the Truth, Justice and Healing Council for the Melbourne Archdiocese.

It was a moment of triumph, an unusual but pleasant change, to hear the Church men silenced. It meant they had no opposition to my words. Or at least, not in front of a public audience. The challenges would come later when no-one was watching.

The judge thanked and excused Anthony and me. As we crossed the courtroom floor, applause and cheering erupted from the public gallery. I couldn't help but smile as I looked at the loving faces of family, friends and total strangers.

The Church representatives sat in continued silence; they had not lost their nerve or thrown away their strategy. Rather, their tactic was to hold fire and do their questioning away from the spotlight. Behind their closed doors, we would soon learn just how they spoke about us when no-one was listening.

# 25

I thought I knew my story. Our story. My daughters' story. I had lived through it, and I had written and talked about it. But I didn't know everything. I couldn't know what the Church hierarchy said or did to us behind our backs. Their silence and stonewalling was a ruse. In reality, they were constantly trying to undermine survivors and families. Behind enemy lines the tactics were more deplorable and sinister than anyone imagined.

After I gave evidence, it was my turn to watch. The rest of the case study would be an examination of how the Catholic Church staged its battle to limit damages. Documents and evidence tendered at the hearing gave us an insight into how we were being viewed by our opponents. It was a strange experience, and shocking.

The next key witness was a man who had fallen victim to priest and family friend Father Victor Rubeo. The rapist priest had ingratiated himself into two generations of a trusting and faithful Catholic family. They called him Gramps. The witness stated he had first been sexually assaulted as an eight-year-old boy. His abuse had continued until he was eleven. When the victim was sixteen years of age, his father disclosed to him that he and his twin brother, the boy's uncle, had suffered years of abuse by Father Rubeo as boys. The witness told of his experience with Melbourne Response.

The third key witness, a victim of Fr Michael Glennon, said he went through Melbourne Response to achieve accountability for the crimes committed against him. After the victim witnesses, those who worked in Melbourne Response tried to explain their roles. Cross-examinations followed.

The truth was unveiled through Church paper trails. Over the course of the next seven days, Anthony and I heard many unpleasant things they had said about us, mostly through letters and notes kept by the Church after private conversations. I sat in the gallery consumed by feelings of disgust and flares of anger.

Day two, the Church-appointed boss of Melbourne Response, Peter O'Callaghan QC, was on the stand when he was questioned about correspondence he'd had with Richard Leder, who acted for the Archdiocese of Melbourne.

Counsel assisting the commission, Angus Stewart (standing in for Gail Furness), asked Mr O'Callaghan questions about a letter he had written to Mr Leder in regard to Anthony and me. In the letter, Mr O'Callaghan wrote about our intentions during the time we were weighing up our legal options, several years after we found out Fr O'Donnell had raped our daughters.

'Just going back to this letter,' Mr Stewart said, 'you ask him for his views as to "whether or not it is appropriate to in effect try to 'flush out' the real intention of the Fosters". Now, what did you mean by that?'

'Well, as to whether they were taking other proceedings,' Mr O'Callaghan said. By 'other proceedings' he meant suing the Church.

Flush out the Fosters! This seemed like subterfuge.

Both Anthony and I were shocked to hear such pernicious intent being used at such a professional level. Long ago I had decided that the men of the Church would not take any more from me than they already had – there would be no tears, just cold contempt.

Day four, Mr Stewart questioned Leder again. There was a long examination of documents that showed an attempt to dismantle the validity of Emma's medical reports in relation to the abuse and her traumatic symptoms. As usual, the Church was trying to minimise its liability.

'So in effect you were calling into question the judgement of the experts [doctors] you referred to earlier,' Mr Stewart said to Leder. 'Is that right?'

'No, I don't think that I was—'

Justice McClellan intervened. 'Mr Leder,' the commissioner said, 'I thought you and I had agreed that you accepted that all of the identified consequences were as a result of sexual abuse?'

'It's possible, sir,' Mr Leder said, 'I was applying the benefit of – some benefit of hindsight in my answer to you. I can see what I said there and, to the extent that what I say there is different from what I said to Your Honour, I was wrong then.'

Justice McClellan continued his questioning. He was always very particular. 'Were you wrong on other occasions about the advice you gave in relation to the relationship between the abuse and Emma's state of health and other issues?'

'I hope not, but it's possible that I was,' Mr Leder said.

I don't know if Leder's reply was seen by some people in the gallery as flippant, but it caused a reaction. A murmuring.

Reacting to Leder's words, Mr Stewart spoke swiftly and force-fully. 'Just on that question of the severity of the abuse,' he said, 'you are aware, are you, that in 2008 – and I accept of course that's ten years after this letter – there was a report from the psychologist which recorded that Emma had said in relation to her abuse by O'Donnell that she had "had enough sex to last a lifetime"?'

'Yes, sir.'

The subdued answer seemed to reflect some shame.

My mind was spinning one way and then the other. Mr Stewart's question had caught me off guard. The sudden reference and defence of Emma, the rapid acknowledgement of her suffering – after years of my and Anthony's voices being the only ones speaking up on her behalf – caused me to burst into tears. Immediately all the wording in the psychologist's report – Emma's entire life after her abuse – came to mind. The report Mr Stewart was referring to had been sent to us by Emma's psychologist a few weeks after Emma's suicide. The seven-page report told us Emma had 'post-traumatic stress disorder. Symptoms included recurrent and intrusive recollections of the past traumatic events, nightmares, flashbacks and intense psychological distress when exposed to events that were reminiscent of the past abuse.'

This was the horror she lived with: 'Emma's drug-taking behaviours were intended to numb the overwhelming and disturbing pain that she experienced. Emma would often acknowledge in our sessions the need to self-medicate for this very reason and that relief would only be found when she was asleep.'

The words tore at my heart.

'In discussing suicide last year, in 2007, Emma again disclosed she would overdose on heroin in particular and also on benzodiazepines. The most important and significant protective factor, however, was her love for her family and in particular her mother. That is, even though Emma wanted to die she would empathise with the devastation the suicide would cause her family and that this knowledge alone would be enough for her not to actively follow through with any plan. Emma often cried when talking about the impact on her family should she die from self-inflicted means and stated she is only "staying alive because of my family".'

Known also to Melbourne Response were the facts that Emma had visited doctors, specialists and pathology services 906 times. And this figure excluded at least seventy-five outpatient psychology appointments and more than fifty-two admissions to hospital and detox or rehabilitation clinics. Emma had suffered. We, her family, had suffered as we witnessed the disintegration of her life. We could do nothing to alleviate her pain, nor erase the memories that tortured her mind and soul.

Then there was Katie, too, driven to the edge of existence.

The Melbourne Response hearing had been harrowing listening to the mechanics of how the Church and its charges schemed against us. How easily they could have made life better for Emma. Nonetheless, I was used to this treatment from the hierarchy. To hear Stewart defend

Emma so promptly in such an esteemed setting impacted me to my heart. I cried for a long time; grateful tears. I was feeling the power of the Royal Commission. Once, we'd had nobody to defend us, we'd been at battle with the priesthood and their legal protectors. We'd had no hope. But now . . . this was a long way from where we'd started.

Another hurtful and enlightening exchange took place on day four. Justice McClellan ran through a series of questions relating to a letter I had sent the vicar general of Melbourne with a letter from Emma's counsellor requesting emergency accommodation for my daughter. Emma's self-destructive behaviour, including drug addiction, was proving too much for her traumatised younger sisters.

The Church had rejected our request through its Melbourne Response system, so I had appealed to the vicar general, a Monsignor Christopher Prowse. I asked that he oversee provision of three months' short-term accommodation for Emma as we were in the process of securing more permanent accommodation in a youth facility for her. Apparently, I had not stated clearly enough that it was only short-term accommodation.

Justice McClellan was examining an internal document written by Leder about my request that led to their rejection of my urgent letter. The judge said, 'And then you go on in the next paragraph: "The request from Mr and Mrs Foster does not suggest that there is any link between Emma's need for accommodation and any treatment that she requires."'

Yet both Emma's psychologist and I had written of the 'link' in our letters. Emma's psychologist's letter also stated: 'The complex symptoms that Emma presents with are a direct effect of the violent abuse she was subjected to as a child.'

The judge continued to Leder, 'Then you say: "Rather, she is homeless because her parents have thrown her out." I take it you accept that's not a fair characterisation of the situation as it was?'

'I do, and I apologise for using that language,' Leder said.

After his testimony, Leder sent Anthony and me a true apology through our lawyer Viv Waller. I was taken aback by this. If he was ashamed of his words, why use them in the first place and why take so long to say sorry? There was no true apology until we heard his words aired publicly eleven years later.

Then there was the vicar general's denial of our accommodation for Emma plea. Everything about the rejection was wrong. Prowse had replied briefly on 11 April 2003 in a conciliatory and humble letter saying he would look into it. Four days later he came back with a flat refusal. It seemed as if someone else had written it. The vicar general's letter stated that Emma could use the compensation money offered to her by the Church, a woeful $50,000, which she had not yet claimed. 'The amount involved would quite clearly address the issues raised in your letter of 2 April 2003, as well as assisting Emma with some of the other issues.'

I had read this last sentence to mean: 'Take the money so you are no longer an ongoing legal threat to the Church.'

Another negative aspect of our experience with Melbourne Response was our request for $7 000 to fund Emma's Division 2 Nursing course, which she wanted to do to become a nurse's aide. It was a one-year course. We saw this as a very positive step Emma was taking, perhaps a way of saving her. Carelink had encouraged us to put in a request for funding. Then in early 2000, our request had been rejected. We thought it typical of Church behaviour so paid the $7 000 ourselves. That was the extent of our knowledge about it. However, the Royal Commission obtained documented evidence that Carelink had wanted to provide funding for Emma's education. But a 'memorandum' dated 10 February 2000 stated, 'Emma could not be funded at Carelink because she had applied for [Church] compensation.'

At the time, we had thought we were talking solely to the professional health providers of Carelink, but unknown to us others, unqualified in the health area, were calling the shots and overriding their own Carelink medical professionals' advice. We had been led to believe that all three sections of Melbourne Response – investigation, ex-gratia payments and care (Carelink) – were separate departments (independent, as Pell claimed) to maintain privacy. 'Chinese walls' was the term used in the commission hearing.

Another lie.

# 26

Cardinal George Pell was also a witness in our Case Study 16. He appeared before the commission on a video link from the Vatican on 21 August 2014. We began hearing him at 4 pm. Normally, the commission would have adjourned for the day, but it was morning in Rome.

When the cardinal appeared on screen, I noticed the curtains behind him. I couldn't help thinking that they had been hung to shield our eyes from the Vatican's wealth.

From start to finish, Pell's two-and-a-half hours of evidence were a defence of himself, his Church and his Vatican. First, when Justice McClellan asked him for the sex offender priest files (the Secret Archives), the witness said the documents were the property of the Vatican and the commission could not have all of them.

He believed the Church had provided enough documents.[124] In a statement he said he was 'aware that the Vatican had provided 5,000 pages of documentation [. . .] but in following international convention they will not provide the internal working documents of another sovereign state'.

When asked by a victim's lawyer if he had listened to his client's evidence a couple of days earlier, Pell implied he had been too busy: 'I have a job here in Rome.' This was infuriating for many survivors and their loved ones, including my family. Then he stunned everyone by likening the Church's responsibility to the child victims of criminal priests to that of a trucking company and its drivers. 'If, in fact, the driver of such a truck picks up some lady,' he said, 'and then molests her, I don't think it's appropriate, because it is contrary to the policy, for the ownership, the leadership of that company to be held responsible.'[125]

There were many problems with the comparison.

The 'trucking company' is not pretending to be a holy institution above the law. The 'driver' is not pretending he is celibate or holy. The 'some lady' the driver is picking up is an adult wanting a lift. The truck driver is picking up a hitchhiker, not invading the bodies of children who are meant to be safe in school or church or home in bed. And the trucking bosses are not hiding offenders, covering up crimes or allowing more offences to occur.

His evidence was tiresome, disappointing, more of the same bullishness. To make things even worse, the cardinal's internet connection was terrible.

The last witness at the Melbourne Response hearing was the Archbishop of Melbourne, Denis Hart. Archbishop Hart had promised in word and writing to hold a consultation with victims to reassess old compensation settlements and remove the $75,000 cap on payments. However, he turned up empty-handed.

He answered questions for hours then asked if he could say something. He was granted this opportunity. Having been pummelled by the forensic examination, he announced that he would hold an inquiry into Melbourne Response. He had just testified at the most powerful inquiry in this country, and now was going to investigate the same thing.

It was laughable. This was his belated 'new era'. Another pitiful gesture from a hollow man with hollow words.

One positive from Case Study 16 was that the Church finally admitted that Fr Kevin O'Donnell, our daughters' abuser, the abuser of hundreds of children over his fifty-year crime spree, had been reported to the Church hierarchy decades earlier. Anthony and I had known this truth for a long time. Only now was the Church making a public concession. It all came down to an internal document, the one that hadn't made it to the Vatican under seal.

The commission's report states: 'In 1958, complaints were made to Monsignor Moran, then Chief Administrator for the Diocese of Melbourne, about Father O'Donnell's interference with a young boy (the 1958 complaints).'[126]

The Church's lawyer, Mr Leder, agreed that 'a senior figure in the Archdiocese had information in 1958 that, properly handled, might have led to Father O'Donnell being exposed and subsequent abuse being avoided'.

This concession under oath meant the world to survivors of O'Donnell's abuse. Their future attempts to gain fair compensation for their pain and suffering would be made easier.

But it was also very painful for me to hear.

It meant that my children and another three decades of other children would not have been sexually assaulted if the Church hierarchy had acted to remove Fr O'Donnell for his crimes in the 1950s.

When the findings of our case study came out in a 179-page report, it referred to our 1997 meeting in Oakleigh with then Archbishop of Melbourne George Pell. The commission's report quoted parts of our sworn witness statement:

> Mrs Foster said that during this meeting a question was asked about known paedophiles still serving in parishes in Melbourne and that Archbishop Pell responded, 'It's all gossip until it's proven in court and I don't listen to gossip.' Cardinal Pell accepted that he may well have used the word 'gossip'.[127]

Two of the 'known paedophiles still serving in parishes' we were talking to George Pell about in 1997 were Father Wilfred Baker and Father Peter Searson.

The Royal Commission unearthed a document from Catholic Church Insurance (CCI) dated 14 February 1997 (four days before our Oakleigh meeting with Pell) entitled 'Confidential Questionnaire'. In writing, CCI had asked the archbishop's office to list the dates at which they, the hierarchy, 'first became aware of any allegations of sexual assault' by the twenty Melbourne Archdiocesan priests that it, the insurance company, had received claims against.

The first name on the list was Fr Baker and the date that Vicar General Denis Hart had filled out that the Church 'first became aware' of allegations of his offending was November 1993. Hart, who signed and dated the document, was a man who would not have done anything without his boss's approval. In 1997, his boss was George Pell.

Joining the dots on this information was not difficult if you knew the names and times referred to in the documents. In short, four days before Pell met us in Oakleigh on 18 February 1997, his vicar general had completed an official and damning concession about the allegations against Baker (and nineteen other child sex offending priests). Pell came to Oakleigh, where we asked him to remove Baker and Searson from their parishes. He challenged our right to make such a plea: where was our evidence? We knew our information – that at least eight current Melbourne priests had complaints against them – was accurate because it had been given to us by the Church's own Pastoral Response Office, a small department within the Melbourne Archdiocese.

In the newspapers, the newly appointed Archbishop Pell was being lauded by anonymous churchmen as a changemaker. 'George is very much a traditionalist,' one senior priest told the *Herald Sun* in February 1997. 'He isn't frightened to kick heads.'[128] I found these words such an unchristian image for a senior priest to use boastfully and a totally unbecoming description of a human being, least of all an archbishop. The only kicking we wanted was paedophile priests down to the local police station.

All this clarity came to me from the evidence given to the Royal Commission. Significantly, I had to wonder where the archbishop's office had obtained the information about twenty offending priests. Some dates of complaints were decades earlier, one being 18 April 1978, eighteen years before Pell and Hart took office. I reasoned that consulting Secret Archives on offending clergy would provide such information.

Fr Baker's crimes had been reported to the Church much earlier than 1993. I knew about a meeting in 1978 between two legal professionals and Archbishop Frank Little, who had flown into a rage of denial and defence of Baker before, nonetheless believing the complaint and transferring Baker unrestricted to a different parish. Hart officially acknowledging the 1993 complaint against Baker implicated former Archbishop Little as being responsible for all the sexual assaults committed by Baker between 1978 and 1993, but Little's death in 2008 meant he would evade punishment by law.

More dirt on Fr Baker was revealed by the Royal Commission after further examination. What Pell knew about Baker was explained to the public when the redacted papers referring to the cardinal were made public years later. The Church hierarchy had found out Baker was likely to be charged by police. This is what the Royal Commission would find after weighing up its evidence:

> We are satisfied that the Curia [selected Auxiliary Bishops and Archbishop of Melbourne] knew in August 1996 that Father Baker would probably be charged in relation to an incident at Brighton in 1965. We are satisfied that Archbishop Pell, Bishop O'Connell, Monsignor Connors, Monsignor Deakin, Mr Exell and Father Waters were at the meeting where this was discussed.

Archbishop Pell had the authority to remove Baker. Despite that knowledge, Pell did not stand down Baker at that point in time. Indeed, Baker remained in his position at North Richmond – a parish with a primary school attached to it – until May 1997.[129] (This was three months after our Oakleigh meeting.) The commission also determined that Pell attended meetings in the early 1990s when allegations against Baker would have been discussed.[130]

It had taken too long for the hierarchy to act.

The Royal Commission's findings also accepted evidence about Baker by Patricia Taylor, the North Richmond St James Primary School principal. When Baker had arrived at the parish and its school in June 1992 the Catholic Education Office staff gave Ms Taylor four very particular warnings about him: one, not to let children be alone with Fr Baker, ever; two, not to let children go into the confessional behind closed doors with Fr Baker; three, not to provide Fr Baker with the contact phone numbers of female school staff; and four, that she should never be in a room alone with Fr Baker.

The CEO, charged with the education and wellbeing of children, went to great lengths to allow Baker to stay in his exalted position while he was a threat to children (and women) at the school. Baker did not have to change his behaviour, but the school did!

On 8 June 1999, Baker was sentenced to four years jail for child sex offences. More victims came forward, but the dangerous criminal died before another case went to trial.

The Royal Commission revealed our 1997 'gossip' was truth. Another thing that I cannot forget in Ms Taylor's testimony is when she went to her local auxiliary bishop Peter Connors (before he became Bishop of Ballarat) for help after more disturbing information came from a victim who told her of Baker's sexual abuse of him as a child. Connors' uncaring and dismissive response to Ms Taylor's legitimate concerns was: 'Once a paedophile, always a paedophile.'[131]

## 27

Earlier, in the lead-up to our case study, it was my job to read through hundreds of pages of documents subpoenaed by the commission. I did this with Anthony and our lawyers. These documents and another 1 313 exhibits, which the commission could call upon, were all evidence for Case Study 16. They were organised into 'tender bundles' and contained all manner of written communications relevant to us and our case. It wasn't a difficult job to go through the evidence, although it took up a lot of time and effort.

Our barrister Tim Seccull, his assisting lawyer Viv Waller, Anthony and I sat at a dining table in a quiet spare room at home. The table was left for weeks in its state of organised chaos, a sea of lever-arch folders both thick and thin, notebooks containing our observations and comments, and my hundreds of documents accumulated over the years. We were all studying the paperwork before us.

We weren't necessarily looking for anything damning or shocking, but I always kept an analytical eye on the words on each page. You never know whether you'll find something hiding in plain sight.

One July 2014 afternoon, as I commenced reading yet another tender bundle of documents, I saw something that stopped me dead. A little alarm sounded in my brain. Within seconds I realised what I was holding. It was the psychiatric report on Fr Kevin O'Donnell, written in 1995 by a Professor Richard Ball, who would later become manager of Melbourne Response's Carelink section. This wasn't a moment of despair. It was exciting. I understood this was the very report I had tried, in vain, to obtain from the Office of Public Prosecutions almost twenty years earlier.

In November 1996, a police officer had told us that Ball had written a psychiatric report for O'Donnell in 1995 while the priest was facing the County Court on child sexual assault charges. The report was used by defence lawyers as an attempt to get O'Donnell a reduced jail term. The trial judge referred to it in his comments, Ball pointing out that O'Donnell was contrite for his past behaviour, was old and lacked libido, and would suffer depression and dietary problems if incarcerated.

Much of this was nonsense. Ludicrous, even. I understood it was every suspected criminal's right to have professional or character witnesses as part of the sentencing process; Professor Ball had also written psychiatric reports on other major paedophile priests and Brothers in Victoria, including Fathers Glennon, Gannon and Ridsdale, and Brothers Best and Dowlan. For the author of these reports to also be placed in a position of overseeing 'care' and psychiatric needs for victims of these sex offenders was a terrible breach of trust, logic and perhaps even process.

As for the full report on O'Donnell, I had never seen it until systematically going through the tender bundles. It was an astounding find.

I remembered eighteen years earlier when we were told by a policeman from the DPP's office of Professor Ball's defence reports for major clergy offenders and that he was now going to head up Melbourne Response's Carelink. I could not believe such a betrayal could happen, yet the simmering anger I felt told me otherwise. First, I had to check that this Carelink Professor Ball and the O'Donnell court case Professor Ball were the same man. Seconds passed as I frantically searched the documents with a growing rage inside me, cutting my finger on the metal suspension-file clip as I went. Seeing my blood didn't slow me down. I found O'Donnell's sentencing transcript, flicked through its pages and found confirmation. Professor Richard Ball.

Some words stay with you. The 1995 court transcript lauded Ball, with O'Donnell's defence lawyer boasting of Ball's extensive credentials: 'It may have some significance, but Dr Ball talks about his position as he, Dr Ball, is an authority I think, your honour, in relation to these sort of matters and frequently gives evidence in these courts.'[132]

O'Donnell had pleaded guilty to sex offences against ten boys and two girls that covered 1946–77. Rape charges were dropped in a plea deal because police wanted to avoid any delay. They wanted him in jail as soon as possible. He had not been charged with offences against our daughters because his case was dealt with before their disclosures. He died in March 1997. But his abuse of Emma and Katie was proof that he had still been criminally active by sexually assaulting children in the 1980s and 1990s, right up until his retirement in 1992.

Now, in 2014, sitting in my home, I held Professor Ball's psychiatric report on O'Donnell in my hands. I read the two-page report with an eighteen-year thirst. I recognised the professor's words of assessment on O'Donnell that had been used by the judge.

The soft language annoyed me once again. Contrite. Sick. It was pathetic.

Fortunately, in 1995, Justice Kellam had not accepted Ball's claim that O'Donnell was contrite. In sentencing, the judge said to the priest: 'Professor Ball expressed the opinion that you are contrite for your past behaviour. There is no direct statement from your mouth of or any act of contrition which might demonstrate substantial remorse for or concern or understanding of what your victims endured at your hands.'[133]

After I finished reading the entire report, I picked up the next document in the bundle. To my astonishment, it looked identical to the Professor Ball report I had just read. Same unique typeface. Addressed to the same solicitor. Same date: 2 August 1995. Signed by Professor Ball. But it was different – two pages instead of one. The psychiatrist had written two separate reports. I read on. Ball was addressing O'Donnell's lawyer with instructions on how to use this letter. 'I am writing this as a general background to what you asked me to assess,' he wrote. 'And this is not – repeat NOT – the letter which you wanted. That will be attached as a separate missive.'

These words indicated this second report was private, a secret alternative assessment of O'Donnell. It exposed details of O'Donnell's offending up until 1991 or 1992, which was withheld from the judge in the first report.

The two reports differed in the following ways. For the judge, Ball stated: 'I will not direct my attention to the offences as such because I have had insufficient time to carry out a formal and detailed assessment.' The secret report to the solicitor stated:

> In order to get some idea of the whole situation I did of course have to go into the background, the nature of the offences, the duration of them and the frequency of them.

For the judge:

> Fr O'Donnell – presumably associated with his age, if nothing else – has little or no libido and there are no inclinations, much less opportunity, to offend again.

The secret report to the solicitor:

> He claims that he has not been sexually active for the last three to four years [i.e. 1991 or 1992, not 1977 as claimed in court] and has little or no libido now.

For the judge:

> He does express contrition for his past behaviour.

The secret report to the solicitor:

As is not uncommon with priests, he has a peculiar, naive lack of insight and a paradoxical tendency to justify, including statements like: 'I nearly always stopped when I realised they were becoming sexually aware.'

For the judge, Ball mentioned O'Donnell's many physical health problems and expressed concerns about his being incarcerated. These pleas for compassion were extensively cited, but offending information disclosed to Professor Ball was not passed on.

For the secret report, Ball did not mention the physical health and incarceration concerns, rather he talked extensively about the offending information he had obtained from O'Donnell. 'He [O'Donnell] had some early involvement with young folk but nothing much until shortly after Ordination [1942], and from then on until three or four years ago [1991 or 1992] there was a series of paedophilic activities, sometimes going on for a reasonably lengthy time with particular individuals.'

In the secret report Ball finished with a line referring the solicitor to the other letter, 'which is the one you want to use for official purposes'.

That last sentence speaks of the deception to mislead the trial judge, the County Court, victims and the people of Victoria over the defendant's criminal activities right up until 1991 or 1992. I wondered if this was legal.

And misled the judge was. By not seeing Ball's secret report, Justice Kellan stated, 'It is in the order of eighteen years since the last offence [1977], for which I am required to sentence you, occurred and it is of great significance in your favour that you have not offended against the law over those past eighteen years or so.'

Despite Ball's contradictory reports and his inappropriate appeal for compassion for the child abuser, O'Donnell went to prison in August 1995. At seventy-eight, he held the distinction of being the oldest man ever to be incarcerated in the state of Victoria.

Discovering this second secret letter felt like finding a silver bullet. It was proof of the behind-the-scenes injustice that caused us years of pain and outrage. Our daughters' rapist was never sorry.

I am not blinded to reality. I understand that clinicians, like child sex abuse expert Ray Wyre, whom I had great respect for, can work with both victims and offenders of the same crime. Their work potentially gives them and society understanding. But Ball was in a different position. Church victims were to be placed under his supervision through Melbourne Response. It was another nail in the coffin around George Pell's argument that his set-up operated independently of the Church, and another slap in the face from the hierarchy.

Long before we read these two letters, we had protested about the Ball appointment. Anthony had said to Pell in 1997, 'It's a conflict of interest.' I had asked, 'Why is he in charge?'

'Because he's the best man for the job,' was Pell's retort.

Years later, Pell was asked by a reporter about Professor Ball's role.

He replied words to the effect of 'We are happy with him.'

The Church hierarchy knew it was untouchable.

After I read Ball's two reports, I submitted a complaint to the Royal Commission. I believed Ball should be questioned about his secret 'separate missive'. Compelling Ball to explain himself publicly would have been a meaningful conclusion to this longstanding deceit. Alas, Ball did not front the commission. He claimed he was too unwell to testify. However, he did make a six-page statement that included: 'My role involved attempting to understand what may have led to an individual acting in a particular way and to make that known to the Court.' It was hard to see how that was true when he had withheld vital information from the court.

In his statement Ball said, 'I have some memory of Father Gerard Ridsdale and giving evidence at a criminal hearing but I do not recall assessing, or giving expert evidence in relation to Father O'Donnell or Brother Best.'[134]

With that convenient statement and 'I do not recall' he was excused from questioning about his two opposing reports on our daughters' rapist.

Regardless, Case Study 16 progressed. Later, the commission made findings in a preliminary report. It contained more information about Ball that I did not know. On 13 March 1997 Ball had told Leder of a national program that had been established for the treatment of priests, including those who had sexual 'difficulties', and that he was the Melbourne director of it. This treatment centre became known as Encompass Australasia. It was the first time I had heard of a Melbourne branch of Encompass Australasia (the Church-funded offender treatment centre Bishop Robinson helped create).

Anthony and I had tried to refuse to have anything to do with Ball from the start because we saw him as part of the hierarchy; we believed that's why the Church used his professional reports – the reports worked for them but were utterly adverse to victims. Yet eventually we had been forced by the hierarchy to meet with him. I didn't want to. Up until then, we had dealt with others in the Carelink office. The meeting took place on 29 July 1997. I have a 21-page transcript of the meeting because Ball insisted on its recording. For eight of the twenty-one pages, both Anthony and I argued with him about his involvement in ensuring O'Donnell received the minimal jail sentence he did. We argued without knowing what his entire report said. We obviously didn't know about the secret missive.

Our instincts were correct in not trusting Ball or his employer. He died in 2017. *The Age* ran an obituary months later – apparently, he had been a pioneer in transgender health studies. Nowhere in the half-page obituary did it mention Professor Ball's many years working for the Catholic Church as its head of Carelink, nor did it mention his role as Melbourne Director of Encompass Australasia, save to say, '[He] continued to contribute in academia and clinical roles, including forensic services and consultant to victims of sexual abuse.'[135]

# 28

It was time to get away.

After our case study, Anthony and I flew to the Northern Territory for a break from the stress of the previous two weeks in court. We landed in Alice Springs and made our way to Uluru. There we met our friends Annie and Bryan. The four of us spent many relaxing hours together talking and sightseeing.

This was good for my soul. We would get up early and walk beneath the cloudless sky. The desert sand would turn our shoes and socks the same red. One morning, we walked all the way around Uluru – 10.6 kilometres – taking in its majesty, finding shaded waterholes.

After several days we said goodbye to the beauty of our brief getaway. On the way home I felt like a recharged battery, ready to resume our life. We had left Katie in the good hands of her kind and loving Transport Accident Commission–funded carers, who look after her 24/7. This allowed us to get away, but it is one of the heartbreaks in our lives that Katie has such a life.

Anthony and I were both receiving invitations to contribute to public discussions about the issue of child sexual abuse. He attended a Royal Commission roundtable discussion on redress. What did real compensations look like? He was firm in his mind that any redress for victims should not be capped by institutions. We had seen how cruel that was for survivors.

I was a guest presenter at the Victorian Women Lawyers Forum. Standing up in front of people and speaking my mind was still challenging for me, but I was getting better at it. In my downtime I continued being a researcher. After all these years, I am still as curious as ever about how the Church works.

Anthony and I attended a Catholics for Renewal evening where Kieran Tapsell was the speaker. Mr Tapsell was an ex-seminarian, retired barrister and acting district court judge in New South Wales. He had written a book called *Potiphar's Wife: The Vatican's Secret and Child Sexual Abuse*, a hard-hitting exposé on the Catholic Church's 1700-year-plus history of clergy child sexual assault. Something in Mr Tapsell's speech stunned me. He referred to canon 1321, which seemed to be a 'catch 22 defence'. He said 'a priest cannot be dismissed for paedophilia because he is a paedophile.' This piece of insanity explains a lot.

Mr Tapsell used two cases in Ireland to illustrate his point. Two notorious paedophile priests were dismissed by a Dublin canonical court, he explained. The appeal court in Rome, however, set aside the dismissals because the clergy had been diagnosed as paedophiles.

It seemed incredible. Once more I consulted my canon law book. There it was in black and white. Page 901, canon 1321 states:

1) No-one is punished unless the external violation of a law or a precept committed by the person is seriously imputable to that person by reason of malice or culpability.
2) A person who has deliberately violated a law or a precept is bound by the penalty stated in that law or that precept; unless a law or a precept provides otherwise, a person who has violated that law or that precept through a lack of necessary diligence is not punished.
3) Unless it is otherwise evident, imputability is presumed whenever an external violation has occurred.[136]

Canon 1321 has not been changed. As long as this canon law exists, the priesthood will retain its paedophilic clergy.

We celebrated Christmas with a large family get-together at Tonimbuk. Anthony and I always looked forward to a new year. It promised a new phase of life and activities. And at this point in our lives, the Royal Commission was at the forefront of everything. It promised so much.

In the middle of January 2015, Anthony and I travelled to the Maitland Bowling Club in New South Wales to celebrate the policing career of former detective chief inspector Peter Fox. The party was a great surprise for him, and some welcome fun. He had endured the legal stresses of the Cunneen Inquiry and a difficult resignation from the police service. Thankfully, he seemed to have an internal fire burning for justice. Survivors were fortunate to have him as an advocate.

The Royal Commission was an examination of many institutions, not just the Catholic Church. In February, the commission began looking into the injustices of Yeshiva Bondi and Yeshivah Melbourne. Manny Waks, who had been a vocal advocate for victims in the Jewish community for some years, was a witness. Manny had been abused as a young boy by two paedophiles in his community, and he and his family had faced a community backlash when they reported the abuse. Manny met Anthony and me at the Parliamentary Inquiry and we became friends.

After the two-week hearing, Anthony and I packed our bags again. This time we were travelling overseas; our good friends Cathie and Mick were coming with us to France.

I loved travelling overseas. Of all my trips since the age of nineteen, my favourites were the island of St Kilda off the west coast of Scotland, Antarctica, Japan and France. I believe these places will forever hold special moments, happy memories and beautiful imagery. This time we were off to France again. We were going to spend all our time in

Paris and the Champagne region with Cathie and Mick. It was going to be terrific.

Five days before departing Australia, busy with preparations, we received some surprising news. A close friend contacted us to say a young relative had seen George Pell dining at a restaurant in the Melbourne suburb of Carlton. Several other people were dining with him. Pell was meant to be in Rome working as the Vatican's treasurer. The source of the news was reliable. There had been nothing in the media about the cardinal's visit, which seemed odd. We didn't give it another thought.

France felt like a homecoming. The four of us had spent a week together in Paris many years earlier with two other couples, moving on to Le Puget, an ancient hill town in the south of France.

The first five days in Paris were spent shopping and seeing the sights. We then drove to the Champagne region, where we stayed in Château d'Étoges. Breakfast was accompanied by glasses of champagne. For champagne lovers like me and Cathie it was a little slice of heaven. Cathie and I were smiling every morning.

As usual, Anthony was the most wonderful travel companion. But that didn't mean he could completely switch off from the news of the world. He checked his computer regularly to keep up to date. One night he told me of a story he was reading. 'St James Church in Brighton has burnt down,' he said. 'They think it was an arson attack.'

We immediately thought it might be a revenge against the Church. The parish had previously been home and hunting ground for Fr Ronald Pickering. I asked Anthony to read the story to me:

Police confirmed the fire, which largely destroyed the 123-year-old St James Church in Brighton (a suburb of Melbourne), was being treated as suspicious. Detectives are now investigating if the fire is linked to the crimes of Ronald Pickering, who served as the church's parish priest from 1978 to 1998 before he fled to Britain, fearing prosecution.[137]

Next night, Anthony was again reading from the laptop. Another church had been set alight: St Mary's in St Kilda East, another of Pickering's old haunts. It was looking like a series of planned attacks.

Sure enough, the third night another church was the victim of arson. It was St Mary's in Dandenong. This time it was personal. This St Mary's was one of the parishes controlled and dominated by our daughters' rapist, Fr O'Donnell.[138]

'The Dandenong fire caused $250,000 damage,' the news story reported. 'O'Donnell, who served there as parish priest from 1956 to 1969, was jailed in 1995 aged seventy-eight after he admitted abusing ten boys and two girls.'[139]

We wondered if on the fourth night we would read that Sacred Heart Church in Oakleigh had also been burnt to the ground but there were no more church fires. As far as I know, police did not apprehend anyone for the arson attacks.

After our French breakfast we drove though the loveliest country-side to find champagne cellar doors for tastings. The samples were generous. Each champagne tasting was almost half a glass. Morally, how could we not drink all of it? Cathie and I were in our element. Anthony and Mick were less enthusiastic about tasting the bubbly, which worked out perfectly because they were doing the driving and navigation.

We were on the move one day when from the front seat our navigator Anthony raised a question and his computer screen for us to see. 'How would you like to stay in a castle on the Rhine in Germany?' He'd found a place called Schönburg Castle.

Cathie and I looked at the photo of the stunning medieval castle Anthony was showing us; a fairytale mansion perched on a hill looking over the Rhine River. With great enthusiasm and excitement, we both said yes. From France to Luxembourg to Germany. Everything seemed relatively close – nothing like Australia and its endless expanses. Schönburg Castle was even more astounding in real life.

Our accommodation of four medieval rooms per couple was amazing. The cosy rooms had long, narrow windows displaying a mixture of plain and beautiful stained glass. The castle was magical. We stayed there five days and loved every minute.

From Schönburg Castle we drove through the Black Forest and made our way to the border town of Strasbourg on our way back to Paris. On one memorable day during our travels, we dropped in to visit Manny Waks and his family who were living in a country area. We spent the day with them and chatted over lunch in a little restaurant in a nearby town. It was good to see Manny again and to meet his family.

Too soon we were returning to Melbourne. Our trip away seemed sandwiched between Church matters. The day after we left for France, Br Dowlan (offender from St Alipius, Ballarat) was sentenced regarding further offences, and the day after we returned the Archbishop of Adelaide, Philip Wilson, stood trial in New South Wales for failing to report child abuse by a colleague in the 1970s.

# 29

Soon after, we celebrated the special milestone of our youngest daughter Aimee graduating with an Arts degree from Monash University. In doing so, Aimee became the first member of our family to receive a university degree. That she earned this academic recognition under such difficult circumstances made it even more impressive. Her eldest sister Emma's life began spiralling out of control when Aimee was only ten years old. Katie's terrible accident pulled Aimee further away from her life and study when she was fourteen. In 2008, on the day Aimee was accepted to do a double degree in Law and Arts, Emma died. We were all debilitated. Childhood, teenagerhood and early adulthood had been a hard road for Aimee. Her graduation ceremony was held at the university in Clayton, not far from our Oakleigh home. We were and are so very proud of her.

A monumental hearing was looming for the Royal Commission. Case Study 28 Catholic Church Authorities in Ballarat was to get to the bottom of crimes and cover-ups in that region. The town had been awash with paedophile priests and Brothers who wreaked untold damage on children. Many victims had not survived their trauma.

The Ballarat hearing was scheduled for two long sittings, one in the town itself, the other in Melbourne later in the year. The Royal Commission wanted to train its spotlight on a children's home, two primary schools and a secondary college, St Patrick's. The press ran preview stories with headlines to make your skin crawl, such as SPIDERS' PLAYGROUND[140] and RETURN TO THE HOUSE OF DEVILS.[141]

The abuse in Ballarat was considered 'historical' but there was nothing old about the trauma. I felt the pain whenever I visited. It existed in the streets and buildings and in big Catholic families. Three brothers and a cousin from one family had been abused in the 1970s; one of the boys survived, the others died by suicide.

On the morning of the first day of evidence, Anthony and I drove to Ballarat from home. By now we didn't think about why we had decided to go to all the hearings. We just turned up. It felt right.

I will never forget the evidence from survivor Phil Nagle. Looking tortured by his experience at the hands of a paedophile at St Alipius Boys' School decades previously, he held up his old classroom photo to the court. He pointed out that of the thirty-three primary school pupils in the picture, twelve had died by suicide. Phil asked for a minute's silence following his testimony.

Each day of the hearing, I looked at the witness list. I knew many of the Ballarat survivors. For many years, Anthony and I had been meeting victims from Ballarat. They were all lovely men who had been given an unfair start to life by God's flock of servants. Devils in sheep's clothing.

Given his standing in the Church, Pell's time spent as a priest in Ballarat was of great media interest.

One day I saw Gerald Ridsdale's name on the witness list. Ridsdale was the most notorious of several predator priests at St Alipius. This almost took my breath away. Three years earlier I had written to the Victorian Parliamentary Inquiry: 'If the Committee wishes to know the inner workings of the hierarchy's dealings with paedophile priests, I very strongly recommend you call for evidence, by way of interview, laicised priest Fr Gerald Ridsdale.' Ridsdale had admitted to sexually assaulting so many children he had lost count. Probably hundreds. Maybe a thousand. Who knew? He had been moved so many times by the Catholic Church hierarchy that his reign seemed boundless. Complaints came in but were never given to police. The cover-up of Ridsdale would amount to one of the worst criminal conspiracies in Australian history. When my submission was published on the Parliamentary Committee's website, the above passage was redacted, making me believe they were going to interview Ridsdale in prison, but I never found out if they did so or not. I had since raised the same suggestion in my submission to the Royal Commission. Finally, we were going to hear him answer questions. I was pleased that we might learn more of what went on behind the Church scenes. I hoped the commission had not let this information filter through to the bishops but I supposed they knew what was coming.

Ridsdale was booked in for two days of forensic questioning.

Pressure was also building for the old cover-up bishop of Ballarat, Ronald Mulkearns, to take the stand. He had dodged the Parliamentary Inquiry, but the commission carried more weight. The word was Mulkearns might die soon. There was furious agreement among the gallery members of the Royal Commission in Ballarat that the so-called Keeper of Secrets ought not be allowed to take all his memories of betrayal with him to the grave.


The Ballarat courthouse was packed every day. The Royal Commission used the largest courtroom on the third floor. People crammed in. An overflow room was available in a separate building nearby; on the day of Ridsdale's reckoning, even the extra space was crowded.

Ridsdale's evidence was scheduled to be given via a video link from Ararat Prison, where he would likely spend the rest of his days. I was pleased by this proposition. As much as I wanted to hear from Ridsdale, I didn't think I could stand to be in the same room as him.

We understood the Royal Commission's request to hear from the paedophile was part of its exploration of how the Church had covered up complaints of abuse. Then, out of the blue, the *Herald Sun* newspaper published a telling story. A priest had come forward with information. A Father Eric Bryant stated he had been present at a 1982 meeting of clergy, during which Ridsdale was discussed.

George Pell was among others at that meeting. It was a gathering of the college of consultors, all the bishop's men.[142]

Fr Bryant said that at the meeting concerns about Ridsdale 'committing homosexual acts' were 'explicitly discussed'.

Bryant's account seemed explosive. At last, a priest who had a memory. I was sure he was a good man who in 1982 had listened with horror as his bishop 'explicitly discussed' the homosexual acts. The significance of this testimony was that if there was an admission by the Church that its clergy had been discussing Ridsdale's crimes as early as 1982, everyone at that meeting might face allegations of culpability for subsequent crimes committed by the paedophile.

Fr Bryant would now be compelled to appear before the Royal Commission in December (seven months later) to give evidence.

Publicly, the heat was now on Pell to give his account of the 1982 meeting. From the Vatican, he released a statement. 'My recollection is that Bishop Mulkearns did not raise any paedophilia allegations against Ridsdale at the Consultors meeting I attended or at any time before or after such meetings.'

I repeatedly read the newspaper reports of Bryant's evidence and Pell's statement. As usual, I was examining specific wording. Or should I say word games? Bryant had not mentioned 'paedophilia allegations'; rather, he had quoted Bishop Mulkearns in 1982 saying 'homosexual acts'.

I believed the 'homosexual acts' *were* 'paedophilia allegations'. I believe Pell was using a play on words from different eras to put the media fire out and divert accountability. Ridsdale 'committing homosexual acts' (in 1982) equated to Ridsdale committing paedophilia acts (in 2015). The 1982 'homosexual' terminology fitted in with society's inadequate vocabulary for child molesting and rape back then. Personally, the first time I heard the word paedophile was when I travelled to England in 1977. Many years earlier while attending my Catholic primary school in the 1960s an altar boy warned my older brother to stay away from our parish priest because he was a 'poofter'. The child had no word for paedophile at the time.

I wrote to the Royal Commission about my concerns over a possible priestly wordplay. But, of course, the commissioners were already one step ahead. Their questioning suggested they were not buying it.

With the Fr Bryant bombshell all but echoing around the courtroom, Ridsdale faced his second day of questioning from prison. It was 28 May 2015. Anthony and I were sitting in the gallery, watching and listening to the paedophile on the TV screen.

Counsel assisting Gail Furness had been asking Ridsdale about his time as assistant parish priest in Horsham. Ridsdale seemed to be suffering memory lapses. He was evading full answers, omitting detail. The pressure this reticence, forgetfulness or obstinacy placed on those sitting in the court was immense. It was giving me a throbbing headache. Our forced silence within the formal courtroom didn't help, instead it magnified irritations. It would have been better if we could scream at Ridsdale to tell the truth.

Some people left the gallery to take a break outside. I imagined them out front on the footpath, wanting to break something.

Ms Furness finally came to a point where she felt it best to spell out details for Ridsdale. 'And you left parish work because of a string of complaints that you had been offending against children for in fact decades?' she said.

'Yes,' Ridsdale said.

The mood in the room seemed to change. We all felt it, although we didn't know why. Immediately after Ridsdale's single-word response, Justice McClellan called an adjournment.

After the break we were cast into a courtroom drama akin to something you are more likely to see at the movies. Justice McClellan was now taking charge of the questioning. 'Mr Ridsdale,' he said, 'just before Ms Furness continues, I want to ask you this: during your life in the Church and offending, did you tell lies about your conduct to people who asked you about it?'

'Well, I don't remember anybody asking me about it but, if they had, I certainly would have told lies about it or minimised what I was doing,' Ridsdale said.

'Are you familiar with the principle of mental reservation?' Justice McClellan said.

'The principle of what, your honour?'

'Mental reservation.'

'I can't really remember what it – I think it . . . I think it was something we used to talk about in priesthood, but I can't remember what it is now.'

'You used to talk about it, did you?' Justice McClellan asked.

'I think it was part of – it's an expression that I know from the past but I can't think what it is.'

'Do you remember that it might have something to do with justifying you not telling the whole truth when asked a question?'

'No, I didn't know that,' Ridsdale said.

'What do you remember the principles of mental reservation being?' Justice McClellan said.

'I don't know,' the paedophile answered. 'I remember the term, but I can't remember what it was about.'

I was astonished and delighted this was being discussed. I had learned about the practice of mental reservation while researching *Hell on the Way to Heaven* in November 2009. Better known as 'lying without lying', it had been attacked in Ireland during that nation's child sex inquiries. In short, mental reservation is the priesthood's way of lying through not telling the whole truth. That it was taught to trainee priests as a standard part of clerical education made me suspicious.

It is my experience that people learning of mental reservation remember the principles of it without the name. Ridsdale, on the other hand, was doing the opposite. He remembered the name but not the concept – almost certainly a lie, I felt.

At this curious point, after Ridsdale's last answer, Justice McClellan fell silent. Looking away from Ridsdale, the judge's stern expression was fixed on the back wall. He had our undivided attention.

We waited for him to speak. Slowly he turned back to Ridsdale's image on the screen.

'Answer this for me: you spoke with me in a private hearing some weeks ago, didn't you?'

'Yes, in Ararat when we had the private closed hearing.'

This was big news to me. I knew there were private hearings, but I didn't know that a prison witness could be called to undergo a private hearing before a public one.

'Had you spoken to anyone about the evidence you might give in that hearing before you came to that private hearing?' Justice McClellan asked.

'No, I've spoken to no-one about it. I was told not to,' replied Ridsdale.

'Since that private hearing, have you spoken to anyone about the evidence you might give in this public hearing?'

'No,' the paedophile said. 'Again, I was told not to say anything about it.'

There was a stirring in the court. Had Ridsdale changed his evidence?

'Have you had any phone calls with anyone when you might have discussed the evidence?' Justice McClellan said.

'No.'

'Not at all?'

'No, I haven't.'

'Do you have people who make phone calls to you in the jail?' Justice McClellan said.

'No, no-one can make a phone call to me,' Ridsdale said. 'I have to phone out.'

'Do you have people who you regularly phone out to?'

'The one I would phone most regularly would be one of my sisters.'

'Who else do you phone out to?'

'Occasionally I phone Father Brendan Davey,' Ridsdale said.

'Yes,' Justice McClellan said, suggesting with his tone that he would wait patiently for any other names.

'And my solicitor, Michael de Young, when I have to,' Ridsdale said. 'There's a Father in New South Wales that I might phone about every three or four months. My sister.'

The air was electric. You could have heard a pin drop between the judge's questions and the inmate's answers. Where was this heading?

'Since the private hearing, when you spoke with me in the private hearing, have you had visitors in the jail?' Justice McClellan said.

'I forget what date . . . was that— Could you remind me how long ago that was, your honour, please?'

Gail Furness said the private hearing had been on 17 March.

'Have you had any visitors in the jail since then?' Justice McClellan said.

'I think the only visitor I've had since then would be a Father John McKinnon.'

'Anyone else?'

'No,' Ridsdale said. 'I don't know whether my sister was here in that time. I don't think so. She was due to come last weekend but we put it off.'

'Where does Father John McKinnon come from?' the judge asked.

'He's retired, he lives in Hamilton.'

My mind began racing. Who was this other priest? What business did he have visiting one of Australia's worst criminals?

The judge was done with his questioning. He handed it back to counsel assisting.

'Yes, Ms Furness.'

'Thank you, your honour,' Gail Furness said.

Everyone exhaled.

By now I believed Ridsdale had changed his answers, and it was disturbing because his words at the public hearing were the only ones that would go on record. Any truth or accountability that might come from the paedophile's role as witness was being diminished, if not lost. A lot of questions were coming to mind. Who could make Ridsdale change his evidence? Importantly, why would somebody want Ridsdale to change his evidence? Most of all, to whose advantage was this changing or hiding of facts? We had no prior knowledge of Ridsdale's private hearing on 17 March. Things must have changed significantly to prompt the ire of the commissioner.

In my mind, one thing was sure: the telephone calls would be a dead end. Ridsdale's suggestion that the commission check his phone records was the giveaway. I was also convinced that anything Ridsdale said to the Royal Commission was Church business, pointing to the visiting priest, Fr John McKinnon. Plus McKinnon's name had had to be extracted from Ridsdale: he had tried to conceal this visit. Unless somebody else turned up in the visiting records, Fr McKinnon needed to be questioned by the commission.

My radar on priests' movements was already alert, with Anthony and me recently reminded of Pell's recent return to Australia when he had been spotted in that Melbourne restaurant. We weren't the only ones who knew about the cardinal's fly-in-fly-out visit. A Ballarat resident had given me a printout of a page from a Ballarat college magazine with Pell front and centre after he was photographed visiting St Patrick's College on 27 March. The dates and events told us that Ridsdale gave evidence in his private hearing on Tuesday 17 March; Pell, at some stage, left the Vatican and secretly flew to Australia; Pell was seen on Saturday 21 March dining at a restaurant with friends in the inner Melbourne suburb of Carlton; on Friday 27 March Pell was photographed in Ballarat at the college. When Ridsdale gave evidence two months later on 28 May, he'd changed it to such a degree that he provoked the ire of the Royal Commission.

Pell's visit to Australia two months previously had been without fanfare and so private that even Francis Sullivan, chief executive of the Truth, Justice and Healing Council was not aware of it. Asked about the visit on ABC TV, Mr Sullivan said: 'That's news to me. I didn't know that, so obviously it was part of a private mission.'

My co-author, Paul Kennedy, was in Melbourne watching online as Ridsdale gave evidence. Paul discussed the evidence with colleagues in his newsroom. They decided to get some reaction by sending a reporter and camera crew to the Fairhaven house of Ronald Mulkearns, the old Ballarat Diocese boss. Perhaps he would give an interview, Paul said, although that seemed a long shot. The reporter was Margaret Paul; she was based in Geelong. Margaret drove to Fairhaven with her cameraman and knocked on the front door but no-one answered. She waited outside the property. To Margaret's surprise, a man walked out of the Mulkearns home. Almost unbelievably, it was McKinnon! If he lived in Hamilton, McKinnon was a long way from home.

Margaret interviewed the priest out the front of the house. It was all recorded. McKinnon did not object. I watched it later on the nightly news. During their interview, Margaret was stunned to hear McKinnon admit that Mulkearns 'probably' knew about Ridsdale's treatment of children, adding, 'We didn't understand the effect it [rape and sexual assault] would have on them [children] back then.'

'But it's a crime,' she said to the priest. And then she repeated it.

Never had I heard or read anyone challenge a priest, bishop or archbishop over this decades-old and outlandish we-didn't-understand-the-effects excuse. Used since 1996 by members of the hierarchy, it was an admission that they both knew about offending and did nothing to stop it. But here was Fr McKinnon face to face with an intelligent young woman who wanted an explanation. So he went on to defend his statement, adding his own cocky embellishment.

'It is clearer it is a crime now because we know the effect,' he said. 'Then, I don't think even the psychologists or the psychiatrists knew the effects of it. Just as you wouldn't go to the police if someone was an alcoholic or something, in the wisdom of the time.'

What fools they are to peddle such rubbish. Raping a child – boy or girl – has been a crime since the 1830s in Australia and for centuries before that in other parts of the world. For McKinnon to utter those words and plead such ignorance in 2015 was utterly ridiculous, misleading and wrong.

I was impressed with the ABC reporter's challenge to this clergy propaganda. The interview would later be nominated for a prestigious Walkley Award for its journalistic excellence.

In contrast, no journalist seemed to follow the story of Ridsdale changing his evidence. One report, however, stated, 'Cardinal Pell is known to be close to McKinnon.'[143] Most media instead pursued a call for Pell to return to Australia for the next Ballarat hearing in December.

I have never been able to shake off my disappointment at not knowing what Ridsdale originally told Justice McClellan in the private hearing on 17 March. The criminal held knowledge of abuse, complaints about himself and cover-ups. Perhaps he knew more than anyone. But now it is lost. If only details of Ridsdale's private hearing could be released. Perhaps a freedom of information request could be exercised in this case. Or with Pell's influence now removed, perhaps Ridsdale will feel free to speak.

# 30

Meeting survivors in Ballarat was always a positive experience and a chance to speak with good people who were still hurting. Our undeserved circumstances bound us all and was the glue of precious friendships. No need to explain, no need to justify. We were in the same fight. One friendship we made was with John, a farmer. He was not a survivor, yet he walked the road with us because he was appalled by what clergy had done to the children of his hometown. Unlike clergy, he had empathy. He had turned his back on the Church. We caught up with John often at the Ballarat hearings and enjoyed his company. He is a man of quiet wisdom. John was the man who had shown us the photo of Pell at the local college a few weeks earlier.

In the hearings, my role was observer. I took the emotional hits like anyone else in the courtroom, but there was a level of detachment I could not be spared in the Melbourne Response case study. It was a surprise and disappointment when this changed, and I felt a personal level of betrayal in Ballarat.

One of those long days, while Anthony and I were sitting in silence listening to evidence, a document flashed on screen. It was a CCI document marked 'Confidential'. Its heading read: 'Report from meeting held ▮▮▮▮▮▮▮ 1994 with Bishop Mulkearns'. Following the name of Mulkearns were the names of another three men. They were CCI representatives on the insurance company's Special Issues

Committee. ('Special Issues', the Royal Commission had established, was a code used by the Church hierarchy to refer secretly to child sexual assault without alerting others to the nature of its criminal content.)

One of the three CCI representatives on the Special Issues Committee was known to me. I will call him Patrick. It made me sick to see his name. Patrick and I had worked together on an inter-denominational church council from the late eighties to the early nineties. This was before I knew my daughters had been abused by Fr O'Donnell; I was still playing my role as a dutiful Church volunteer. Part of our council duties was to visit local churches of all denominations promoting unity rather than division through friendly contact. We would meet with a variety of ministers from different religions and attend a mix of religious services.

Patrick was a devout Catholic and lived in a neighbouring suburb. For five years, he was president and I was secretary. At my first meeting I was talked into the position, but I was happy to oblige and work for the cause. During our outreach work we had to sometimes meet and talk with O'Donnell. Patrick had already met O'Donnell before I joined the council. Towards the end of my time as secretary (August 1992), O'Donnell retired. Unknown to me, his lifetime of child sex crimes was about to catch up with him.

After my last council meeting early in 1993, I did not see Patrick again until three or four years later, after Emma had disclosed that O'Donnell had sexually assaulted her. It was before we knew Katie was also a victim. I bumped into Patrick at the local shopping centre. We said hello. I was reluctant to say much to him. The most devout among us were still not allowing themselves to comprehend that a priest could sexually assault a child.

Despite my trepidation, I told Patrick about what had happened to Emma. I believed all Catholics needed to hear the truth – especially the devout ones. Patrick's reaction to my news was surprising. Expecting a rebuttal, I watched as he took in a sharp breath, tilted his head back and looked up to the sky saying, 'Oh no!' By now

I had told several people of our situation. Most of our friends had displayed shock, a delayed comprehension, a disgusted shake of the head. None of them had reacted like Patrick. It was out of the ordinary and made me wonder, but at least he believed me.

I ignored his reaction because I had other things on my mind. Questions. I had recently learned of CCI's insurance cover for the Church's paedophile priests. Rape seemed like an insane and impossible thing to insure. How can any organisation obtain an insurance policy for the sexual assault of children?[144] It was infuriating. (In fact, this was simply Church business. The first Special Issues liability policies had been issued as early as 1991.)

I asked Patrick if he knew anything or had any information on O'Donnell from his dealings with CCI. The look on Patrick's face told me he didn't want to talk about what he did and didn't know, so I said goodbye. The only other time I saw his face was when he unexpectedly turned up to my book presentation at Parliament House in April 2011. Surprised to see him, I said hello. He and his wife bought a book and quickly left without explanation.

Now, eighteen years after our chance meeting in the shopping centre, I could see Patrick's name on the Royal Commission document screen. He had been one of the men responsible for meeting Mulkearns in respect of victim payouts concerning Gerald Ridsdale. Meeting notes proved they talked about Ridsdale's other victims in Warrnambool, Apollo Bay, Sydney and 'a new one' in Inglewood. Comments such as 'trying to stay out of court' were in the notes. 'Would not want to go to court on any Ridsdale matters' was another numbing sentence. Patrick had been dealing with the Church's insurance business on clergy paedophilia in conferences with the Special Issues Committee. Yet another document showed Patrick did have direct involvement in the management of claims against O'Donnell. It was a letter from a chartered loss adjuster, addressed to Patrick, Special Projects, Catholic Church Insurances Ltd. and dated in August 1994.

It was so hurtful. This man, who was a father and grandfather and acted like a holy and reverent Christian, had been working against what I considered to be the best interests of children. One document, dated after I had left the Church council, made it clear that Patrick had been doing this work while I was volunteering alongside him. Quite possibly he was still dealing with payouts for Church paedophiles when I spoke to him in the shopping centre.

Suddenly his 'Oh no' reaction took on a whole new meaning. My customary fury reached its highest level. Patrick *knew* me. He *knew* I had three young children at the primary school with O'Donnell. I have never spoken to Patrick about what he knew, and probably never will. One thing is certain: he didn't chance sending his children or grandchildren to Sacred Heart Primary School, Oakleigh in the seventeen years O'Donnell was roaming the classrooms and playgrounds.

Why hadn't he warned me? Warned the school? How did he sleep at night, this devout Catholic?


It was half-time in the case study. It had been a gruelling period for all of us. Ballarat was in pain. I hoped the second phase of examinations, to be held later that year in Melbourne, would somehow ease this suffering, although I did not know how. I suspected Cardinal George Pell would be called to give evidence one more time. Maybe this was how? When it was eventually announced that he would be questioned about his actions in Ballarat, it felt like a slice of justice.

The case study so far had only heightened tension in the region. Being on the receiving end of clergy abuse made you stand apart from the rest of society. We were outcasts in a way, carrying a truth that nobody wanted to hear, least of all our Church. Clergy got in first with their propaganda, handed down from their elevated status. I always felt that the hierarchy liked to hint that victims and families were money-grubbing liars. When this first happened back in the early 1990s other people believed them. That perception was difficult to change, particularly among churchgoers. Reputations, *lives* depended on the truth emerging from the Royal Commission. When that path of truth and justice was obstructed by poor memories, lies and mistruths, it hurt. It was another axle-breaking pothole in our progress. While the Ballarat hearing was well awaited, the enlighten ment was too slow. All we had was hope.

One of my top hopes was for Ronald Mulkearns to be compelled to take the stand before he died and took the details of his wickedly corrupt and unholy actions with him. He was the Church convener of the Ballarat cover-up. It was vital he answer questions about his many transfers of paedophile priests. I feared he would say he was too sick to give evidence in person.

At the very least, I was comforted that the Church's broadscale stonewalling I had encountered since the 1990s no longer seemed to be holding up. The examination of documents was dismantling the hierarchy's see no evil, hear no evil, speak no evil defences. Ironically, a highly informative source turned out to be the very same CCI that had recently made me so upset. While many Secret Archives had been sent to the Vatican, other records existed, diligently collected and retained by the Church's insurance company. The files were turning out to be a goldmine for the Royal Commission.

Earlier in the year, the commission had issued a summons for 1 500 CCI claim documents (these were only for the assaults against children the commission knew about). A two-month limit was placed on the summons. It had expired. On 10 July the commission held a 'directions hearing' to address the summons breach. Anthony and I did not attend the hearing and I'm not even sure it was open to the public, but it was a short hearing in Sydney.

The transcript reveals the commission's strength and determina-tion. Here is Justice McClellan questioning Church lawyer Peter Gray, trying to access the 1 500 files. Justice McClellan: 'I want to know when there was a claim made, Mr Gray, and I want to know what has happened to that claim so that I can sort out those where prior knowledge was accepted and where prior knowledge was rejected as a proposition.'

Mr Gray: 'The current summons doesn't do that, your honour.'

Justice McClellan: 'Maybe that's right, Mr Gray. I have said three times now I will write a new summons.'

Mr Gray: 'We are happy to cooperate in that. CCI wants me to say—'

Justice McClellan: 'I'm sure they do. I've had many discussions with CCI and I respect their willingness and indeed the assistance they have given the commission so far.'

Mr Gray: 'Thank you, your honour.'

Justice McClellan: 'We have to solve a practical problem: what is the formula of words that will get me all those files?'

Mr Gray: 'That I would need to take instructions on and discuss with Ms Furness, but that can be done, your honour.'

Justice McClellan: 'Let's do it right away. I will take a short adjournment; you can sort out the formula of words and you can expect to be asked to provide those files within a matter of days.'

Mr Gray: 'I will take instructions, your honour, but I think that will be impossible.'

Justice McClellan: 'No, it won't be, Mr Gray. If they have been identified, they will be somewhere where they can be collected together and brought to the commission.'

A 'no' from the Church to Justice McClellan's request for the files was not on the cards. I was in awe of the Royal Commission, its leadership and its willingness to extract all evidence. Without it, victims would have no hope of gaining such knowledge.

My everlasting fury was exhausting me – even though it was the healthy choice – so Anthony and I went on another mini-break. To spend some days under another sky would be like rehabilitation. Also, it was our thirty-fifth wedding anniversary. We went to Queensland's Hamilton Island with six family members and Katie's carer. It was a beautiful week spent overlooking the Coral Sea.

Anthony and I were so used to following the Royal Commission that we began looking forward to certain case studies. Number 35 was circled on our calendar for late 2015. It was to examine the Catholic Archdiocese of Melbourne and its worst paedophile priests, including our daughters' rapist, O'Donnell. For many of us, the hearing was long awaited, and as it was being held in Melbourne we did not have to travel interstate.

Each day of the hearing, Anthony and I would walk down to Oakleigh Station, travel by train into the city and head to William Street to the County Court. I carried with me a notepad and pen. I was not going to miss anything.

Appalling statistics were read out about the abusers and their abuse. Each offender priest's background was exposed. What was apparent in the extensive overview of the archdiocese was the pattern of repeated abuse and the hierarchy's protection of clergy offenders. It seemed to me the safest place for a paedophile was to be a member of the clergy in the Catholic Church. And for children? To be a child in this archdiocese was to unknowingly play a game of Russian roulette with bishops and archbishops holding the gun against their heads.

My mind turned constantly to Emma and Katie.

Once more, mental reservation (lying without lying) was examined by the commission. 'We were certainly taught mental reservation as a way to convey a meaning to a person who is asked a question that gives an answer that is not reality,' former priest Phil O'Donnell (no relation to Fr Kevin O'Donnell) said in evidence.

He also testified to another cover-up element. It dealt with the seal of confession. 'I had a situation where a paedophile priest did come to confession to me. I had a victim come to see me the night before with his wife; he then contacted this priest and said, "I've told Phil O'Donnell about you," and this priest was on my doorstep at eight o'clock the next morning, sat on the chair, and then dropped on his knees and went into the confessional mode, and I was a bit shocked, and I gave absolution, and as he walked out the door he laughed at me. In other words, he had made sure that I couldn't speak to anyone, and it was— I felt totally entrapped by that situation.'

Here was proof that the seal of confession had protected the paedophile and silenced a priest who was going to report the abuse. This was a hammer blow to the Church, which was desperate to keep its religious exemption to mandatory child abuse reporting laws.

I wrote more than forty pages of notes. One word I scribbled down was 'blackmail'. Did some criminal priests use blackmail to protect themselves from detection or ousting? This question has intrigued me since I heard a professor give evidence to the Victorian Parliamentary Inquiry in 2012.

Professor Desmond Cahill was an ex-seminarian who had attended the Corpus Christi seminary in Werribee in the 1960s. He had shocked me by speaking about our daughters' abuser, 'who often made visits to the Werribee seminary during the 1960s with carloads of young altar boys and girls as part of the grooming process – little did we young seminarians know what was really happening'.[145]

I did not know that O'Donnell was in the habit of taking carloads of children to the Werribee seminary. Who was he grooming, children or seminarians? I immediately remembered something a survivor had told me years earlier about his experience at a seminary. Instead of being taken to Werribee, the survivor I met had been taken to the Glen Waverley campus of the Corpus Christi seminary. It was in 1972. The survivor, who made a private submission to the Royal Commission, was a former altar boy.

At fourteen, he was taken to Glen Waverley by a priest called Father Terrence Pidoto, who paraded the child in front of several trainee priests sitting in their underwear. 'He's the one I was telling you about,' said Fr Pidoto. 'Isn't he cute?'[146]

Frightened, the boy said he wanted to go home. Instead, Pidoto later raped him 'in the seminary dining hall'.

If seminarians took part in sex crimes with children supplied by career paedophile priests, then those paedophile priests had knowledge of the seminarians' crimes. These facts would never go away. Is this how blackmail could be used to protect and sustain some paedophile priests? Is this what O'Donnell was doing in Werribee?

Case Study 35 continued along these harrowing lines.

Thankfully, there was some light in all this darkness. After the first week of hearings, our friend Judy Courtin held a celebration in an inner-city vacant lot to mark the completion of her thesis for her doctor of philosophy degree. Titled 'Sexual Assault and the Catholic Church: Are Victims Finding Justice?', her PhD thesis had just been published and we all received a copy of her 260-page book. Next step for Judy was to become a lawyer and represent survivors. We were very proud of her. She would be a formidable opponent to the Church's most expensive silk.

# 31

Through the Royal Commission's work, I learned many things, not least the startling statistic that each child victim endured approximately 2.2 years of sexual slavery. Bishop Peter Connors, who had told a school principal, in reference to Fr Baker, 'once a paedophile, always a paedophile', gave evidence in Case Study 35 concerning the Melbourne Archdiocese. Connors had held positions such as Secretary to Archbishop Frank Little (1974–76), Vicar General of Melbourne to Archbishop Little (1976–87), Auxiliary Bishop at Altona to Archbishop Little (1987–97), then Bishop of Ballarat (1997–2012). He was also Chairman of the Special Issues Committee, established in 1988 by the Australian Catholic Bishops Conference. Documents show Connors led the body from at least 1992 until after 1994. A previous chairman was Mulkearns.

Two years earlier, during the Victorian Parliamentary Inquiry, Connors had given sworn evidence claiming that Mulkearns was naive in his treatment of offenders. Connors reckoned Mulkearns had some sort of God-given innocence. Again and again, Connors used the word 'naive': 'I think he got bad advice'; 'He very naively accepted that advice.' Another time he said, 'I think he was naive about it all.' And: 'I am just reading what Bishop Mulkearns has done. I think he was being very naive.'

This 'naive' bishop was a canon lawyer – an expert on Church law! – an esteemed bishop for twenty-six years, and first chairman of the Special Issues Committee. Mulkearns was not naive at all, rather he was clinical in the way he dealt with paedophiles in his enormous diocese. Bishop Ronald Mulkearns was a good and faithful foot soldier for the Pope. He obeyed canon law.

Once upon a time, a cover story of naivety may have passed by unnoticed. But the Royal Commission had opened the public's eyes. On the penultimate day of the Archdiocese of Melbourne hearing, Bishop Peter Connors took the stand and spoke about his job as chairman of the Special Issues Committee from 1992. This was a privileged role, placing him at the forefront of Australia-wide information on the depth and breadth of clergy offenders and their cases. He was working under Archbishop Sir Frank Little. I was looking forward to hearing what he had to say.

Counsel Assisting Gail Furness asked Connors about a documented note from a discussion he had had with the vicar general of Melbourne, Gerry Cudmore, in 1993, about an offending priest. 'Scrolling down,' Ms Furness said, directing Connors to some words on a document that they were both looking at, 'you will see under a line there's "discussion with", and that's you, I take it?'

'That's me, yes,' Connors said.

Ms Furness then started listing the items and words on the document.

'One,' she began, 'don't admit accusation. Two, indicate that Archbishop has asked for resignation i.e. out of parish life. Stopping there, the first point, "don't admit accusation", it's clear, isn't it, from this document that he'd already admitted the accusation?'

'Yes,' Connors said. 'I think that was referring to what the Archbishop should do.'

'Can you explain that?'

'In other words,' Connors said, 'This was the advice which we were receiving from Catholic Church Insurance, I mentioned that in the Parliamentary Inquiry, and it was advice which I think was very inapp— It was very bad advice.'

Here we have an insurance company having enormous influence on the hierarchy's – the supposed moral authority of society's – decision-making. Yes, it was bad advice, but it was only advice. Little was free to protect children. Connors was free to urge his boss to protect children.

Connors was also asked by Ms Furness to explain meeting notes from 16 November 1992. He had been chairman of the meeting, whose purpose was to discuss Fr Brian Lucas' recent fact-finding trip to the USA and Canada. Lucas, known as the Church's Mr Fix-It for this issue in Australia, had travelled abroad to understand how the North American hierarchy was handling its large-scale abuse problem. The entire eight pages of meeting minutes were under the heading 'Father Brian Lucas's Report and Recommendations Arising out of his trip to USA and Canada'.

The United States, in particular, was qualified to pass on ways of avoiding liability, responsibility and accountability because their exposure to their own child sex abuse history had started in the 1980s. In October 1985 in the State of Louisiana, Father Gilbert Gauthe had pleaded guilty to eleven counts of molesting boys. Families of the boys had successfully sued the Church for millions of dollars.[147] There were lessons to be learned about avoiding the same fate of monetary loss.

One part of Fr Lucas's report for Australia stood out to me: 'It was agreed that there are serious "time bombs" ticking away in a number of Dioceses at the present time.'

'Serious time bombs' was a reference to active paedophile priests working in Australian parishes. I suppose he meant time bombs for the Church to defuse, not time bombs for children. There was no concern for children. Again, this exposes their knowledge of offenders and offending around Australia. Lucas also told the gathering. 'It is very important that the alleged offender be given every opportunity to provide all the facts and be questioned very fully by an expert investigator.'

When Lucas said 'expert investigator' he was not referring to police. He was talking about an unqualified, Church-minded amateur investigator. He was talking about himself.

Bishop Connors was also questioned by the Royal Commission about two priests, Fr Gannon and Fr Pickering, being awarded distinguished Church honours after they were belatedly stood down because of child sex assault allegations. Both men were given the title of pastor emeritus, meaning distinguished pastor, akin to an Order of the British Empire (OBE) in the Catholic Church, according to one priest. Pastor emeritus bestowed on them a larger Church pension in their retirement.

I knew all about the meaning of pastor emeritus because the Church had given Fr O'Donnell the same title and benefits at the celebration of his fifty-year anniversary in the presence of Archbishop Little. O'Donnell was one of the Church's most explosive (and expensive) time bombs.

After Little's death in April 2008, *The Age* ran an obituary that quoted Ballarat bishop Peter Connors. 'I had thirteen lovely years sitting opposite him at breakfast every morning,' Connors told the newspaper about the cover-up merchant. 'He was a holy man. He loved God and God's people. He was always fearful of hurting priests, and found it hard to correct or reprimand a priest.'

Little was not a holy man. Contrary to the impression Connors intended to give of his old boss, Little was cunning, alert and efficient – a real piece of work, a danger to children.

After Connors gave evidence to the Royal Commission, we heard testimony from retired bishop Hilton Deakin, once the vicar general of Melbourne. He was questioned about his role in the Church cover-up of offender priests by claiming they were stepping down due to ill health instead of allegations of child sexual assault. This was another Church tactic used worldwide.

Ms Furness took up the questioning. 'What part did you play in the cover-up?'

'Well, there were meetings, for instance, where everybody voted on things,' Deakin explained. 'Like, for instance, when a priest was moved or retired, it was because of ill-health or something, when in fact it was because of child abuse.'[148]

Significantly, Bishop Emeritus Deakin had just admitted that the Archbishop of Melbourne and auxiliary bishops – the curia – had moved offender priests because the priests had sexually assaulted children.

'I didn't understand the people who were ahead of me in seniority who decided that this should be the policy,' Deakin said. 'But that's the way the culture, as Peter Connors so often said, the culture of the day required of us—'

'When you say the culture of the day required it of you,' Ms Furness said, 'Are you saying the culture of the day required you to cover up priests who had been accused or accepted offending of child sexual abuse so that others outside the church wouldn't know that that was the case; is that what you're saying, that was the culture?'

'Yes, that is the— at the time, I wouldn't have been thinking along those lines, I feel confident [. . .] but I'm absolutely aware of it now, because of what I've heard and read.'

'But at the time, if you knew that a priest was resigning because they had offended or had been accepted as offending,' Ms Furness continued, 'how could it not be that it was a cover-up to say and agree that they were resigning on ill-health grounds?'

'I've conceded that,' Deakin said. 'I knew that, but it wasn't with all the cases, and everybody who was at the meeting made the vote and it was the same, and I felt at the time reasonably comfortable about it.'

Bishop Emeritus Deakin and his colleagues had normalised the obscene. To me, they were spineless men.

Hilton Deakin had been Vicar General of Melbourne from May 1987 until 1992. The curia he referred to included Archbishop Sir Frank Little, the Most Reverend Bishop Joseph O'Connell, the Most Reverend Peter Connors and the Most Reverend George Pell. These were the most reverend Catholic Church yes-men.

This testimony gave new insight into the curia's workings. When Sir Frank Little died, another member of the hierarchy, Hart, said the 'former archbishop kept reports of sexual abuse to himself'.[149] This kind of statement let the rest of the hierarchy off the hook; they were free of blame for any cover-ups. Dead men cannot speak for themselves. Yet here was a different scenario from Deakin, who revealed his hierarchy's actions fitted perfectly with a letter from Church lawyers to a victim's lawyer in 1994 (a letter I discovered during my research). The lawyer had asked about Archbishop Little's responsibility relating to Fr O'Donnell's child abuse complaints. The church lawyers responded:

> (vii) Under canon law, the Archbishop had the responsibility to deal with complaints. He would do so under his general power of governance; see canon 391. In practice, he shares it with his Vicar General, his Episcopal Vicars and any adviser to whom he delegates it. If the complaint involved the possibility of an offence, the process described above would be invoked.[150]

This evidence shows it was a group effort.

Deakin was questioned about the minutes of a curia meeting on 16 June 1988. Item 12 of the minutes was 'Sexual Molestation' and referred to setting up a committee; this would later become the Special Issues Committee.

'In 1991, Archbishop Little established a Victoria-wide regional committee on special issues,' Ms Furness said to Deakin. 'And you were the first chair of that committee?'

'Correct.'

It was not brought up in the hearing but when I later examined the June 1988 document, item 12 listed the members of the child 'Sexual Molestation Committee' whom the hierarchy had chosen for the role: '12 SEXUAL MOLESTATION: Committee: P. O'Callaghan legal; E. Seal, psychological; Fr. Dan Torpy; Vicar General. Committee to meet, draw up guidelines.'[151]

'P. O'Callaghan, legal' referred to Peter O'Callaghan QC, who was later chosen by Melbourne Archbishop George Pell to lead the investigation arm of Melbourne Response. Pell had called Mr O'Callaghan the 'Independent Commissioner' and ludicrously tried to pretend he was akin to a 'royal commissioner'.[152] Now we could see Mr O'Callaghan had been on a previous secret church committee.

Listening to all this evidence and joining the dots on a map of betrayal was gruelling. I was relieved when it finished on 4 December. The following evening, Anthony's cousin Meg arrived from England to visit us for four days. On Sunday 6 December, two significant things happened. Firstly, we were surprised by the front page of the *Sunday Age*. I recall shopping in the Gembrook supermarket when I noticed a stack of newspapers. The cover story was illustrated by $100 banknotes in the shape of a cross. THE $62M SAVING, the headline said. HOW THE CATHOLIC CHURCH SHORT-CHANGED ABUSE VICTIMS.[153]

I bought three copies for us to read.

The article reported that the Church had avoided paying up to $62 million in compensation to sexual abuse victims by creating the controversial Melbourne Response. 'Internal documents also show church leaders ordered written records about sex abuse be "kept to a minimum" to avoid losing lawsuits,' the story reported, 'and hired one of the country's best spin doctors in a bid to prepare for the scandal in the early 1990s.'

The $62 million saving to the Church applied only to priests in Melbourne. The Towards Healing system for the rest of Australia would have provided similar savings but on a national scale. It was very consoling to read and know that investigative journalists were putting together information from documents obtained from the Royal Commission's case studies and exposing the truth.

The second significant event on that day came while we were watching *60 Minutes*. Anthony and I had been interviewed for it a month earlier. Once again, it was a show of diligent investigation. The TV program posted on its website: 'New documents have revealed a conflict of interest between Cardinal George Pell and the experts he appointed to investigate child sexual abuse allegations in the church.' The 'new documents' related to Fr Kevin O'Donnell, in particular Professor Ball's two conflicting reports. British abuse survivor Peter Saunders had also been interviewed for the program. He was a member of the Pontifical Commission for the Protection of Minors, and had been increasingly frustrated by that commission's lack of action. In his interview, Peter spoke out very strongly against the Church.

Anthony, Meg and I watched the show on Channel 9. Often when you are interviewed by the media you are not certain which other elements of the wider story the journalists are looking at. You don't know which comments the producers will use. You watch the final product go to air with as much curiosity as other viewers.

For me, this exposé on Professor Ball was exceptional. I hoped it would have some effect on public understanding.

Two months later, we were sad to read that Peter Saunders had been 'dismissed' from the Pontifical Commission.

# 32

The morning after *60 Minutes* aired, on Monday 7 December, Anthony and I travelled into Melbourne with Meg to the second part of Case Study 28: Catholic Church Authorities in Ballarat. Up until earlier in the year, Meg had been a minister in the British Parliament. She was interested in our Royal Commission, so she attended it for three of her four days in Melbourne.

Holding the Ballarat hearing in Melbourne caused disappointment and distress for many survivors from the town. We didn't know why the location was different to part one of the hearing. Cardinal Pell was supposed to return to Australia to give evidence in part two. Was that why?

Nonetheless, having Pell return to be questioned by the Royal Commission again felt like a triumph because as the commission moved forward, everybody's knowledge grew and it became apparent that the cardinal had often been in positions of power in trouble spots. Unfortunately for us (yet fortunately for him), Pell had moved himself a long way from Victoria. I doubted whether he would come back to Australia to give evidence, but now it was only days away.

This particular part of the Ballarat hearing would hear from five survivors: David Ridsdale, Timothy Green, BWE (some survivors were never named publicly), BWA, Paul Levey and his mother Beverley. I had first heard of David Ridsdale in 2002. David was

Fr Gerard Ridsdale's nephew. He had previously claimed that he had made a 1993 telephone call to then Auxiliary Bishop George Pell to tell him about his abuse at the hands of his uncle. David Ridsdale said Pell responded by saying, 'I want to know what it will take to keep you quiet.'

David was about to repeat the same accusations under oath. He was the first witness for the day, but before he was called to the stand, Counsel Assisting Angus Stewart raised an item of interest: 'The Royal Commission received a statement last night from the Reverend John Thomas Walshe, dated 5 December 2015,' he said. 'He states his occupation as parish priest, St Patrick's Mentone, [and] Parkdale.[154]

'In this statement, the Reverend Walshe gives evidence in relation to his recollection when living with Bishop Pell when he was an assistant parish priest and Bishop Pell was the auxiliary bishop. He gives evidence about what he recalls in relation to Bishop Pell following, as he says it, a discussion that Bishop Pell had with Mr David Ridsdale.'

Mr Stewart stated, 'The Royal Commission would require Father Walshe to give evidence.'

Sitting in the Royal Commission courtroom upon hearing Fr John Walshe's name, Anthony and I looked at each other. Years earlier, we had received a letter from the parents of a victim. They had told us that when their son was eighteen years old, he had claimed he was sexually assaulted by Walshe in the Corpus Christi seminary.

Fr Walshe was now the parish priest in Mentone and neighbouring Parkdale, bayside suburbs not far from where we lived. And seemingly coming to his former housemate George Pell's defence over the David Ridsdale telephone accusation.

This was going to be interesting. Perhaps Walshe thought he could just send a letter to aid his friend and his word be taken as gospel truth and nothing more would happen. But now his claim was going to be forensically and publicly examined by some of the best legal minds in the country.

That night Anthony rang the mother of Father Walshe's victim to tell her what had transpired in the hearing.

On the second day of the Ballarat hearing, ex–Victoria Police detective Denis Ryan took the stand. Ever since he'd lost his job in Mildura in 1972 after trying to arrest Fr John Day for sexual assault offences against sixteen of the parish's primary school children, Ryan had been trying to achieve some form of justice. The young detective had suffered in the 1970s and ever since. He had lost his career and it had traumatised his family to go up against the Church and Victoria Police's Catholic Church–defending element. Meanwhile, the priest that Denis Ryan had been trying to prosecute, Fr Day, and the cover-up bishop, Ronald Mulkearns, had seemingly prospered in their positions. When allegations had begun piling up over Day, Mulkearns had moved the prolific paedophile to Portugal. Later, when the uproar had settled, he welcomed Day back into the diocese and appointed him parish priest in the small country town of Timboon. The bishop promoted Day to monsignor status. Monsignor Day kept his parish and promotion until he died in 1978.

When Day died, Mulkearns said his late employee had 'faithfully fulfilled his ministry in God's name'. Day had lived the last decade of his life accused of buggery, attempted buggery, indecent assault and acts of gross indecency against potentially hundreds of children. He was protected from prosecution by corruption within the Church and by the police service.

Following Ryan's evidence was former chief commissioner of police Mick Miller, who said he believed his 'predecessor Reginald Jackson helped thwart an investigation into Mildura paedophile priest Monsignor John Day'.[155]

In the Royal Commission courtroom that day was our newly appointed chief commissioner of Victoria Police Graham Ashton. Anthony and I approached Mr Ashton in one of the breaks and told him Denis Ryan should be given a medal for what he had tried to do in upholding the law. It seemed Mr Ashton was already on a mission to right the wrong. He spoke to Ryan after the proceedings. The following year Denis received an official apology from Victoria Police and, two years after that, in 2018, he was compensated. It had taken forty-six years.

The hearing continued with evidence from clergy who had served in the Ballarat Diocese. Bishop Brian Finnigan, the former adviser and secretary to Mulkearns, was one of them. After one of the lunch adjournments, the commission chair referred to an application being made by Pell to give his pending evidence online from Rome. The courtroom rumbled with disapproving mutterings from the public gallery. We had all anticipated that Pell would present in person at the commission. It was Friday and the cardinal was due to appear on Monday. He was claiming he was too unwell to travel to Australia.

I was disappointed. During our case study, Pell had appeared via video link and come across as pompous, uninterested and flippant. To make matters worse, the communications were patchy at best.

The Pell no-show was a dismal development.

The hearing continued with Bishop Finnigan, but for me dark thoughts lingered. Instead of Pell getting on a plane, he was getting off the hook. Ours was a glum house on Saturday, but on Sunday Anthony came to me with a smile. 'What if I told you that I'm going to request that we sit in on Pell's interview in Rome for the Royal Commission hearing to give it some gravitas?'

'Oh, yes,' I said.

# 33

L ike a mystery movie, the Ballarat hearing continued with more twists and turns.

On Monday, Bishop Finnigan's examination recommenced. By the next morning's news reports, his name was mud. Different media outlets had reported Finnigan was accused of 'lying to the Royal Commission'. The current auxiliary bishop of Brisbane and Mulkearns' former secretary had insisted under oath that he had only learned of Ridsdale's horrific crimes against children in 1993, when Ridsdale was charged by police. However, the *Herald Sun* found evidence that Finnigan had admitted in July 2015 that he had known of abuse complaints against Ridsdale more than ten years earlier.[156] In the private hearing by Gail Furness SC, Bishop Finnigan confirmed he had known of complaints against now-jailed child abuser Ridsdale, eighty-four, back in 1981 and 1982. His game was up.

Queensland media demanded Finnigan's removal as an auxiliary bishop of Brisbane.[157] Four days later, on 31 December, the liar retired.[158] When he bowed out, the press revealed that Finnigan had written a letter to serial offender Fr Gerald Ridsdale in 1994 stating, 'Some of these fellows [victims] now see the opportunity to obtain some easy cash.'[159]

Why Finnigan had been sucking up to Ridsdale, who seemed bound for a lifetime in prison, was unclear.

Anthony rang the Royal Commission to make his request that we attend George Pell's hearing in Rome, saying we would pay our own way if granted permission to attend.

In the meantime, the Ballarat hearing in Melbourne continued. After Finnigan, we heard from other priests, including Fr John Walshe, who had written the letter to support Cardinal Pell in regard to David Ridsdale's bribe claim. The commission would later find David Ridsdale's allegation of attempted bribery was 'unlikely'. But that had nothing to do with Walshe, whose evidence was problematic.

'Cardinal George Pell's former housemate has been accused of lying to the child abuse royal commission to "save" his friend from accusations that he tried to bribe a survivor to keep quiet,' *The Age* reported.[160] A Catholic priest who had defended Pell at the Child Abuse Royal Commission the previous week 'was himself the subject of a historical sexual abuse claim'.[161]

On the same day as the ABC reported that Walshe's sexual assault victim had been compensated $75,000 by the Church, an online news report referred to a mysterious request from Victoria Police's SANO taskforce – the squad born of the Victorian Parliamentary Inquiry to investigate historical child sexual abuse – in relation to St Patrick's Cathedral. 'The allegations relate to fourteen-year-old boys who may have been abused at the cathedral in the later 1990s,' the report said. 'Detectives would like to speak to anyone who was a victim of a sexual assault, or anybody with any information relating to any alleged sexual assaults, committed at the St Patrick's Cathedral between 1996 and 2001.'[162]

It was two days before Christmas, a busy time of the year with so much happening. The article barely registered with me at first. Then I thought about the time and place. St Patrick's Cathedral. Between 1996 and 2001. I said to Anthony without suspicion, 'They are the years George Pell was archbishop.' I wondered who police were looking for. I wasn't the only one. Next day the police appeal was on the front page of a major newspaper with a large photograph of the cathedral.[163]

We had no idea whom the accusations were made against, but it sounded like somebody who had worked with George Pell. Then everything stopped for Christmas.

There was no New Year revelry for the priesthood. With the Royal Commission unearthing documents and testimony, coverage of the cover-ups multiplied. I felt thankful because this meant many people were now talking about a critical part of Australian life: child safety.

We celebrated Anthony's birthday in January but there seemed no time for parties. Another appeal for witnesses by the SANO taskforce went out, this time in Ballarat. The appeal referred to the Eureka Stockade Swimming Pool in the 1970s. It stated there was an investigation into allegations of historic sexual abuse against boys as young as eight.[164] Again, we wondered where this was leading.

All this time, Rome was calling us. But we weren't sure whether the Royal Commission would allow us to witness Pell's evidence and cross-examination in person. One Australian tourist in Italy had spotted the cardinal dining al fresco in Rome, eating a large plate of chips and steak.[165] The photo did not seem to tell a story of a man too sick to fly home. Two doctors offered to travel to Rome and accompany the cardinal back to Australia to ensure he was okay during the flight.[166]

Out of the searing summer heat in February came a scorching musical hit. Tim Minchin released a song in support of Church victims called 'Come Home (Cardinal Pell)'.[167] The cheeky, catchy song reflected the population's unrest at Pell's sudden inability to appear before the commission owing to health reasons.

All the commotion over the song led Anthony to do a string of interviews. On the same day, a crowdfunding page was set up by *The Project* television show to raise funds for abuse survivors to travel to Rome. It raised almost $130,000 in a day. The survivors, affectionately known as the Ballarat Boys, were amazed at the public's generosity.

Now events were happening at a dizzying pace. Next day the *Herald Sun* ran a bombshell story: POLICE PROBE PELL: TOP-SECRET

INVESTIGATION INTO SEX ABUSE CLAIMS AGAINST CARDINAL.[168]
Reporter Lucie Morris-Marr had written:

> A Victoria Police taskforce has been investigating allegations that
> Cardinal George Pell sexually abused between five and ten boys.
> Detectives from SANO taskforce have compiled a dossier contain-
> ing allegations that Cardinal Pell committed 'multiple offences'
> when a priest in Ballarat and when archbishop of Melbourne.

It was barely believable. The pre-Christmas and January police
appeals had not been referring to somebody who worked with Pell but
the church leader himself. Then again, I remembered Pell had faced allegations before. In 2002 he had been compelled to stand aside as Sydney
Archbishop. A man had accused Pell of the abuse of two thirteen-year-
old boys, himself and his friend, at a Phillip Island camp for altar boys
decades earlier.[169] Pell had been a seminarian. Our prime minister John
Howard had come leaping to the defence of his archbishop friend.
A retired judge, Alec Southwell, sat on a Church-convened inquiry
and eventually found he believed the stories of both the victim
and George Pell.[170] Southwell found he was 'not satisfied that the
complaint has been established' but also found the complainant 'gave
the impression that he was speaking honestly from an actual recollection'.[171] I have always seen this as an open finding.

In February 2016, Anthony and I drove to Ballarat for the
beginning of the third hearing of Case Study 28. The Christian
Brothers were first up, and we had hoped to arrive before the 10 am
start. Despite our best efforts we arrived a little late. By the time we
parked the car and raced up the several flights of stairs in the Ballarat
courthouse to the third-floor commission hearing room, the doors
were closed. Proceedings were underway. We stood outside the
courtroom watching the live stream with many others. Justice Peter
McClellan was speaking.

'The Royal Commission has received requests from some survivors that they be able to be present in the room where Cardinal Pell

will give evidence in Rome next week,' Justice McClellan said. 'The commission considers that to be a reasonable request.

'It's important to understand, though, that the Royal Commission will be sitting in Sydney, not in Rome, and will be receiving the Cardinal's evidence in Sydney, transmitted from Rome. With the assistance of the Australian Embassy in Rome, we have located a room in a hotel in central Rome which, I am advised, has the technical facilities to ensure an effective signal to Australia.'[172]

We were blown away. I did some counting in my head. The hearing in Rome was due to start only six days away. At the lunch break, Anthony booked return tickets to Rome.

My farmer friend John, who had shown us the photo of Pell at St Patrick's College, now gave Anthony, myself and many other commission attendees colourful ribbons to tie on fences belonging to churches, schools and orphanages throughout Ballarat. It was a show of support for victims who had suffered as children in those Catholic properties. Later in the day, John asked me where I had tied my ribbons. I answered I still had mine because I was going to tie them in Rome. He was touched by my words, and I could see how deeply this awful issue had affected a good man.

The colourful ribbons were part of a new movement called LOUD Fence, created by Ballarat woman Maureen Hatcher.[173] Seeing the ribbons and knowing so many people cared about what happened to them was comforting for victims. For everybody else it was a stark reminder of the extensive and ungodly clergy crimes against innocence.

Ballarat ex-bishop Ronald Mulkearns finally appeared as a witness via video link before the Royal Commission. He admitted he had failed children. Faced with the evidence, what else could he say? During his ninety minutes on the stand, he stated fifty times he couldn't remember details of his time as bishop.[174] The 'I can't recall' mantra was still grating. But the ageing boss did remember to use the old excuse. 'We had no idea, or I had no idea,' he said, 'of the effects of the indecent [assaults] that took place.'

Just before we left for the airport, we watched the evening news and saw a report that Cardinal Pell's secretary had sent out an invitation to seminarians and other clergy to attend the commission's hearing in Rome to support him.[175] I listened with dread, thinking the venue would now likely be filled with clergy and religious enthusiasts who still maintained the fantasy that victims were liars after money.

I took this trepidation with me onto the plane. We took off at 3.30 am. It would be our most exhausting journey. It would change our lives.

# 34

We were in the air all night and all day. I slept for between thirty and sixty minutes. Nothing unusual there. I think the most I have ever slept on one of these long-haul flights is about three hours.

ABC foreign correspondent Lisa Millar had arranged to meet our flight in Rome at 7.30 pm. I was so tired, and a certain dread was creeping in. We were in Pell's place now. We made our way out of Italian customs and were shuffling along with all the other travellers when I spotted one person facing the opposite way to everyone else. It was Lisa Millar, with a huge warm smile. Despite everything I smiled back.

Lisa put us at ease. We had an interview then chatted for a while longer before making our way to a taxi to head to our accommodation. We spent a restless night in a room just big enough to hold a queen-size bed. The following morning we booked a room in the Hotel Quirinale where Pell would sit to answer the commission's questioning. The grand old hotel was huge. Our room was on the first floor at the front of the building, with windows looking onto the street.

We walked to St Peter's Square. The last time I had been in the square was in 2011, holding a copy of my book. Today we were to meet a London journalist for an interview. Other interviews followed. Channel 9 News London. *The New York Times*. SBS

Australia. Channel 9 News. Channel 10 News. Sky News. *Herald Sun.*
Channel 7 News. An Italian newspaper, *La Stampa.* The BBC. Radio
3PR. Some other interviews were done with news crews I did not
know. The media interest would proliferate in the coming days.

We were joined in Rome by the Ballarat Boys, some of their
partners, their counsellor from the Centre Against Sexual Assault
(CASA), a psychologist, a lawyer and a reporter from the Ballarat
*Courier.* It was wonderful to see their smiling but tired faces. They,
too, were swamped by questions from journalists.

Anthony and I had arranged to meet ex-Detective Chief Inspector
Peter Fox, his wife Penny and their friend Pat Feenan (author of *Holy
Hell*) at a central point in Rome. Many months earlier Peter had gone
to a survivors' charity fundraiser and won a week's holiday at a large
villa in Tuscany in a silent auction. Peter, Penny and Pat being in Italy
at the same time as us was a complete coincidence, and one we cher-
ished. We had lunch and talked as we always did about living life in
the shadow of clergy sex crimes. It somehow helped.

The hearing would take place in the Hotel Quirinale's Verdi
Room. It seated 220 people and was decorated in soft shades of green
and white. Pell, we were told, would sit at the front so he could look
at a screen projecting the proceedings from the Royal Commission
room in Sydney. Royal Commission staff would sit in the front seats
near Pell and we, the survivors and supporters, would be in the front
two rows across the aisle.

We planned to be in the Verdi Room at 9.15 pm that evening for
the 10 pm hearing commencement. For some reason Pell had chosen
the strange 10 pm start time, meaning the four-hour hearing would
finish at 2 am. In Rome, home of the Vatican, the Catholic Church
is big news. To have a foreign government's inquiry there, by order of
the Queen of England (head of the Church of England), was a sensa-
tion. The city wouldn't sleep until the hearing had concluded.

Curt Italian police officers greeted us with frowns at the Verdi
Room. Pell's private bodyguards and hotel security were also present.
So many guards – it was overkill. Armed forces for whom? Priests?

Journalists doing their job? We victims and supporters were the only perceived threat. There were nineteen of us; we were harmless.

They patted us down.

The late start time was not a deterrent for journalists. About sixty turned up to sit in the reserved media area. That left another 140 seats in the room. These became occupied by priests, monks, seminarians, nuns, men in dark suits and a few others I assumed were of bishop status. A sea of black with white collars. I tried to ignore our intimidating surroundings. The survivors must have been feeling enormous angst.

Anthony and I sat alongside Peter, Penny and Pat. Chattering filled the room before a chime rang through the speakers. It was Sydney calling for our attention. The commissioners were about to file out of their chambers and into the courtroom on the other side of the world. After three years of attending various hearings, we knew the drill. Chime. Silence. 'All stand, please.' Bow. Wait till the commissioners sit down. 'All be seated.' I looked with some strange kind of nostalgia for the familiar faces back in our beautiful Australian city of Sydney. Justice Peter McClellan bowed to us. Nobody else in the room stood when we, the survivors and families, did. The Italian clergy remained seated. They must have all looked at us wondering what we were doing. However, our dignity and respect to the commission must have impressed them. By the third night, everybody in the Verdi Room would be following us in the ritual of honour to our Royal Commission.

Staying awake during the hearings was a problem. During the day, we would be out and about doing interviews, discussing the proceedings with the Ballarat Boys or seeing a little of the city instead of resting or sleeping. I dozed only two or three hours a day, with jet lag also playing havoc with my body clock. When it came to 10 pm, sitting still and quiet was difficult. Sleep came for me. Sometimes I would be taking notes without the ability to finish a word or a thought. I had concrete eyelids.

News was passed to us that the Hollywood film *Spotlight* had won the Academy Award for Best Picture.[176] Although *Spotlight* was set in the USA, it highlighted the same hierarchical deception and fight we had faced in Australia. The movie not only gave victims of clergy great consolation that the truth about the priesthood was being told, but was received with critical and popular acclaim. Now it was an Oscar winner. I doubted that any of our group had not seen it. As depicted in *Spotlight*, Cardinal Bernard Law, the Archbishop of Boston, who fled the United States in 2002 due to the *Boston Globe*'s scandalous revelations of the child sexual assault cover-up system he managed, now lived in exile in Rome. Cardinal Law had protected almost 250 paedophile priests during his eighteen years as archbishop. The story of one priest he had protected is a mirror-image of Victoria's Father Gerald Ridsdale: Father John Geoghan was alleged to have raped or molested more than 130 children in six different parishes in a career spanning thirty years.[177]

The *Boston Globe* journalists had been exactly on target when they went after the system instead of individual paedophile priests, because it was the priesthood's system, one it created, installed and maintained in secret, that kept offender priests offending. Just like in Australia. And here we were in Rome with a similar quest to establish truth through forensic examination from our own country.

The questioning of Cardinal Pell went into his history in Ballarat. From 1973 to 1984 he was the Episcopal Vicar for Education, chaired the Ballarat Diocesan Education Commission and was Chairman of the Board at Sacred Heart Teachers College (now Aquinas Campus of the Australian Catholic University) making him the top clergyman for education in Ballarat. He once described his role as 'the essential link between the Bishop, priests, parents, teachers and students'. When quoted these words by Ms Furness he replied, 'I think it somewhat overstates my role.'[178]

As the Episcopal Vicar for Education in Ballarat for eleven years, it was Pell's job to manage and oversee the Catholic schools in the diocese. It is only logical to believe that if he had not performed his duties effectively, he would not have held the position for so long.

We heard that in January 1977, four years into his tenure as Episcopal Vicar for Education, Pell was promoted to a position as one of Bishop Mulkearns' consultors for the college of consultors in the Ballarat Diocese. This promotion also indicates he was working efficiently and effectively at his job.

St Alipius Boys' School, workplace of several paedophile priests, was another topic of questioning.

The following day, Pell was photographed in the Italian newspapers entering the Royal Commission hearing. Also in the paper was an article on our family and *Spotlight's* Oscar win.[179] Back home, coverage featured the Ballarat group walking along Via Nazionale towards Hotel Quirinale, which became their daily habit.

One Cardinal Pell comment that caused a stir was that his memory was 'not infallible'.[180] In Rome, survivor Gordon Hill said, 'I wish I could give him some of my childhood memories of being abused by priests [. . .] because I tell you what, those memories are unforgettable.'

Pell told the hearing he considered the Church's failures to protect children human error: 'Faults overwhelmingly have been more personal faults, personal failures, rather than structures.'[181] He was wrong. Structures are inert: they do not function without people. People drive, uphold and enforce structures. With 'personal faults, personal failures' comes structural corruption.

The second evening of the Royal Commission hearings saw the crowd of journalists outside Hotel Quirinale almost double. The timing of *Spotlight's* Oscars success and Pell's questioning had drawn journalists not only from the USA but also from Europe and South America to our Royal Commission. The Ballarat group walked up Via Nazionale to be greeted by a wall of at least a hundred journalists and cameras. Survivors said a few words before entering the hotel. It was overwhelming to witness. Our Royal Commission had captured the world's attention.

Pell arrived with an announcement that he had 'the full backing' of Pope Francis.[182] He had stated the previous evening that he would update the Pope after each session of the hearing.

Counsel Assisting Gail Furness asked Pell about Fr Gerald Ridsdale: 'Did you subsequently know, not that he offended at

Inglewood [a small Victorian town in the Ballarat diocese] – leave that to one side – but that it was common knowledge of his interfering with children at Inglewood?'

'I . . . I couldn't say that I ever knew that everyone knew,' Cardinal Pell said. 'I knew a number of people did. I was— I didn't know whether it was common knowledge or whether it wasn't. It's a sad story and it wasn't of much interest to me.'[183]

When Pell uttered these cruel, dismissive words, our mouths fell open. I believe the intimidation and isolation we felt in the room full of clergy prevented any sound of protest escaping us. In the split second that we hung suspended, a loud gasp of horror rushed through the speakers all the way from Sydney. The sound filled the cavernous Verdi Room. It was as though victims and supporters who were sitting in the gallery back in Australia gave audible reaction when we could not. It was a haunting moment.

Oblivious to the fact that his words were so offensive, Pell seemed startled. He cast his eyes around the room, as if he were searching for the sound's origin. I could see on his face that he had no idea of the pain his heartless words had inflicted.

'What wasn't of much interest to you, Cardinal?' Ms Furness asked, cool and calm as ever.

The penny dropped.

'The suffering, of course, was real and I very much regret that,' Cardinal Pell said. 'But I had no reason to turn my mind to the extent of the evils that Ridsdale had perpetrated.'

In 1984 Father Pell had left Ballarat and gone to the Melbourne Archdiocese. In 1987 he became a Melbourne Auxiliary Bishop stationed in the Melbourne bayside parish of Mentone. Three short years later, in 1990, he was appointed to the Congregation for the Doctrine of the Faith, which oversaw sexual misconduct, including child sexual assaults and also laicising priests for such crimes. He served on this body for ten years with Cardinal Ratzinger.[184] Within six years of leaving the paedophile-infested clergy of Ballarat, Pell was plucked out of Mentone to lend his assistance in the Vatican on international clergy child sex crime matters. This makes no sense to me, because in Ballarat, Pell apparently would not deal with clergy sexual assault. How did this churchman qualify for the elite Vatican job dealing internationally with paedophile priests when he hadn't liked turning his mind to the extent of such evils back home?

After each day of the Rome commission hearings, Pell would go to the top floor of the hotel to debrief with his staff. He would then descend to the ground floor with his bodyguards to be driven home. On this second night, he came downstairs alone and Anthony, not knowing this was the witness's routine, was going up the same stairs on his way to our room. This is where they met. Anthony told me later he extended his hand. They shook. Anthony said he would like to talk about Melbourne Response; Pell said he couldn't do that and tried to walk away. Anthony looked the man of God in the eye and tried to make a human connection. He told me and then later the press that he had said to Pell, 'You are looking at a broken man.'[185] My husband also told the cardinal he had the influence to change things. Apart from two negative responses, Pell would not engage. He went on his way.

It was a brush-off. In other words, nothing would change. After almost twenty years of Anthony's valiant efforts to repair the Church scheme in order to help survivors achieve fair compensation, he finally had an answer: a big no. It was a much different one to Pell's response only two years earlier in Sydney, at the end of the Ellis Defence case. Perhaps he felt untouchable now that he was in the Vatican, and could at last be truthful to Anthony that he had no intention of ever changing the system he had installed.

Anthony was visibly disappointed and disturbed at failing to reach Pell on a personal level. He regretted sharing his heartfelt feelings with the churchman because he could see it meant nothing to him. I tried to console my husband later, but it was a deep hurt. The whole encounter took Anthony a long time – many months – to get over. And, of course, it was the end of achieving a better deal for victims, something he had pursued passionately since 1996.

One front page criticised Pell's evidence with the headline SEE NO EVIL, HEAR NO EVIL, STOP NO EVIL.[186]

Author David Marr wrote, 'George Pell wasn't much interested in stories of abuse by priests. Which was lucky for his career. Had Pell made a big fuss about the abuse going on all around him as a young priest, he would not be at the Vatican.'[187]

One of the interviews Anthony and I gave was with an Italian journalist. I took to the interview two copies of my book *Hell on the Way to Heaven* (English and Italian versions). I asked if he had seen or heard anything about the book *Così in terra*. I could see his mind translating my question, then his face lit up. 'Ahh, your book,' he said. 'Every time this issue comes up on television, they show your book.' I was amazed. A photo of Emma and Katie was on the cover of the Italian version. I was pleased to know people in another country recognised their faces.

On the third evening, Pell was questioned about his time in the Melbourne Archdiocese as auxiliary bishop from 1987 and then as archbishop from 1996 to 2001. It was another four hours of excuses and blame. Between his bad memory and everybody else deceiving him, we were supposed to believe this great intellectual warrior of the Church was either naive or ignorant.

The following exchange took place between Ms Furness and the witness. Ms Furness: 'So now we have the education office deceiving you, and the archbishop deceiving you . . . as well as Bishop Mulkearns and one or more of the consultors in the Ballarat diocese.'

Cardinal Pell: 'That is correct.'

Ms Furness: 'It's an extraordinary position, Cardinal.'

Cardinal Pell: 'Counsel, this was an extraordinary world, a world of crimes and cover-ups and people did not want the status quo to be disturbed.'[188]

It was an appalling indictment of the Catholic priesthood and their education structures. (The 'people' Pell spoke of could only be other priests and the hierarchy.) Parents trusted them. We trusted them. Pell was admitting that what we had been saying for many years was true. His only explanation was that he was not at fault.

In Rome each morning I would go out and buy the major Italian newspapers then go through them over a coffee looking for articles on the commission hearing. I could not speak or read Italian, so I searched for pictures and certain words I came to understand. Back home, I had friends and family collecting Australian coverage for me to read when I returned home. And for updating my scrapbooks.

On the morning of the fourth day, Anthony and I had completed a few interviews, both television and newspaper, to which I had brought some photos of Emma and Katie. One was a class photo of two happy little girls smiling in their school uniforms. At 11 am, while I went up to our room, Anthony silently studied the photo. Without a word to anyone, he took it outside to the crowd of more than one hundred reporters and camera crews, who were staking out the hotel. Anthony got their attention and held up the photo of our beautiful daughters. 'These are my girls,' he said. 'A Catholic priest was raping them when this photo was taken. This was my perfect family. We created that. The Catholic Church destroyed it.'[189] I was not there to witness this. I was told later Anthony went back inside and cried. The Ballarat Boys were there to offer their kind comfort.

The men from Ballarat had been amazing during our time in Rome. They had moved as a group and had grown in confidence and strength with every passing day. It was wonderful to see them smile and feel a modest pride in their huge international achievement of recognition. Their dignity and courage under stress was impressive. As hard as the hearings were to sit through, they sat in silence, absorbed everything, and later discussed the evidence. Australia could be proud of the band of survivors from Ballarat. We were.

I tied my colourful ribbons on an old cast-iron street lamp outside Hotel Quirinale for the LOUD Fence movement. Peter and Penny Fox and Pat Feenan went one better: they tied a few ribbons to a gate close to where Pell lived. We hoped he could see them.

The final night of evidence examined Pell on a range of issues. Lawyers at the commission were able to ask questions about previous evidence. Barrister David O'Brien, who had sat on the Victorian Parliamentary Inquiry committee and was now representing a Ballarat victim, asked the cardinal about Br Ted Dowlan, the violent child rapist who had first assaulted children at St Alipius Boys' School before attacking students at St Patrick's College. 'What did you hear about Dowlan?' Mr O'Brien asked.

'I heard that there were problems at St Pat's College,' Cardinal Pell said.

'What sort of problems?'

'Unspecified, but harsh discipline and possibly other infractions also.'

'When you say, "possibly other infractions", you mean of a sexual nature?'

'I do.'

Justice McClellan intervened at this point and took over the questioning, asking Cardinal Pell why he had done nothing about it. 'Well, you didn't go straight to the school and say, "I've got this allegation, what's going on?"' Justice McClellan said.

'No, I didn't,' Cardinal Pell said.

'Should you have?'

'With the experience of forty years later, certainly I would agree that I should have . . . should have done more.'

'Why do you need the experience of forty years later? Wasn't it a serious matter then?'

'Yes, but people had a different attitude then. There were no specifics about the activity, how serious it was, and the boy wasn't asking me to do anything about it, but just lamenting and mentioning it.'[190]

Bloody hell. Even the child knew it was wrong – that's why he was reporting it. It was obvious that only clergy had a 'different attitude then' about child rape and sexual assault.

Evidence presented told us several children had approached Pell over the years to talk about abuse. Regarding St Patrick's College and Br Dowlan's behaviour, he said that he knew something from 'perhaps as early as the 1970s'.

'I could have heard it from one or two of the students and certainly I think one or two of the priests mentioned there were problems,' he said, agreeing the 'problems' were of a 'sexual nature'. The evidence included testimony from a boy who had spoken to Pell at the Eureka Stockade Swimming Pool. And another boy who had approached Pell at the college as stated by Pell. They were brave boys who were let down. Nothing had happened to stop further assaults. From evidence given to the Royal Commission we knew the accusations had the following in common: the boys knew the sexual assaults were happening, they knew the assaults were wrong, and they reported the sexual assaults to someone they saw as possessing the authority to act.

After four days of evidence, it was clearer now than ever that child sexual assault and rape had *thrived* in the Catholic Church in Ballarat and Melbourne because no clergyman had bothered to stop it despite receiving complaints.

The following day, some of the Ballarat survivors met with Pell. A few others rejected the invitation. Anthony and I said we didn't want to meet with him. We didn't want any photos to give the impression Pell had made amends. He had not.

Pell read a statement at the end of the meeting to the gathered media. He said he was committed to helping the victims in their goals to combat the 'scourge of sexual abuse', with a focus on Ballarat. He mentioned supporting a victim research centre.

Years later, nothing has come of the cardinal's commitment.

I was flattened by the evidence we heard in Rome. Anthony and I had no energy to continue travelling north to join Peter, Penny and Pat for a week's holiday. We just wanted to go home. Getting back to Australia, however, was no easy matter. It was difficult to change our flight and we had to wait four days. We arrived in Melbourne at 1.50 am on 10 March, pleased to be with family. But Rome had left us under a cloud of gloom. After holding high expectations, there was no accountability for the likes of Cardinal Pell.

The Rome hearing had been the best and the worst. It had been amazing to be there and achieve such a worldwide focus on clergy child sex crimes, but it had been exhausting and emotionally draining and left us with the sense of making no progress.

Back home, debate and analysis continued for days in the Australian newspapers. One cartoon by Matt Golding in *The Age* captured the moment. It showed a stooped Pell in his black soutane and pink skull cap walking off, briefcase in hand. Behind him was the word 'Ruthless' next to a crucifix, below which the meaning of the word ruthless was spelled out. Synonyms enriched the understanding: merciless, pitiless, cruel, heartless, callous, unmerciful, unfeeling. That just about summed it up.

# 35

Anthony seemed particularly burdened by the memories of Rome. He could not shake them. I believe it made him depressed for about nine months. He had little energy for life and so I waited for my Anthony to return to his old self.

Ronald Mulkearns died in April 2016. The Ballarat bishop had sheltered and protected numerous paedophile priests and brothers in his diocese from May 1971 until he stepped down in May 1997. He was responsible for likely thousands of children being sexually assaulted during his 26-year Catholic stewardship of half the state, stretching west from Ballarat across to the South Australian border, up north to the New South Wales border and then down south to the Southern Ocean. He caused suffering that remains mind-boggling in its breadth, criminality and total disregard for human life. His actions caused countless deaths. Nobody will miss him. Usually, no matter how many crimes they commit, all is forgiven by fellow clergy. But Mulkearns, the faithful, loyal and devoted priest of sixty years, was buried in a common grave.

We should never forget that his priesthood brothers, some of whom made him the scapegoat, were supporters of him and his actions during his reign.

What brightened our lives were our daughters, Katie and Aimee, and our wonderful little grandson. Two months after we returned to

Melbourne, towards the end of April, we had another momentous event, the arrival of a second grandchild, this time a little girl. Again we experienced the loveliness of grandparenthood as we held in our arms the tiny person who looked like her big brother. They are a beautiful joy.

I loved to take them for a walk in the pram down the street or in the park, proudly showing them to friends I met at the shops. We would stop at one of the cafes and have a babycino, usually with a big marshmallow – a treat that lit up their faces. The little ones sat at the big table with their legs dangling. When they could speak, they called me Chrissie-gran and Anthony was their grand-dad. I remember one morning I was at Aimee's house when Anthony walked in; our granddaughter was only about nine months old and on her tummy on the floor. Seeing Anthony walk past, she began to follow him: not yet crawling, she pursued him with a propelling slide along the floor. 'Dan-dad, Dan-dad,' she said. I was so excited at her words, I told Anthony, who immediately turned around and picked her up, making a big fuss of her. For Anthony and me, the arrival of our two little ones kept us grounded and brought a joyful new dimension and purpose into our lives.

In the middle of 2016, the Royal Commission issued a request for submissions to 'Issues Paper 11' – opinions on canon law, clericalism, operation of the sacrament of confession, the use of secrecy (including the practice of mental reservation) and many other points. It was an invitation to write to the commission on virtually any aspect of the Church relating to the sexual assault of children by clergy. Anthony and I spoke about it. We were very keen to make a submission, but he was still suffering from our experience in Rome. He said he wanted to write but did not have the energy. I asked him what he would like to write and he told me that what he couldn't get over was the way George Pell had repeatedly wriggled out of his responsibilities.

I told Anthony that I would write our issues paper for him, and began almost two months of research and writing. The Royal

Commission had provided many Church and insurance documents relating to the abuse. These telling documents proved who had said what and when in meetings, notes, letters and memorandums. Anthony and I already had copies of 'tender bundles' from our own case study. I had another folder full of documents, all of which related to Pell as an auxiliary bishop in Mentone with Sir Frank Little as archbishop. To complete my library of learning, I had decades of newspaper articles and recent information on Ballarat, plus my own twenty years of records and documents. There were many hundreds of documents, all in order and ready to go.

Injustice stoked the old fury inside me and that turbocharged my fingers as I tapped at the computer keyboard. Writing came naturally. The story was there. Seven weeks later, on 20 June, I finished my 42-page document. I gave it to Anthony to read for the first time. When he finished, he looked at me with soft eyes.

'I'm proud of you,' he said.

It made all the effort worthwhile. It helped alleviate some of his gloom. My writings said what he had been too tired to say.

Because my paper was largely based on Pell, it was not fully published on the commission's website with other submitted papers. I was disappointed and did not understand why. I later learned it was because police were investigating complaints involving the cardinal. However, the commission did publish two parts of my submission, one on mental reservation and the other on confession. On mental reservation, I wrote: 'The sole purpose of all this deception and secrecy is for them to hide the truth; basically, mental reservation exists and is exercised because they don't want certain truths to be known. It enables them to contain, control and hide the truth.'

My submission also covered the Christian Brothers, Salesian Brothers, St John of God Brothers, the Church's Secret Archives and the seal of confession, and ended with an appeal to our Australian Government to act and enact to protect children.

*

More and more survivors were finding their strongest voices.

Our dear friend Joan Isaacs had been busy writing a book, *To Prey and To Silence*, over the previous year and now we were going to attend her book launch in Brisbane. It was an exciting time. Joan had detailed her life from childhood to bruising encounters with the Catholic Church in Queensland. Her efforts were nothing short of courageous.

The book launch was a happy event, a lovely evening of moving speeches and conversations with supportive and like-minded friends and relatives. Joan and Ian, their sons and daughters-in-law and grandchildren, and Joan's dad were all there to enjoy the momentous occasion.

Joan had been silenced by going through the Church's Towards Healing scheme, which had handed her a small, confidential sum of money. She had been forbidden to speak about it, even to her husband, for thirteen years. This had been the case right up until one week before she spoke at her Royal Commission hearing in December 2013. As it was a lifetime contract, she had to seek permission to speak about her case from the Archdiocese of Brisbane.

This is the burden the Church places on its victims for crumbs of compensation. Joan had already taken her abuser to court, and he was in prison. The Church couldn't argue that the abuse wasn't true.

Peter and Penny Fox also attended the book launch. The following evening, we had a quieter get-together when the six of us went out to dinner. It was so good to see our friends again and to celebrate the publication of a new book, another piece of the puzzle in understanding how the Church really works.

When in Queensland for Joan's book launch, Anthony and I had decided to visit Fraser Island and Lady Elliot Island, both amazing tropical places of beauty. Our travels continued in September when we attended the Royal Commission in Sydney for an examination of the Armidale and Parramatta dioceses (Case Study 44) and allegations of child sexual abuse made against Father John Joseph Farrell. Farrell had been known as Father F when news of his crimes was first made public by the ABC's *Four Corners* program in 2012. At that time, the laicised Farrell was living as a prominent member of the community in Armidale. The story had caused journalist Paul Kennedy and the *Sydney Morning Herald* to publicly call for a royal commission into the Catholic Church.

Now the Child Abuse Royal Commission was doing exactly that – taking a forensic look at Father F and the priests and bishop around him.

Most alarming to me was the revelation that in 1992, after complaints of child sexual abuse were made against him, Farrell had been called to St Mary's Cathedral in Sydney for a meeting with the Australian Catholic Bishops Conference Special Issues Committee, where he made a damning disclosure. The two priests of the Special Issues Committee in charge of interrogating alleged paedophile priests were Rev. Brian Lucas and Rev. John Usher. Rev. Wayne Peters also attended as a representative of Armidale's bishop. All three men held prominent positions of power within the Australian arm of the Roman Catholic Church.

At the meeting, Farrell was questioned by Frs Lucas, Usher and Peters about the sexual abuse of boys. Eight days later, Peters penned a report of the meeting and addressed it to the Bishop of Armidale, Kevin Manning:

> He [Farrell] admitted that there had been five boys around the age of ten and eleven that he had sexually interfered with in varying degrees in the years approximately 1982 to 1984 while he was the assistant priest at Moree.
>
> He admitted that over a period of approximately twelve months he fondled the genitals of each of the boys and 'sucked off their dicks'. As far as [Farrell] can remember this was done on about a monthly basis over a period of twelve months. It was done only when each boy was alone with him. The boys were never together whenever an offence took place.

Without a word of concern for the boys, Peters went on to make an observation he knew would be critical to his Church employer:

'The possibility always remains that one or some of the boys involved may bring criminal charges against Farrell with subsequent grave harm to the priesthood and the Church.' Peters signed his report: 'Judicial Vicar'.

Despite Farrell's disclosing multiple crimes of child sexual assault, the Special Issues Committee of the Australian Catholic Bishops Conference did not report him to the police.

Now, in 2016, we were sitting in the Royal Commission case study investigating Farrell. The testimony from various priests and bishops was disheartening. I sat in the gallery taking notes. 'Crime with impunity,' I wrote. 'Enraging and sickening to listen to their current cover-up for their past cover-up. They've had 2,000 years to fix this problem. Disgraceful testimony. An ecclesiastical view of search warrants: to shred or not to shred, that is the question.'

Another comment I wrote was 'Google George Brandis and George Pell Rome'. Mention of the two Georges must have been made that day, 14 September 2016. I didn't google it back then, but I did four years later, while writing this book. I could find only one reference. It appeared on Ten Eyewitness News, which reported Australia's Federal Attorney-General George Brandis had dined with Cardinal George Pell in Rome. In a 20 July 2015 report, Ten Eyewitness News' Adam Walters stated, 'Although the leader of the Australian Catholic Church has been a key witness at the Royal Commission into Institutional Responses to Child Sexual Abuse, the attorney-general has found time to dine with Cardinal Pell in Rome. Victims were outraged to learn of the secret lunch.'[191]

The lunch had been hosted while John McCarthy was Australia's Ambassador to the Holy See. Walters said an official media release about Mr Brandis' trip made no mention of the lunch with Pell, who was due to give evidence to the Royal Commission for the third time. 'The attorney-general's office denied the lunch was official, leaving lawyers to wonder why the most senior law officer in the land would be meeting the highest-profile witness called so far by the Child Abuse Royal Commission,' Walters reported.

Friends in high places.

Another witness at the Fr Farrell case study was Bishop Gerard Hanna. Hanna's retirement had been approved just two days before his Royal Commission appearance, probably because he knew his testimony was damning. Hanna had learnt about child rapist Farrell. He testified that many years earlier, while a priest, his old boss Bishop Henry Kennedy had said to him in relation to complaints about Farrell, 'Oh you know, Gerry, it's that usual thing – he was messing around with altar boys.' Both the bishop and Hanna knew 'that usual thing' and 'messing around' meant criminal sexual assaults of children.

When Hanna was asked by counsel assisting the Royal Commission what was meant by 'that usual thing', he said, 'It wasn't unknown – that there were priests who used altar boys, that they were paedophiles, in fact.'

Two of Fr Farrell's victims died by suicide when they were twenty-eight years old.

Hanna appeared to be the second bishop to stand down in relation to the Royal Commission. There should have been many, many more. It had taken from 1992 until 2005 for the priesthood to laicise Fr Farrell.

The second week of evidence in the case study was full of clerical attempts to reinvent the facts despite documented evidence of crimes committed. There was a smoking gun – a copy, in civil court records, of Fr Peters' official report to his bishop. In a rare but gratifying piece of honesty from clergy, before his 2015 death, Peters stood by what he had written and quoted in his 1992 report on Farrell.[192]

It was September 2016 and the Royal Commission as it pertained to the Catholic Church was winding towards its finale. All the bosses of the Catholic Church in Australia had been summoned to appear one last time at a hearing in Sydney. The country's largest inquiry was crossing every T and dotting every I before making recommendations that I hoped would make children safer.

It would be sad to see our Royal Commission end. However, despite a lift in my husband's mood, he had not yet recovered from Rome. And he never really would.

The Church was still hogging headlines. Archbishop of Adelaide Philip Wilson was appealing to the New South Wales Supreme Court to dismiss a criminal charge alleging he had failed to tell police about Father James Fletcher's abuse decades earlier. His appeal failed. In May 2018 Wilson would be convicted of these charges,[193] becoming the most senior Catholic clergyman in the world to be convicted of this offence. A jail sentence was a real possibility, although what seemed a victory for victims would be short-lived, as only seven months later his conviction was overturned on appeal. He was a free man.[194]

In other news, Fr John Walshe from Mentone went to Ireland but was banned from 'ministering' because of the abuse of the eighteen-year-old man at the seminary years earlier.[195] Walshe would soon resign as parish priest at Mentone after almost twenty-five years in that position. He then tried to transfer to a parish eleven kilometres away, but those parents protested, negating the move. It is unknown where Walshe ended up.

Then came the biggest news. Victorian police flew to Italy to interview Pell. He repeated his innocence and said he would 'continue to cooperate with Victoria Police until the investigation is finalised'.[196]

On 28 October 2016, Anthony and I organised a trip for our whole family to Byron Bay. While we were there, we watched on television the Federal Government's Social Services Minister Christian Porter announce that the Federal Government would implement a National Redress Scheme as recommended by the Child Abuse Royal Commission. It would be an opt-in compensation scheme for states and institutions. Payments were to be capped at $150,000.

Anthony was devastated by the low cap. He had sat on the Royal Commission's roundtable meetings advocating for the limit on the redress scheme, if there had to be one, to be $500,000.[197] Over months of discussion, the proposed cap had been lowered to $200,000 because the commission needed a figure that government and the institutions would agree on. Anthony had reluctantly gave up his hopes of a higher cap. Now he was learning that it was all done and dusted for $150,000. He rang a state politician in Victoria he had been speaking with about the redress issue.

'What's going on?' he said.

The politician had no idea that the announcement had been going to happen, nor that the cap had been lowered to $150,000. It was a crushing moment.

Two days later, we were back in Melbourne. The Melbourne Archdiocese had issued a press release to announce it had reviewed its Melbourne Response scheme. The Church had decided to change its cap on payments from $75,000 to – surprise, surprise – $150,000. It was also going to review some previous payments. The full Melbourne Response review was not made public.

'This is not good enough,' Anthony told the media. 'There's been an explicit promise all along this report would be released and it should be released.'[198]

Now, all of a sudden, the Church's ex-gratia cap of $150,000 matched the Federal Government's National Redress cap of $150,000. I did not think it was a coincidence. Anthony and I had long conversations wondering about the Church coordinating its response with the conservative Federal Government. We could not rest easy thinking the organisers of such crimes and cover-ups would have a seat at the table with government representatives to dictate compensation levels for victims. The announcements were made two weeks apart, both on Friday afternoons, the worst day and time to attract media attention yet the best for those who don't want to be questioned about their announcements. In time I would learn that this decision and others on redress had come after the Federal Government and Church hierarchy had been in workshops together.[199] Tellingly, the $150,000 also matched insurance cover limits for the Catholic and Anglican churches.

At least the civil law noose was beginning to tighten around the neck of the priesthood. The Victorian Parliamentary Inquiry continued to bear fruit with law changes as recommended in its *Betrayal of Trust* report.

One change to legislation made it easier for people to sue organisations. This of course included the Church, which would now have to prove it had taken all necessary steps to stop the abuse. At the same time, the Child Abuse Royal Commission was about to look at breaking the seal of confession on mandatory reporting of child abuse by removing the exemption the priesthood held. The priesthood saw breaking the seal of confession as an assault on one of its sacraments. The Church's Truth, Justice and Healing Council made a formal submission to the Royal Commission asking that Victorian legislation grant the Church 'occasion of privilege'.[200]

Ireland broke its seal of confession on mandatory reporting in 2012: in the most Catholic country in the world, it was already a crime for anyone, including priests, to not report their knowledge of child abuse.

It was heartening to see the prospect of loopholes that might aid clergy offending being closed in Australia.

In what seemed like no time at all, Christmas was upon us again. We celebrated with a big lunch. This was a beautiful time, although there were concerns and stresses. My father turned eighty-four on 5 January. Dad was very unwell and in a nursing home not far from where we lived in Oakleigh. Ten days later he died. He had suffered in the last months of his life but was now at peace. It was a great sadness for our family. We celebrated Dad's long life at his funeral and laid him to rest at a local cemetery where his parents and sister are buried.

# 36

Finally, the Royal Commission held its last monumental Catholic hearing. It was called Case Study 50: Institutional Review of Catholic Church Authorities. Scheduled for three weeks, it would hear from seventy-two sworn witnesses, including figures from the Church's hierarchy. The last two days would see all seven Australian archbishops sitting before the commission. It would be grim.

Anthony and I embarked on our final mission to bear witness. Every Monday we caught a 7.30 am flight to Sydney; every week we stayed in a hotel until Friday. The 5.30 pm flight back to Melbourne was our relief.

Statistics were revealed in the courtroom. 'Between January 1980 and February 2015, 4,444 people [only those who came forward] alleged incidents of child sexual abuse made to ninety-three Catholic Church authorities. These claims related to over 1,000 separate institutions [various schools, homes and orphanages].'[201]

The statistics continued: average ages of victims were ten-and-a-half for girls and eleven-and-a half for boys. The average time between abuse and disclosure of abuse was thirty-three years (non-clergy abuse disclosure was ten years earlier).

The commission found that each child had been sexually assaulted for an average of 2.2 years.

The worst dioceses were listed on a scale of average of priests were accused perpetrators. Diocese of Sale, Victoria: 15.1 per cent. Diocese of Sandhurst, Victoria: 14.7 per cent. Diocese of Port Pirie, South Australia: 14.1 per cent. Diocese of Lismore, New South Wales: 13.9 per cent. Diocese of Wollongong, New South Wales: 11.7 per cent.

The worst five brotherhoods were Brothers of St John of God (40.4 per cent), Marist Brothers (20.4 per cent), Christian Brothers (22.0 per cent), Salesians of Don Bosco (21.9 per cent) and De La Salle Brothers (13.8 per cent).

There were 1 880 alleged perpetrators identified by the Royal Commission. They included non-ordained religious Brothers (32 per cent), priests (30 per cent), lay people (29 per cent), non-ordained religious Sisters (5 per cent), and known alleged perpetrators with religious status unknown (4 per cent).

I heard these numbers and did my own calculations. If we take the 597 brothers, 572 priests and ninety-six nuns who offended, we have 1 265 religious offenders. Fr Gerald Ridsdale told his family that he'd had 'hundreds' of victims over his twenty-nine years of offending; Fr O'Donnell told the hierarchy of ninety victims over his fifty years, and they were just the names he could remember. If we make Ridsdale's 'hundreds' into a minimum of 200 victims and we make O'Donnell's ninety into one hundred victims, that gives us an average of 150 victims each. One hundred and fifty victims of 1 265 clerical offenders makes 189,750 children molested. This is how my mind worked when trying to calculate the incalculable. I also kept in mind that the numbers of victims would be far greater than those who had come forward to the Royal Commission. One lawyer dubbed O'Donnell 'the two-a-day man'.

As anyone could see, the evidence given in Case Study 50 was earth-shattering.

At the end of the second week I put together my own unofficial press release. I thought I needed to remind journalists of the history of three of the archbishops about to give evidence.

To remind Melbourne's Catholic boss Denis Hart I photocopied an August 2009 *Age* front page whose headline read ARCHBISHOP

TO ABUSE VICTIM: 'GO TO HELL, BITCH'.[202] The archbishop had
made this comment to a victim who confronted him at his home. A
magistrate had labelled his conduct 'appalling'. When *The Age* questioned Hart about what he had said, he replied three times, 'I don't
recall.' To remind people about Sydney Archbishop Anthony Fisher's
behaviour, I cut out another front page that told the story of how
the clergyman had labelled our family too cranky six months after
Emma's death, heartlessly calling our grief 'dwelling crankily [. . .]
on old wounds'.[203] For Adelaide Archbishop Wilson it was the newspaper coverage from 2015 – ARCHBISHOP PHILIP WILSON: 'I DIDN'T
HIDE CHILD SEX'.[204]

On top of these words from three archbishops, there was my experience with Brisbane Archbishop Mark Coleridge. I did not include
details of our interaction in the foyer of the Royal Commission because
there was no headline. Four of the seven archbishops of Australia had
behaved badly towards victims or their families. I handed out my press
release to media in Sydney.

Familiar names of priests rose to the surface of commission
evidence. My ears pricked up when I heard the name Br Robert Best
from the St Alipius Boys' School in Ballarat. He had been jailed for
fourteen years in 2011. What stood out now was that the Christian
Brothers had spent $1.5 million on his legal costs. We had previ-
ously heard that figure to be $1 million. I was surprised by the vast
increase. From my seat in the gallery, I sensed that Justice McClellan
was also perturbed. He asked the person who was giving this
evidence why the figure had increased by $500,000. The nervous
speaker stated that the extra half million was for Best's appeals. We
were all shocked. It seemed incredible that the Christian Brothers
would spend $1.5 million defending one child sex offender who
had pleaded guilty in some cases and been found guilty in others.
If the Christian Brothers had spent the same on all 281[205] of their
offenders it would have cost them $421,500 million. I doubted they
were that generous, so why had they spent so much on defending,
protecting Best? Justice McClellan moved the hearing on.

During a break in proceedings, I was in the hearing room while Anthony was still in the foyer. When he came back, he was ashen. I immediately asked him what was wrong. Anthony told me Father Frank Brennan, Adjunct Professor and Rector of Newman College at the University of Melbourne had approached him. They had never met before.

'I know your face,' Fr Brennan had said to Anthony, trying to remember, then added: 'Your name is O'Donnell.'

'My name is Anthony Foster.'

'Oh yes; O'Donnell was that horrible priest,' Fr Brennan said before walking away without so much as a grimace or apology. To mistake Anthony for the man who had raped two of our children was a disgraceful act.

One pleasant moment during those three weeks in Sydney was in February when we met up with Paul Kennedy for dinner when he was in town for work. He was helping the ABC in its coverage of this part of the Royal Commission. We all had an enjoyable evening breaking the oppression and fatigue of hearing grinding hierarchy testimonies. We also met up for dinner with friends we knew in Sydney – encounters that were a great source of much-needed downtime and comradeship.

When I returned to Melbourne, I wrote an opinion piece for *The Australian* titled PATHETIC EXCUSES FOR THE SINS OF THE FATHERS.[206] At the end of the story, I related Anthony's disturbing experience with Fr Brennan. Brennan then contacted us and came to our home to apologise, though I couldn't help but feel it was more of a PR exercise than a genuine attempt to express regret.

The scrutiny on Pell increased, despite his declaration of innocence.

There was so much attention on this one clergyman that you could be excused for missing other Catholic news. But I missed nothing. I had to buy more scrapbooks to keep up. In Ireland, the bones of hundreds of babies were found at the site of a former unmarried mothers and babies' home in a small town called Tuam. A report from an inquiry the government ordered in 2014 backed up a historian's claim that up to 800 children may be in an unmarked grave (the sewer) beneath the home.[207] Some religious people called those babies 'the spawn of the devil'.[208] In January 2021 a 3 000-page government report would reveal that 9000 children had died in Church-run Irish mother-and-baby homes over an eighty-year period.[209]

We flew home from our marathon Royal Commission journey. This part of our job was done. Being at so many hearings had been a long, enlightening and, at times, wonderful journey. It had proved to be a confirmation of what we had already learned and knew to be the priesthood's attitude and behaviour, but with many more examples. The Royal Commission had confirmed what victims had been saying for decades. I felt vindicated.

During its five years, the Royal Commission had examined 1.2 million documents, handled 42,041 calls, received 25,964 letters and emails, held 8 013 private sessions, hosted fifty-seven public hearings, and made 2 575 referrals to authorities.

This work was a gift to pass on to coming generations of children, keeping them safe because society could now understand.

It had also taken its toll.

# 37

It was always a task getting Anthony up on the dance floor. Neither of us had any worthwhile moves, just awkward motions. But I will forever remember one rare night. We were at a work convention in the US in 2009. The convention related to the air-conditioning side of our business – a fun six-day event for major dealers. We saw it as a good chance to get away.

One of the nights was set aside for wining and dining in an enormous ballroom. Luckily for us, the convention organisers had hired a musical act we recognised – KC and the Sunshine Band. When they played their funky songs like 'Give It Up' and 'That's the Way (I Like It)', Anthony couldn't resist. He loved the music. And when the band played their beautifully slow song 'Please Don't Go', Anthony held me tight and sang the meaningful words close to my ear.

It was a moment in time I treasured, and always will. After all the pain we had been through, and the fact that, as the Catholic, I had brought that pain into our family, it was amazing that Anthony could still love me deeply. And to be able to sing those words to me – about being blessed to be loved – said everything about the man Anthony was. But I was the one blessed to be loved by him.

Eight years later, Anthony and I were closer, and busier, than ever. It was May 2017 – a particularly hectic month. In one week, we attended the book launch of *Cardinal: The Rise and Fall of George Pell* by ABC journalist Louise Milligan. Another day, we had lunch with Peter and Penny Fox, who were down from New South Wales; then came yet another lunch, on the Mornington Peninsula, and that evening we met our dear friends John and Monica in Melbourne to see a preview showing of the new Australian movie *Don't Tell* (based on a true story of child sexual abuse and cover-ups in the Anglican church). That weekend we drove to Ballarat for the Loud Ballarat No More Silence Walk. It started off with a visit to the Art Gallery of Ballarat, which housed an extensive display of portraits of Ballarat survivors. Monday, I drove to Tonimbuk for the day while Anthony went back to the Mornington Peninsula. He'd been working quite a bit at Aimee's new house, helping with renovations.

We were both at home on the morning of Wednesday 23 May. Anthony was leaving early, heading to Bunnings on his way down to Aimee's place. His plan was to install an IKEA kitchen.

I kissed him goodbye. Fifteen minutes later, I went across the street to see Aimee, where she was living before getting ready for the big move. When I arrived, I was surprised to see Anthony again. He was there talking to Aimee about the renovations. After another farewell, he left for Bunnings. Aimee and I chatted. Then Aimee remembered something she had forgotten to tell Anthony. She tried to ring him, but he didn't answer. She tried again five or ten minutes later. This time, the phone was answered, but not by Anthony. It was an ambulance officer on the other end of the line. Aimee did not indicate to me that anything was wrong; she just walked away listening to the phone.

'Mum, sit down,' Aimee said when she got off the phone. 'Dad has had a fall at Bunnings and is being looked after by an ambulance officer.'

I had lived through many medical emergencies. My experience told me to latch onto hope. Doing this allowed me to function. I went home and grabbed my handbag, not knowing what else to take. Luke drove us to the Alfred Hospital, waiting for an update on Anthony's condition. He had been placed in a coma at Bunnings by the ambulance officer. The hospital staff told us he was in the operating theatre. This confused me. I couldn't understand why he needed an operation. I didn't know details of his injury or injuries. I just knew it was serious.

I rang my mum, other relatives and a dear friend.

Eventually, a nurse invited us into a private waiting room. Still, I held onto hope. A surgeon and his assistant entered the room. Their faces were grave. The surgeon told us Anthony had suffered a bad head injury. I was thinking of Katie's brain injury and imagined him being more disabled than Katie, but as I was thinking this, in what seemed a response to my thought, the surgeon clarified.

'Anthony has had a catastrophic brain injury,' he said.

I had a fleeting thought that Anthony would be bedridden for the rest of his life. But it was worse than that. The surgeon told us that Anthony would not survive.

Devastation. The worst thing we could hear. We froze in our chairs. Shocked. Only two hours earlier, Anthony had been fine. We just sat there, trying to understand the enormity of the surgeon's words. Finally, I spoke.

'Anthony was a good man,' I said.

Then tears came to drown us. Anthony was the most patient, intelligent, compassionate and loving man I had ever met. He was the kindest person in the world. The best. He was everything to me. We had been together for thirty-seven years.

We later found out that at Bunnings Anthony had been on the phone to the builder. They were mid-conversation when Anthony didn't reply to a question. The builder thought the phone connection must have dropped out. He rang back several times but there was no answer. Anthony had gone from speaking on the phone to blacking out, falling backwards onto a concrete floor and hitting his head. An autopsy would reveal he had blocked arteries, one of which, I was told, would have caused him to pass out so suddenly and profoundly.

Anthony stayed on life support for another three days, allowing family and friends to say goodbye. Two days after his fall, my wonderful husband was pronounced brain dead, confirmation that it was only life support equipment keeping him alive.

Organ donation was arranged for Saturday.

During the afternoon, we heard about a young teenager with liver failure. He had, at most, forty-eight hours to live. The doctors measured Anthony's liver and found the size was a match, as was the blood type. That night, after Anthony had donated organs, his liver was sent under police escort, sirens blaring, to Melbourne Airport. From there, a private jet rushed it to the boy in need. It was some consolation to us that Anthony was saving a life some-where. And we had to smile – he would have loved the police escort and private-jet flight. Being an ex-commercial pilot licence holder, he loved flying. The transplant operation was a success, and the boy received another chance at life. Anthony's kidneys were also success-fully donated, to two patients, relieving them from further years on dialysis.

Despite the life-giving, I was heartbroken. The love of my life, my best friend, the other half of me, had gone forever. Shattering, too, for the rest of the family – Anthony's siblings, my mum and brothers and their families and all of Anthony's family and friends.

It was torturous for us all. For Katie, it was even worse. Her brain injury prevents her remembering her previous few minutes, but she can remember her childhood years from before the accident. While it can take months for her to recall a new carer's name, some things, like Emma's death, burn immediately into her long-term memory. For the first three mornings after Anthony's collapse, Katie woke feeling something bad had happened, though she couldn't remember what it was. When her carer gently reminded her, she relived the pain all over again.

In the days after Anthony's death, when I saw many of his male friends, I had strong images of the love he had for them. The big man-hugs he had used as a greeting instead of a handshake, and the look of happiness on his face when he saw them. Anthony knew how to love.

His absence was very real. It caused me acute pain. We had spent decades together. Now I felt like an island, surrounded by loving people, yet alone. On my first night without Anthony, I got out of bed and walked into the bathroom, not really knowing why. Next thing I knew I was waking up on the floor. I had fainted.

Anthony died at the age of sixty-four, ten years younger than his father and twenty years younger than his mother. It was an indicator of the stress he had endured: the traumas when Emma's life began to fall apart; the shock of learning of the sexual assaults; the shock of Katie being hit by a car, her twelve months in hospital and her life of disabilities; Emma's death and the nine years of grieving since her suicide; and the 21-year battle against the priesthood, fighting for justice for our daughters and all clergy victims.

I sent a text message to politician Frank McGuire, the member for Broadmeadows who had been on the Victorian Parliamentary Inquiry. Frank was a kind man. I wanted to let him know about Anthony, rather than have him read about it in the newspapers. I did not want to tell him or other people the sad news, yet I had to. Frank's heartfelt response was immediate and humbling.

Paul Kennedy was hosting a national program on the ABC when he broke the news to viewers that Anthony had died. He later spoke about his friendship with Anthony on *News Breakfast*.

Messages of condolence began to arrive; there were hundreds of them – text messages, emails, cards and letters in the post. Relatives, friends and perfect strangers sent their kind thoughts, well wishes and love. Most mornings I would get up early and spend hours replying to texts and emails. It was exhausting, but I had a need to reply to such kindness. Still there were many I couldn't reply to. They were all beautiful messages with heartfelt words of encouragement and love, many with stories of their own memories of Anthony.

Life was hazy amid the shock, but so many loved ones were there to help. We were just beginning to think about the funeral when Ann Barker took me aside one day to ask if I would like a state funeral for Anthony. The Victorian premier, Daniel Andrews, had asked Ann to ask me. I could barely believe it. State funerals were for important people; Anthony had been the most important person in our lives, but this was different. It was an amazing honour. I said yes.

After much searching by Aimee and Luke, the Melbourne Recital Centre in Southbank was chosen as the venue for the funeral. The centre's ceiling and walls are covered in a beautiful timber, and Anthony loved working with timber. He also loved classical music.

Aimee, Katie and I went to the funeral home and sat beside Anthony's open coffin. It was late in the afternoon as we sat talking to him about the funeral arrangements and the beautiful messages we had received. It was strangely lovely to sit with him in the peace and quiet and to just be in his presence. After Katie's carer arrived and took her home, Aimee and I stayed on, making the most of our last moments together with Anthony. Eventually, we kissed him goodbye. Walking out was so hard.

That evening, Tara Brown appeared on *60 Minutes* and paid tribute to Anthony, telling the national audience: 'For the past twenty years, Anthony and Chrissie Foster have been fighting the Catholic Church. They've been battling for the most fundamental rights: recognition and justice for their two daughters and countless other children who are the victims of paedophile priests. Tragically and unthinkably, Anthony's crusade has come to a sudden end. The 64-year-old died last week [. . .] but his tireless work and extraordinary courage will never be forgotten.'

Most of the footage was of Anthony speaking on earlier *60 Minutes* programs and, significantly, they had pieced together controversial footage of George Pell in 2002 and explained how he had committed the sin of lying by denying he had been shown the picture of Emma. This made for a fitting tribute to Anthony. The righting of a wrong inflicted upon us by Pell was appreciated. Anthony would have loved it.

The day before his funeral, our family was invited to Victoria's Parliament House for a condolence session for Anthony. Ann Barker and Paul Kennedy also attended; they were always there for help and support. We sat together in the public gallery. It was a deeply moving formal event that gave solace, love and recognition of Anthony's achievements. It was a profound experience that we could not have anticipated. Daniel Andrews spoke first. Hansard recorded the premier's statement for history:

I only had the privilege of meeting Anthony and Chrissie a handful of times. And it was always Anthony and Chrissie; they were always together. The most recent occasion where we met was earlier this year at a ceremony at Government House for our state's Australian of the Year. Most deservingly, Chrissie had been chosen as Victoria's Local Hero. But, as I am sure she would agree, the very same title could have also applied to her soulmate Anthony, because together they were heroes for justice and heroes for truth. They had faced their own heartbreak – unimaginable heartbreak. But remarkably, despite everything they had endured, Anthony and Chrissie did not resign themselves to silence and solitude. Instead, they dedicated themselves to fighting for their girls and on behalf of every other victim too – for every childhood that had been taken and for every family that had been broken. Together the Fosters challenged a culture of silence and shameful suppression, together they took on those who lied and those who conspired to hide the truth and together they shone a bright light on one of our darkest chapters. Before any royal commission or any parliamentary inquiry there were the Fosters, Anthony and Chrissie. And because of their courage, because of their strength and, as their lifelong friend Paul put it, because of their relentless 'quiet fury', the mood in this nation has profoundly shifted and at long last victims are finally being heard.

I do not think words could ever really be enough, but to Chrissie I say thank you for everything that you have done, and on behalf of all Victorians, the Parliament, all of us, we are eternally thankful. I am just so sorry that you have lost your darling husband, and to Katie and Aimee, I am so sorry that you have lost your darling dad. Today we pause, just as we will tomorrow, to honour him and all he did – a quietly spoken man but a most powerful voice for victims, a tireless campaigner, a hero. And although Anthony has left us far too early, just as he did in life, he leaves us with a guiding light. Anthony Foster will not be forgotten, and our fight for justice will continue.

Frank McGuire and other members of Parliament, including the Leader of the Opposition, then stood and spoke about Anthony.

It was a truly amazing day in Parliament. As sad as I felt, the words spoken about Anthony warmed my heart and brought smiles to me and my family. Now I prepared myself for the state funeral. I had no idea how many people would attend, but I knew they would come from everywhere to say goodbye.

I could hardly believe any of this was real. But it was, and I was lost in shock, grief and a hundred other emotions. I was constantly receiving messages from wellwishers. I felt suspended under an avalanche of funeral plans and other day-to-day necessities. Organising the funeral was a distraction from the death of my beloved husband. I decided to process my situation later, so I stayed in the present as things swirled around me. Since before I had met Anthony I had learned to base things on reality, and the reality was that Anthony had died and there would be a funeral, and the funeral would be a state funeral. I fortified myself by accepting all that was happening and all that I was feeling. I moved forward as best I could. I did not think about my public advocacy during this time; later, when I fleetingly considered the future, I assumed my work would be over. We had always acted together. We could never do that again.

# 38

The funeral was at 10.30 am on Wednesday 7 June 2017. Everyone I knew was there and many more I didn't know. One thousand people packed into the Elisabeth Murdoch Hall at the Melbourne Recital Centre.

One day during one of the Royal Commission hearings, Anthony had been a bit restless, so he used his phone to take a photo of the colourful socks he was wearing. He sent out a tweet with a funny caption; some people liked it. Today for Anthony's funeral, members of Care Leavers Australia Network (CLAN) had travelled an hour from Geelong on the train all wearing colourful socks in memory of Anthony. They took a photo of all their socks as they sat on the train and tweeted it. CLAN members had attended months of the Victorian Parliamentary Inquiry and many more case studies of the Royal Commission hearings. For close to seven years they had always been there, sitting out the front of Parliament or the courts, rain, hail or shine, with their protest posters, always with big smiles and ready to chat.

Seventeen days before the funeral there had been a public gathering in Ballarat called the LOUD Fence No More Silence Walk. I had been introduced to a couple, Patricia and Terry, who had driven from Queensland to take part. I had then introduced the couple to Anthony and told him how far they had driven. Anthony had chatted to them for over half an hour. The same couple had now driven all the way back again to attend his funeral.

So many people had won our hearts and minds over the years. It was a bittersweet shock reunion when they all arrived at once to publicly remember Anthony. I had asked ABC radio broadcaster Jon Faine to be the master of ceremonies. He and Anthony had got on well over their years of interviews and I believed Anthony would have liked Jon being there as MC. Jon had kindly accepted the invitation.

The mourners took their seats and waited in silence for the ceremony to begin. Jon now greeted and welcomed everyone from the stage. Between musical interludes, moving tributes were made by friends and family. Anthony's siblings Carol and Brian made the opening tribute, followed by Premier Daniel Andrews. Alan, a colleague, gave a speech about Anthony's work life. Then came sister-in-law Linda, friend and survivor John, our barrister Tim Seccull and Ann Barker. Paul Kennedy delivered a very moving eulogy for Anthony. My brother Geoff spoke lovingly. The air in the room seemed to stop and listen when Katie and Aimee took their places behind the microphone. Finally, we heard some heartwarming words from Royal Commission chair Justice Peter McClellan. We chose songs Anthony loved: 'This Year's Love', 'Gone', 'Firework' and 'Time to Say Goodbye', which we had played at the funerals of both Emma and Anthony's mother. The Amati Strings, a group of young and talented musicians, filled the hall with beautiful sound.

I wanted to speak at Anthony's funeral but didn't think I would be able to do it. I felt so depleted from the shock of his sudden death, weakened further by feelings of loss and despair. In those first days I didn't know if I could stand, let alone speak at his funeral.

At the end of the service, Aimee bravely bore her father's coffin along with five male friends and relatives of Anthony. As Katie and I followed, I could feel the love in the room of a thousand people. It was an amazing feeling at such a sad time, and I felt I could not ignore them. I paused and looked out at everyone. It is an image I will never forget, seeing all the people who adored Anthony sharing their grief. I just had to give a little wave to acknowledge them, thank them. Their response made me feel their love even more.

One friend later said that he had never seen so many men cry.

Outside the Recital Centre, people lined the street as Anthony's coffin was placed in the hearse. We all watched as the vehicle slowly drove my husband away with a police motorbike escort.

The wake was around the corner at The Atlantic restaurant in Southbank, a venue Anthony would have loved: ground floor, level with the promenade of people walking beside the Yarra River, where boats passed by and seagulls flew overhead. On the other side of the river, trains from Flinders Street Station travelled back and forth, against a background of Melbourne's all-sizes and all-ages city buildings. Anthony would have been in his element mingling with the several hundred friends and relatives.

The last of us left The Atlantic at about 8 pm. The city lights displayed their colourful hues as we drove home. Sadness aside, it had been a wonderful funeral and wake. Everyone had appeared to enjoy the time together in memory of Anthony. As the landscape turned from city to suburbs, I thought back to the Recital Centre and how both Katie and Aimee had bravely stood up and spoken about their dad. Katie's tribute to Anthony was: 'Hey Dad, thanks for always making me feel special. You were such a smart, wise, giving and generous man. Love always, your Katie.'

Aimee's tribute to her father was the best eulogy I had ever heard. Every time I read her words they bring tears to my eyes.

Anthony's intellect and words and the voice he devoted to victims – like his little girls – will be missed forever. To be loved by him made life a joy despite everything we had endured because the one thing they, the priesthood, could not destroy was our love. It was us against them. I did not know how I would continue alone. I loved him with all my heart and still do.

\*

I took solace from knowing we had always said what was on our minds. Now, with Anthony gone, I did not feel there was something I had not told him. More than once, I told him he was my hero. Recently, I had lovingly told him he was perfect. Of course, he couldn't accept it and denied it was true, but I persisted. I took his face in my hands and told him why. I am so glad I did. I know nobody is perfect, but he was as close as I believe anybody could be.

Together we had reached the final hearing of the Royal Commission and, importantly, twice after the hearings we had stopped, held each other, and absorbed the feelings of the five years of forensic examination and the role we had played in it, and acknowledged what a wonderful change it had made to the plight of victims. There was some relief and peace in knowing that those who had come forward had done their best to ensure future children and families would not suffer as we all had.

One night after the funeral, I had a dream that Anthony was outside my office window at home. I quickly went to the window to see him, but he was gone. As my eyes searched the garden, I finally saw him crouched down beside the window, hiding from me with a big smile on his face and holding a big bunch of yellow daisies for me. It was so like him to be playful and with a surprise. It left me happy as it did again the following morning when I remembered the dream.

I tried not to let sadness overwhelm me, because I knew it would break his heart to realise the depth of my despair. Sometimes, when his absence was acute and life ahead suddenly appeared to be unbearable, I would stop the feelings and think *Five minutes ago, I was okay. I can be okay now.* I chose to feel the way I did those five minutes ago because it was possible and because it was where I preferred to be. It was life. I did this several times, stubbornly forcing myself in a direction other than the roads to dark places. I had been there before: they were roads to nowhere. I chose peace over despair, and it became easier as I practised it. I understood the enormity of my situation. I didn't ignore it; rather I chose to go forward as a better way. I had the kindest and most amazing children, grandchildren, mum, brothers, aunt, cousins and friends to be with.

In July 2017 George Pell flew back from the Vatican to face charges of historical child sexual assault. The churchman's lawyer, Robert Richter QC, told media that his client would plead not guilty. The charges were not known due to a suppression order.

A cardinal fronting court for child sexual assault charges was a world first and gained international attention. I suspected it was going to be bedlam at the Melbourne Magistrates' Court for Pell's first appearance, which was a filing hearing.

I wondered whether I should go. I knew there would be requests from media for my comments. If Anthony were still alive, we both would have attended without hesitation. Anthony used to give me the courage to confront these potentially chaotic situations. He was better than me at speaking to the reporters and doing live crosses for television coverage. With Anthony no longer here, I felt isolated and I now hoped the media would not call for comment – but call they did. Pell back in Australia lit up the media and my phone. I don't know where they all got my number. Perhaps it was on a billboard somewhere. It made for a busy time.

I decided to attend the legal first as an observer.

The criminal court was mostly populated by media and police. Citizens like me were few. The hearing was over in six minutes. We didn't learn much. The magistrate ordered Pell to return for another hearing later in the year. There was nothing reported in the press as the case had a suppression order on it and that suppression order had a second suppression order placed on it: we were forbidden from even saying we were not allowed to talk about it – a double whammy. This was to ensure a fair trial, if it came to that.

Three weeks after Pell's brief appearance in court, the Royal Commission released its *Criminal Justice* report with eighty-five recommendations 'aimed at reforming the Australian criminal justice

system in order to provide a fairer response to victims of institutional child sexual abuse'. One of those recommendations was about
breaking the seal of confession. The report recommended there be no
exemption, excuse, protection or privilege from the offence granted to
clergy for failing to report information disclosed in connection with
a religious confession.

This was a serious challenge to Church authority. Clergy, mainly
the hierarchy, came out in strong opposition to the recommendation.

Whenever I heard anyone talking about the sanctity of the confessional, I thought about the case of former Catholic priest Michael
McArdle, who pleaded guilty in a Queensland court to sexually
abusing children. He wrote an affidavit in 2004 stating that he had
confessed 1 500 times to molesting children to thirty priests over
twenty-five years. After being forgiven 1 500 times for his regular
criminal offending in face-to-face confessions with his thirty fellow
priests, he was told to 'go home and pray'.

'I was devastated after the assaults, every one of them,' he wrote
in his affidavit. 'So distressed would I become that I would attend
confessions weekly.' He said each confession was like 'a magic wand
had been waved over me'.

This case was so shocking that three times I published opinion
pieces on it – it was the perfect example as to why priests should
be forced to report cases of child sexual assault that they hear in
confession.[210]

In 2011, when Senator Nick Xenophon released a press statement headlined CONFESSION OF CHILD ABUSE MUST BE REPORTED TO
POLICE, one priest defended the confession seal, saying, 'The proposed
change could scare offenders away from confession, which otherwise could be a first step towards seeking treatment or surrendering
to police.'

This was a smokescreen of nonsense. In the case of McArdle, all
thirty priests over twenty-five years had told him to 'go home and
pray'. Not one of them had suggested he seek help or turn himself
over to police. If the Church had abided by mandatory reporting like

teachers or anyone else in charge of children, the criminal priest would have been stopped from reoffending twenty-five years earlier.

The seal of confession was not the only source of secrecy used by clergy that worked against children being abused and then as adults pursuing justice. Over time, in hearings, I noted many truth suppressors they employed: oath of secrecy; mental reservation; a multitude of 'I don't recalls'; the Secret Archives; the pontifical secret (this was abolished by the Pope in December 2019); *Crimen sollicitationis*; blackmail over sex secrets; victim-blaming; euphemisms; canon 489's destruction of criminal documents after ten years; blaming the dead bishop or archbishop; ceasing written references on the issue; Special Issues Committee; and invoking legal privilege.

What hope did children – and then survivors – have?

By the end of the Royal Commission, I was frustrated with the clergy's multitude of 'I don't recall's, and noted that the men under questioning were not saying 'I don't remember', as would be normal. I looked up the meanings of 'recall' and 'remember'. Recall means to bring something to mind – to access your memory – whereas remember means to hold something in mind, to have not forgotten. In repeatedly opting for the first word over the second, I believe that instead of answering the questions, these men were stating that they would not bring the information to mind, yet giving the impression they couldn't remember.

I held great faith in the state governments around Australia to take up the Royal Commission's recommendation to seek out the truth for protecting children now and in the future. At that same time, my annihilated faith in the hierarchy of the Catholic Church meant that I had no confidence that they would do the right thing by treating children with respect and victims with generosity.

# 39

Before Anthony passed away, we had planned a trip to Kangaroo Island in South Australia with Cathie and Mick. We had already booked and paid for the holiday. Now, I had to decide if I still wanted to make the journey. After some gentle encouragement from Cathie and Mick, I decided I would go. I didn't know how I would feel on my own, stepping back into life without Anthony, but having them by my side was a good place to start. I appreciated their friendship and companionship.

When I was about to leave Melbourne, Paul Kennedy called to say he was planning to make a documentary for the ABC about the Royal Commission. The hour-long program, to be titled *Undeniable,* would serve as a reminder to politicians and the public as to why the five-year inquiry was so important, and equally important would be the implementation of the upcoming recommendations.

Paul's words sounded wonderful as he explained to me what he envisaged the message of his documentary would be. But he needed a clincher – he felt the program would only be approved if he could secure an interview with former PM Julia Gillard, who had called the Royal Commission. I wished him luck.

I was at Kangaroo Island's Southern Ocean Lodge with Mick and Cathie having a glass of wine before lunch when my phone rang. It was Paul; he had good news. Ms Gillard had agreed to be interviewed

for the documentary. She had had many television requests for interviews, seeing as the closing ceremony of the Royal Commission was
coming up in December, but had said no to all the others.

With the documentary now approved, Paul and the film crew
would travel around the country to interview people who had helped
spark the Royal Commission through their actions in standing against
corruption and cover-ups. I was smiling at Paul's enthusiasm and
the thought of such a powerful documentary being produced. It all
sounded very exciting. Towards the end of our conversation, Paul
said, 'And you will be doing some of the interviews.'

I was silent for a moment, processing his words. I wondered if
I had heard his unnerving suggestion correctly. Yes, I had. I would
have to front the camera for some interviews. After another pause,
and with most of the wine in my glass gone, I replied, 'Okay.'

Afterwards, my friends and I had a celebratory toast to Paul and
his project. The thought of being a part of it was amazing and scary at
the same time, but I let the fear slide away and replaced it with cheerful
conversation about the documentary over a second glass of wine.

We enjoyed our five days at the lodge, though I would often
look out on the Southern Ocean and wish Anthony was with me.
The sadness of his absence was always felt.

Not long after returning home, I received a call from a Royal
Commission staff member whom I had spoken to many times at
hearings. She told me that one of the commissioners had been hearing
private sessions in Perth when a survivor had asked after me. The
survivor, Ballardong Noongar woman Dallas from Goomal Koomal
Boodjar, had made me a traditional message stick: a message of
courage. My heart melted when I was told the touching story of how
Dallas had made the message stick out of a piece of her daughter's
kitchen table, because the table was where they all gathered to eat,
talk, laugh and cry. The table had been part of their family's life and
therefore the message stick she sent was part of them too. Such an
amazing gift, and wisdom. (Little did I know I would soon be receiving the message stick in person.)

Less than a month after returning from South Australia, I met the ABC film crew who would be working on Paul's documentary. The crew consisted of two cameramen, Dan and Kyle, a sound technician, Stuart, and senior producer Ben Knight. It was 9 October 2017, and the documentary had to be ready to air nationally on 12 December, two days before the closing ceremony of the Royal Commission. We had only sixty-four days to make this film – it was going to be a tight schedule.

The following day we started filming in West Gippsland, where we interviewed survivor John and his wife Monica. I felt nervous but the crew was friendly, calm, confident and experienced, so I went with the flow. I had known and been friends with John – a Fr O'Donnell survivor – and Monica since 1996, so it was a good place for me to start.

A week later we had the great honour of interviewing Julia Gillard at my home. The family were all part of the filming. Julia was lovely, and so down to earth. 'Thank you for having me here,' she said. 'I'm really sorry I didn't get to meet Anthony. I feel like I kind of know him a little bit. I was broken-hearted for you when I heard the news.' She explained the public's overwhelming reaction to the Royal Commission. 'I've met so many people and many of them will say that it was the single biggest thing that the government I led ever did. That was the thing that mattered to them the most.'

It really was a pleasure to be in her company. In her interview she spoke of her reasons for calling the Royal Commission, and said she had 'faced widespread opposition into holding a royal commission into child abuse'. 'Perhaps there was a sense at some point that institutions were going to respond, and respond in a meaningful way,' she explained. 'I think it was becoming more and more apparent that that kind of institutional response was never going to be sufficient.'

Hearing of her experience, I was filled with admiration. Julia Gillard had persisted against the odds to make justice happen for victims. It always staggered me that for so long, those who spoke up against such a terrible crime had failed to garner support. But

Julia believed, held out and courageously made real our Child Abuse Royal Commission.

The next day our crew flew to Mildura to interview ex–police detective Denis Ryan, who had lost his job after trying to arrest paedophile priest Fr John Day. We were moving at a hectic pace. The day after we got back from Mildura, we all drove to Ballarat to meet lawyer Dr Judy Courtin and two survivors. One of the survivors, Rob, told me, 'It's been hard. I think the burden is heavier now because we now know more about the abuse, and the cover-up.'

Three days later, we flew to Newcastle and interviewed Peter Fox, the former detective chief inspector. We also met Lou and Pam Pirona, whose survivor son had died by suicide.

Each day raced by. After every interview, we wiped away tears and kept travelling.

After meeting the Pironas, we interviewed *Newcastle Herald* journalist Joanne McCarthy, now the author of more than a thousand articles on paedophile priests in the Hunter Valley. Next up was ABC journalist Suzanne Smith, who had covered many clergy abuse cases and would go on to write a powerful book, *The Altar Boys*.

I was in awe of all these people who had contributed so much to fighting clergy child sexual assault. Paul had chosen our subjects well; each person represented a battlefront that had chipped away at the Catholic Church and its many hidden crimes. The collective efforts of these survivors and advocates had exposed the need for our Child Abuse Royal Commission – and helped make it a reality.

Back in Melbourne, Paul and the crew interviewed ex–Victorian premier Ted Baillieu about Melbourne Response. 'The Melbourne Response left the solution to what was criminal behaviour in the hands of an institution which probably never wanted to reveal that,' he said. Later that day, I met up with the crew and we interviewed former Liberal MP Ken Smith in the Assembly Chamber of Parliament House. Ken told us about a mid-1990s parliamentary inquiry into clergy sex abuse and cover-ups, which was never properly acted upon. He was very emotional about this inaction. 'Part of our report was adopted but it was a long way short of the 130 recommendations that should have all been adopted,' he said. 'There was a lot of pressure that went on from the Catholic Church.'

Days later, we visited the State Library of Victoria, where we filmed our research relating to historical records on the crime of child rape and the fact that it had been a hanging offence in Australia since at least 1833 – busting the ridiculous and dishonest priesthood myth that they didn't know raping children was a crime or wrong. I found this claim an endless source of torment and a damning indictment of the priesthood that we needed to work so hard to prove the fact that child rape was indeed a long-established crime.

With our deadline looming fast, Paul and I pushed on with filming. We had more places to visit and revisit. In Ballarat, we interviewed Paul Tatchell at St Patrick's College. Paul had attended St Patrick's as a young boarder. Not long after he arrived, he was sexually assaulted by Christian Brother teacher and boarding-house master Ted Dowlan.

On a tour of the school, Paul took us into classrooms that had once been the boarding bedrooms. He showed us where his bed used to be. Then he went into what was once Dowlan's bedroom, where he told us of his nightmare experience at the hands of the Christian Brother: a pants-down caning punishment that quickly turned into rape. Paul Kennedy and I were appalled as we listened and watched this brave survivor recounting the event. He told us that after the rape, his anger boiled over and he yelled at Dowlan. The boy then began punching the supposed holy Brother hard, until the cowardly criminal lay crying on the floor.

Witnessing Paul's account of taking back his power from a child rapist was both heart-rending and uplifting. How many times had I, as a parent, wished I could have a moment alone with Fr O'Donnell – just one minute. By the time I knew what he had done to my daughters, my children's abuser was in prison. Still, the opportunity probably would not have arisen because O'Donnell, like so many, was protected by his bosses, the all-knowing hierarchy.

It was in 1997, at our Oakleigh meeting, that Archbishop Pell himself had told us a sob story by way of protecting Fr O'Donnell. Pell said he had visited O'Donnell in the prison hospital, where the priest kept repeating the same incoherent words, apparently on his death bed. Pell claimed the criminal was saying, 'I'm sorry, I'm sorry.' It sounded like rubbish at the time (and still does). Pell's claim enraged me so much that about three days later I rang the prison section of St Vincent's Hospital, where O'Donnell was supposedly dying. A nurse answered and to my inquiry after O'Donnell's health said she'd put me through to him! I couldn't believe it and didn't want to speak to him, but curiosity made me wait. After a couple of rings the spritely and lucid voice of O'Donnell came down the line: 'Hello?' Shocked, I immediately hung up. My overwhelming thought was that Pell had tricked everyone at the meeting into thinking O'Donnell was on his deathbed and therefore how dare we demand he be punished with laicisation. So we had been lied to and deceived into shamed silence. Betrayed, again.

The day after Paul Tatchell's powerful interview, our film crew was back in Melbourne for an 8 am interview with Senator Derryn Hinch. Immediately afterwards, we got word of a funeral for Father Guelen, a friend and former colleague of O'Donnell. We drove directly to the service at St Mary's Church in Dandenong.

In the 1960s, when Fr Guelen had walked into Fr O'Donnell's bedroom during one of the older cleric's sexual assaults, Guelen had just shut the door and walked away. Many years later, in 1994, after O'Donnell had been charged over his years of sexual offences, Guelen had played detective for Archbishop Little and begun snooping through an old complaint. He went and interviewed a man he thought might be able to hurt the Church with evidence that would reveal the cover-up. (The man was one of two from the local scout group who had taken the sexual assault complaint of a young O'Donnell victim to the archdiocese hierarchy in 1958.) An official church document confirmed this; twenty years later it would be revealed to the Royal Commission.

Now Guelen was dead. We filmed mourners coming and going. It was a small turnout, and all of Guelen's former parishioners and friends were wary of our camera crew. It felt daunting just being there with multiple priests, but at the same time I felt a resentment towards this priest who had turned a blind eye to O'Donnell's crimes and then worked against victims seeking justice. Minds like his were hard to fathom.

The next day, at the office of lawyer Viv Waller, I met survivor Dallas and her husband Thomas, who had flown in from Perth for the documentary. It was lovely to meet in person and talk to them. Dallas then gave me her message stick. It was so moving to receive such a meaningful gift from the heart. She had carved, painted and decorated the stick herself and written strong and healing words about Anthony and me; the last words were 'Warriors for Justice'. It was very humbling.

Dallas told me that her family had lived on a farm. Her father worked as a slaughterman/butcher and was only allowed to take offal for the family, while her mother grew vegetables. Her father set traps and snares for extra food. Dallas remembered it as a good life. Then a Western Australian Government order saw people taken to the Goomalling Native reserve where many families were places in basic tin sheds and given ration orders. Life changed dramatically while living on the reserve, as all poor people were controlled by the Native Welfare Act.

Cruel government policies that forcibly removed children from their families caused a world of suffering and broke the hearts of thousands of children and their grieving parents. Not only were the children ripped from their parents, they were also placed with clergy, some of whom were sexual predators. Other mistreatment came in the form of beatings, malnourishment, hard labour and removal of language, breaking their connection to Culture and engendering intergenerational trauma. It was the damnation of a people from shameful halls of power.

A terrible and shocking reality.

That evening in Melbourne I joined Dallas, Thomas, Viv and some of her office staff for dinner. Dallas told me that message sticks are meant to stay beside your front door so you see their message every time you leave your home; my message stick remains there to this day.

The next morning, Paul flew to Sydney to interview lawyer John Ellis from Case Study 8 of the Royal Commission. Then in Melbourne he interviewed the former premier Jeff Kennett about his Victorian Government's inaction over clergy sex abuse in the 1990s.

'The thought of the state getting involved in a Church matter didn't appeal to me very much,' Mr Kennett stated.

By early November, our filming was complete. Participating in the making of *Undeniable* was one of the most exciting and rewarding things I have ever done. Having a common goal, working together and being part of such a great team was the best thing that could have happened to me after Anthony's death. I know he would have loved to have been a part of it too.

On Sunday 12 November, I hosted an end-of-production barbecue at Tonimbuk. The weather was warm and sunny, a lovely spring day for our gathering. Being together without a schedule to maintain gave the day a relaxed feel. Added to that was the good feeling you get when the job is done and you're pleased with your work. We talked about the documentary and toasted its completion. As the afternoon wore on, we all walked down to the English garden, where Anthony and I had planted the Royal Commission tree, a red oak gift from John and Monica to celebrate the announcement of the Child Abuse Royal Commission back in November 2012. More toasts were made. 'Cheers to the Royal Commission.'

Soon, the documentary would go to air and the Royal Commission would hold its closing ceremony and hand down its findings. I couldn't wait.

# 40

I took a phone call from Australia's twenty-ninth prime minister, Malcolm Turnbull, on 28 February 2018. He invited me to be a member of the National Apology Reference Group, a gathering of people who would inform what survivors would like to hear from Mr Turnbull in a National Apology to victims of child sexual abuse. More than one hundred Royal Commission recommendations were sent to the Federal Government; one of them was to give a National Apology.

During our conversation, Mr Turnbull said something out of the blue: 'Many bishops have told me that they have lost all credibility.'

I paused before responding.

'Their own actions have rightly made people believe that they have no credibility – they have brought this crisis upon themselves through their actions and inaction,' I said.

Mr Turnbull agreed with me, but his mention of 'many bishops' was troublesome. I had a lot of questions I didn't ask – it felt rude to grill a prime minister. Later, they came back to me, one after the other. Did he often talk to bishops? Did the Church hierarchy have one-on-one access to Australia's highest elected official? Was I meant to care about the bishops' loss of credibility? What else had they said to the prime minister? What had followed that self-pitying sentence? (At about this time, I read a newspaper report stating the Catholic

Church was Australia's second-largest landholder, with a nationwide worth of more than $30 billion.[211] The poor bishops were not so poor.)

A week later I wrote a two-page letter to the PM asking to meet with him, insisting that if the bishops can have their say, 'my voice to you is of importance too'. I offered to meet him anywhere, and an appointment was made for 11 April in Melbourne.

Cardinal Pell's four-week committal hearing began in Melbourne. The first week would be held behind closed doors, suppression order still in place. I attended as many days as I could. It felt important to be there.

While attention was on the legal precinct, across the other side of the city important things were happening too. I met Ann Barker outside Parliament House. We had a coffee then returned to the steps of Parliament for a press conference with Premier Dan Andrews and Attorney-General Martin Pakula. Mr Andrews was announcing that a new law was being passed in Parliament that day. Legislation had been drawn up to overcome obstacles faced by child abuse survivors who wanted to sue organisations for their abuse. The bill would counteract unincorporated organisations from relying upon a legal technicality to fend off lawsuits.

Our state of Victoria was dismantling the Ellis Defence![212] The new Victorian law was an enormous slice of justice for victims and an equally enormous blow to the Catholic Church. The number of law changes happening in Victoria was growing, all of them protecting and advancing the rights of children.

I didn't have much time to enjoy the moment as I was soon due to give evidence to a Senate hearing in the form of an address to the Legislation Committee of the Standing Committee on Community Affairs. It was one of the most stressful speeches I have ever had to deliver. Months earlier I had written a thirteen-page submission to the Senate regarding the National Redress Scheme. It was a desperate plea for governments to avoid tampering with the Royal Commission recommendations. I had then been asked to address the Senate hearing. To educate the federal politicians, who had probably never attended a Royal Commission hearing, I chose to speak of my daughters and our family's nightmare experience. This was distressing enough. Without Anthony by my side, it was traumatic.

I told the politicians about Fr Kevin O'Donnell and his horrific criminal history covered up by the hierarchy. I quoted one of Emma's old psychological reports to teach them about the trauma that follows abuse – for primary and secondary victims.

'Yet now I am forced to take this re-traumatising action of speaking here because – at this very first implementation of a Royal Commission recommendation – the Redress cap has been reduced from $200,000 to $150,000. We have been betrayed,' I said. I questioned why the Federal Government was even speaking to the Catholic Church. 'They are the biggest criminal offenders of child rape and sexual assault in this country of all the institutions,' I said. 'If they didn't understand the obscenity of their actions over child rape then, how can they understand now? You should be telling them what to do.'

I outlined the riches of the Catholic Church. 'In addition, more billions are given to the Catholic Church by the government for their health and welfare agencies,' I said. 'In this multibillion-dollar merry-go-round between the Church and the Federal Government, they have decided that the victims must suffer a $50,000 cutback when one of the players is one of the richest organisations in the world. The Federal Government must restore the Royal Commission redress recommendation to $200,000 and our confidence in them to protect children now and in the future via unchurched Royal Commission recommendations. Thank you.'[213]

There was applause after my speech, which was consoling even in my state of extreme stress.

Three days later I was up early and out to Melbourne Airport. I had to be at the jet base at Gate 24. I didn't even know Melbourne Airport had a jet base, nor a gate 24. Gate 24, as it turns out, is the space occupied by the prime minister's Australian Air Force jet.

Ann Barker and I boarded the PM's plane with the premier and the attorney-general, joined by a few other Victorian child abuse advocates. We were on our way to Kirribilli House to meet the prime minister and the New South Wales premier for the announcement that both Victoria and New South Wales were opting in to the new Commonwealth Redress Scheme.

From Sydney Airport, we travelled in a guarded convoy to Kirribilli House. I had only ever seen the PM's official residence on television. The 1866 Victorian-era home was beautiful, with the most breathtaking view of Sydney Harbour. The sun was shining brightly in an endless blue sky. We spent some time in the garden absorbing the warmth and beauty while waiting for the media conference to begin.

The very same day, Federal Attorney-General Christian Porter, who had previously announced redress would be capped at $150,000, issued a media release about the National Apology. He mentioned our working group had been organised to help the government with its wording.

I attended most days of the Pell committal hearing, and bit by bit, from the words said in court by both defence and prosecution lawyers, we learned a little more about the charges. There were multiple allegations against the defendant, involving a family's holiday to rural Victoria, a swimming pool and picture theatre in Ballarat, and choirboys at St Patrick's Cathedral in Melbourne. In a few days, another would be added to the list. Pell said all the allegations were false. The hearing was examining evidence to see whether there was enough to go to trial. If not, the charges would be dropped.

Each time the cardinal appeared outside the court he would be surrounded by twenty police officers, his legal team and dozens of photographers and journalists. They ferried him in and out of the court forming a big human ball slowly moving up or down the stairs then along the street. It was a ridiculous spectacle. If you took away all the police, photographers and journalists, he could have walked effortlessly with his legal team in and out of court.

Pell's four-week court journey was soon over; he was ordered to face a jury trial in the County Court. Some of the charges were struck out. Magistrate Belinda Wallington committed Pell to trial on the case relating to the Ballarat swimming pool and the choirboys at St Patrick's.

I did not express my opinion on the case in any media, nor did I speak to anyone publicly about it. I knew it was a legal minefield, and there was no way I wanted to damage the chances of a fair trial. There was too much at stake for everyone involved, including the cardinal's accusers.

My advocacy had not ended after Anthony died, nor had I made a conscious decision to keep working at it. Things just kept surfacing. If anything, I became busier because I took on Anthony's role as spokesperson for interviews with television and radio news. I had been in pursuit of justice for decades and could not stop. Participating in these events was satisfying, as they were offshoots from our nation's inquiries. But I was still waiting for the hierarchy to be dragged into the courts to face charges over their part. That day still hasn't arrived. Archbishop Wilson, the one and only case, had his conviction overturned on appeal.

The National Apology Reference Group met for the first time. It was decided that we would run several meetings in our own states with Department of Social Services staff and a psychology team. In all, there were fifty-seven public consultations to organise and attend. Our job was to gather opinions from victim survivors and advocates as to what they would like to hear the Prime Minister say. The National Apology date was set for 22 October, to be held at Parliament House in Canberra.

A week later, I had my appointment with Prime Minister Turnbull. On a sunny autumn day in Melbourne's Treasury Place, I was able to speak to our nation's leader for fifty minutes. It was a pleasant and down-to-earth meeting during which I shared with him what life was like for my family. At the end of our meeting, I gave Mr Turnbull some colourful socks as a reminder of Anthony. We said goodbye. I admired Mr Turnbull; he seemed a genuine and kind man.

*

Life at home without Anthony was very quiet. The void in my heart was immense. Not having him by my side after so many years together, doing so much together, took a lot of getting used to. It felt strange going out to family and friends' homes alone when we had almost always gone together. I felt isolated and awkward. When I married Anthony, I had felt complete. He had made me feel that way. What I hadn't been good at, he was. Life together was all I could wish for. Now I had to fill the empty spaces of long days alone. My memories of him have helped me cope.

I have met some impressive and life-changing women in my time as a child protection advocate. Dallas was proving to be one of them. Wanting to reach out to other victims, she organised a peaceful demonstration called Walk-2-Heal in her small and remote Western Australian town of Goomalling. Dallas invited me to be a speaker, and I accepted. On 31 May 2018 I flew to Perth with Viv Waller and we hired a four-wheel drive to get to Goomalling.

It was good to see Dallas again and be in her beautiful country town. She had hoped Walk-2-Heal would encourage other Aboriginal people to come forward to tell their stories of abuse by various churches or institutions. While some of us had been talking about the abuse issue for many years, it was still very much a taboo subject for Aboriginal people; Dallas wanted to help her people overcome their reticence and gain the freedom she had gained by telling her story to the Royal Commission.

Late in the morning after we arrived, there was a gathering of about twenty people, including two local politicians, at the town's footy ground. We all walked and talked through the streets of Goomalling to the old railway station in the town centre where Dallas held a smoking ceremony of welcome. After sharing in this traditional rite and listening to speeches, we lunched together and mingled with the crowd.

Next day Viv and I drove to New Norcia, a monastery town north-west of Goomalling. New Norcia is Australia's only monastic town. Basically, it is a Benedictine monastery with buildings established in 1847, built on fertile land far from any other settlements, that was a Catholic mission industrial school, orphanage and home. New Norcia Mission was the collective name for St Mary's Mission for boys and St Joseph's Native School and Orphanage for girls. These institutions were run by the Benedictine monks and the Missionary Sisters from 1848 and 1861 respectively until they closed in 1974.

Today New Norcia is a skeleton of its old self, with a total of thirteen or so elderly monks and their younger abbot. Viv and I met the abbot. In her role as a lawyer, Viv had been speaking to a number of Aboriginal people who were at the institution as children and had been sexually assaulted. Less than a year earlier, in December 2017, the Royal Commission's final report had stated that among the Benedictine community of New Norcia's priests and monks, the proportion of alleged perpetrators had been 21.5 per cent. What hope had the children had?

The abbot gave us a guided tour. Our first discussion was about the many unmarked graves of Aboriginal children who had died in care. The dirt graves of the children differed greatly from the grand marble tombs erected for past abbots and the modest graves for monks. The abbot began by asking us what he should do about the unmarked graves. I found it incredible that in 2018 he had to ask *us* for advice on such an issue. The monks should have already shown respect to the deceased children. The abbot held a list of the buried children's names. We visited the cemetery. I could see from slight mounds in the red clay that there were dozens and dozens – probably over a hundred – of the unmarked graves. Too many to comprehend. My heart broke for those precious children. We suggested the abbot make public the children's causes of death.

Then we were taken to the monastery chapel, where the abbot told us how monks used to stop work eight times a day, gather in the chapel then pray for twenty minutes.

'Praying every two hours,' I said, disgusted by what I was hearing. 'It's a wonder they found the time to sexually assault the children in between.'

The abbot laughed. But it was not funny. Such ungodly monks – sexually assaulting trapped children separated from their parents and with no way of escape.

What was no laughing matter were the monks and their warped sense of Christianity that allowed them to stop work, gather in chapel and pray to God eight times a day and still have their minds bent on violence against children. Supposedly celibate monks stuck out in the middle of nowhere since 1848, volunteering to look after and educate children, committing sex crimes on a grand scale? What had they done for sex before they cared for children? Had their order provided care for schools and orphanages in remote areas with the intent to rape First Nations children? These are questions that must be answered.

I ate lunch in the New Norcia dining room, a strange experience. The tables were set in the shape of a horseshoe. One of the monks walked to a pulpit next to where I was sitting and began reading aloud the diary of their founding father, who had sailed to Australia in the early 1840s. I am not a fast eater, unlike the monks. At one point during the meal, I became aware of a stillness in the room; I was the only one making a noise with my cutlery. Looking up I saw that all the monks were staring at me: they had all emptied their plates and were waiting for me to finish so they could tuck into dessert. Viv finished before me: I felt very pressured to eat quickly. To make matters worse, the reading was now finished so every noise my knife and fork made on my plate echoed.

After lunch, we visited the churches and a museum, established in the old dormitories where the children used to sleep. One large dorm contained an exhibit of the history of New Norcia consisting of long canvases on tall posts with historic photos and expansive captions. There were about twenty of these information banners. I read a few of them but learned nothing about the Aboriginal children who had suffered in this place. Eventually I found one banner at the back of the room that made mention of the abuse. Being one of the last banners in the sequence, it seemed to be of lowest priority. Some of the buildings contained exhibitions and displays about Aboriginal history and art. This was a portrayal of positive and happy Aboriginal culture, not the hell children had lived in. Dallas was one of the children who had suffered in New Norcia. The modern portrayal struck me as a kind of cover-up. I was glad to leave.

# 41

South Australia was the next state to scrap the seal of confession relating to mandatory reporting of sexual abuse.[214] Buoyed by this news, I went back to Canberra for our second National Apology Reference Group meeting. Less positive was the consternation over redress. Disappointingly, I was asked to address another Senate committee meeting. Things were moving too slowly and with no clear direction. This went against what the Royal Commission had determined.

The compensation of survivors remained one of the last standing issues of the post–Royal Commission years. Victims in Australia and around the world were taking notice of how our country looked after abused children. America, for one, was following our plight.

On invitation from SNAP in the United States I attended a conference in Chicago. SNAP wanted to give the ABC documentary *Undeniable* its international premiere.

It would be my first overseas trip without Anthony, and I thought deeply about not going. But my friend Cathie helped make up my mind. 'I'll go with you,' she offered. It was the encouragement I needed to book the flights.

Cathie and I wore custom-made T-shirts that read 'Ontologically Challenged'. These words had been used by a priest to put a survivor, Mike, in his place about the priest's superiority, but Mike had decided to own it and make T-shirts to counter the insult. We thought they were brilliant.

The SNAP conference was held over three days in July 2018 at the Palmer House Hilton. The 30,000-member organisation was celebrating its thirty-year anniversary – '30 Years Strong – We've Only Just Begun' was the theme. The thirty years of victims' advocacy showed the extent and history of Catholic clergy child sexual assault in the USA.

Cathie and I were welcomed by the kind members of SNAP, with convener Steven Spanner taking us under his wing. The esteemed child protection advocate Father Tom Doyle delivered a speech entitled 'How the Wound that Will Not Heal Has Changed History'. Later that afternoon Terry McKiernan, President of BishopAccountability. org, spoke on the topic 'Takeaways from a Crucial Year: Chile, Australia, Pennsylvania'.

It was amazing to meet Terry because for years Anthony and I had been reading BishopAccountability.org's Abuse Tracker, which collated the endless number of newspaper articles from around the world on Catholic clergy child sexual assault. The site has blogged more than 100,000 news articles since 2002. In the past, especially in early years when all had seemed lost, I had found consolation in the constant stream of worldwide evidence shared by BishopAccountability.org. It had been the reality check against the hierarchy's spin.

I made a short speech to introduce *Undeniable*.

Our Australia-wide Royal Commission was the envy of survivors in the USA. They all knew about it, with speakers at the conference praising it and referring to it in their presentations. They all wanted a similar inquiry. It made me feel proud of my country, politicians, survivors and journalists.

'Your history here in the United States of child sexual assault by clergy within the Catholic Church is basically a blueprint of our history in Australia,' I said in my speech. 'Our [Australian] inquiries have led to extensive law reforms, which allow churches and other institutions to be held to account for their crimes against children.

Only four weeks ago the Australian Capital Territory announced it will extend its mandatory reporting laws to break the seal of confession. This was a Royal Commission recommendation. Since then, the South Australian, Tasmanian and Western Australian governments have also stated they will remove the mandatory reporting exemption currently allowed for the confessional.'

It was wonderful to stand in front of the conference and present my and Paul's documentary. I was the living example of someone who had attained a measure of justice. Australia had made so much headway. We were miles ahead of other countries in making the Catholic Church's priesthood accountable under civil criminal law, as all institutions should be.

There were handouts given to those who attended the conference. One of them detailed a list of 157 new names of accused clergy child abusers in the USA reported by survivors in the past year. The names would be added to a database of a further 6400 accused priests in the US. Because the United States has a statute of limitations on child sex offences – which varies from state to state but expires between ten and twenty-one years after the event – by the time victims feel they can complain about their abuse the time frame for reporting it to police has vanished. They can do nothing to have their perpetrator punished or exposed, leaving a situation where the offender may simply continue to work in parishes or schools. And the hierarchy's history is that it will not act against its priests or Brothers, leaving the status quo to thrive.

Our Royal Commission had already recommended that all jurisdictions in Australia remove their statute of limitations on reporting child sexual assault. Victoria had done it in 2015.

Cathie and I went to a Chicago cathedral and tied LOUD Fence ribbons from my farmer friend John. We visited New York, found another cathedral in Manhattan, and tied more ribbons.

Meanwhile in Melbourne, Archbishop Denis Hart had retired. New to the post was Archbishop Peter A. Comensoli.

An event called Lunch with the Archbishop was going to be held by the Melbourne Press Club. Tickets cost $60. I attended and sat at a table at the back of the room with my lawyer friend Dr Judy Courtin; one of her clients (also a friend), 94-year-old Eileen Piper; and journalist Tess Lawrence. Judy and Eileen were there to try to speak with the new archbishop about Eileen's long-running case. Eileen's daughter had been sexually assaulted by a priest and later died by suicide in 1994. Eileen had been fighting for justice over her daughter's abuse and further ill-treatment by the Church both prior to and after her death.

The Press Club was an organisation I had often heard about but never had anything to do with. Earlier, in March, I had been to the Quill Awards, a state version of the prestigious Walkley Awards, in which the *Undeniable* documentary was a finalist. This is where I had learned that the Church's longstanding lawyer Richard Leder was club secretary and a board member. I was shocked. It did not sit right with me because the Press Club's championing of quality journalism seemed to me to conflict with his work for the Church hierarchy, whose misdeeds had been exposed by hardworking journalists. (Later, in September 2022, I was to read that his law firm billed over $4 million annually for this work acting for the Church.[215])

I went to the Press Club lunch function for the archbishop because Judy invited me. At question time I decided to ask the new archbishop if he had read my book *Hell on the Way to Heaven*. Comensoli was from New South Wales, and I thought it would be beneficial for him to read my book so he could understand a bit of history regarding the Melbourne Archdiocese. It is good to know bad history so it is not repeated.

I waited for Judy to go first. She stood and spoke about Eileen's case. (The following year, Eileen had a successful settlement with the Melbourne Archdiocese after thirty years.) When it was my turn, I stood and asked my question. Comensoli replied that he had 'read parts of it'. So obviously he knew me and knew what it was about. He paused, smiled and continued, 'It's just that I'm a slow reader.'

His table of guests all laughed loudly; some others seemed to politely follow suit. Annoyed at the archbishop making fun of the issue, I waited for the laughter to finish.

'Well, I suggest you do read it,' I said with the help of a microphone. 'Because it's about the Melbourne Archdiocese and you might learn something.'

After question time, the archbishop came to our table to speak to me. By this time, I was angry. I immediately had words with him about his comment. My words continued for some time. I raised with him the criminal behaviour of priests who sexually assault children and how it wasn't funny. I am sure he regretted coming to speak with me, but maybe in the future he would act with more empathy.

It was not right of him to humiliate me publicly then try to apologise privately.

The criminal trial of Cardinal George Pell began in the County Court. The public had no idea it was happening because suppression orders were extended.

I had purposely avoided Pell's court case until the closing arguments, which I was invited to attend by journalist Lucie Morris-Marr. I thought this legal process would last a few hours; instead, it took two-and-a-half days, after which time the jury withdrew to consider its verdict.

Seventeen days earlier we had suddenly found ourselves with a new prime minister. During the second day of arguments, 11 September 2018, a media statement was released by Federal Attorney-General Christian Porter to announce our new Prime Minister, Scott Morrison, would make the National Apology the following month. Up until this point I had not been sure it would go ahead. Our National Apology Reference Group knew Mr Turnbull had a keen interest in the issue of child sexual abuse and survivors, but Morrison's opinion was unknown. Thankfully, the media release put everything back on track and our minds at ease.

On 20 September the jury in Pell's trial returned. The jurors had deliberated for five days without reaching a unanimous verdict. There would have to be another trial. Not a word of this was made public.

My focus was on the Melbourne hearing of the Joint Standing Committee on Oversight of the Implementation of Redress Related Recommendations of the Royal Commission. The address I wrote and delivered was eight pages. Alterations to the Redress Scheme by the Coalition Federal Government were complex. It was hard to understand, describe and compare the changes to the Royal Commission's recommendations. I found it extremely stressful and difficult to succinctly tell politicians what was unfair about the many changes. It felt like individual advocates and victim support groups were suddenly going up against the Federal Government to restore the Redress Scheme to how the Royal Commission had intended.

One disturbing thing I had learned since the last Senate redress hearing was that any money-related changes made by the Federal Government were secret. It was now a criminal offence under Commonwealth legislation to 'reveal any knowledge of how these payments are calculated'.

'We must ask who the winner is because of these changes in the redress recommendation,' I told politicians who attended the Senate hearing. 'Follow the money. The offending institutions are the winners; they are the beneficiaries.'

# 42

It had been seventeen months since Anthony passed away, and I was glad to be busy. The activities I chose to do were a distraction from missing him and I know he would have been there with me in all the things I was doing. We were still one.

I had thought about having some counselling. I even went to the effort of arranging it. But it didn't eventuate so, in the end, I left it. I believed I was doing okay. I was beginning to enjoy life again.

My commitment to the ongoing child abuse developments gave me purpose. Watching my grandchildren grow was also a thing of wonderment. They were always loving and entertaining and kept me busy whenever they were within cooee.

I had mixed feelings about the National Apology, even my involvement in it. On one hand the Federal Government was apologising to victims, and on the other they were taking money away from victims by lowering the redress cap and other alterations, seemingly to appease the churches. Try as I might, I could not sway those in power to reverse their decisions. It was galling to think the cap decrease was to fit in with the Church's insurance policy limits. In the end, I gave up. No more stressful Senate inquiry speeches. I turned my back on the issue. The Church has too much influence within governments, especially, it seemed, the Federal Government. But our apology group did have a little bit of power. At least we could help decide who was not invited to the apology.

Nonetheless, I believed there should be an apology from the government so I worked hard to collect as many victims' and their supporters' opinions as possible. I felt so sad Anthony would miss out.

The National Apology was to be made special because it was a family affair, albeit without my husband. I travelled to Canberra with my mother Dawn, now eighty-seven, and Katie, who came with her longtime carer, Corinne.

Months earlier, I had spoken to former prime minister Julia Gillard on the phone about attending the National Apology. In our conversation she said she wanted to sit next to me in Parliament House when the apology was being read out. I was taken aback by her words and felt very humbled. I said I would let the organisers know.

Much closer to the date, I rang the responsible government department contact to let them know Julia's wishes. I suspected they were not going to believe that Julia wanted to sit next to me. When I started to explain it on the phone, the voice at the other end said he had been in contact with Ms Gillard's office.

'The message from her was that, "If Chrissie sits up the back, I will sit up the back; if Chrissie sits up the front, I will sit up the front; if Chrissie sits in the middle I will sit in the middle,"' he said.

'Oh, okay, thank you,' I said, almost lost for words.

We arrived in Canberra the day before the Prime Minister was to make his speech. It allowed us to catch up with some of the people Anthony and I had met and formed friendships with over the years. We all came together, warriors for justice. Peter and Penny Fox. Ian and Joan Isaacs. Dallas and Thomas. John and Monica. Denis and Bev Ryan. The sun was out. We were in a pretty garden at the hotel and enjoyed time together. That night I met with the other members of the Apology Reference Group to relax and talk about our big day, one sleep away.

Next morning, we went for morning tea at Parliament House. In attendance were Justice Peter McClellan and his other distinguished royal commissioners, Julia Gillard, Ann Barker, Dr Viv Waller, John and Nikki Ellis, and other friends and advocates. Then Julia, the

Reference Group and Katie and I made our way to the floor of the House of Representatives. It was a treat for me to have Katie at my side for the late-morning commencement.

Mum and Corinne sat in the public gallery upstairs. Downstairs we sat in a row of seating on the edge of the chamber. Julia sat on one side of me and Katie on the other.

Prime Minister Scott Morrison began his apology.

Today the Australian Government and this Parliament, on behalf of all Australians, unreservedly apologises to the victims and survivors of institutional child sexual abuse. For too many years our eyes and hearts were closed to the truths we were told by children.

For too many years governments and institutions refused to acknowledge the darkness that lay within our community. Today, we reckon with our past and commit to protect children now and into the future.

After the enormous rush and bustle of months of work and travel, it was amazing to be in the seat of power in our country, listening to the leader of our nation speak these words, which should have been said decades ago. It was a poignant moment, a tearful one. Any official recognition or understanding of what children had suffered – *my children* – made me cry. There are few more moving experiences than for the silenced to be heard.

Today, we apologise for the pain, suffering and trauma inflicted upon victims and survivors as children, and for its profound and ongoing impact. As children, you deserved care and protection. Instead, the very people and institutions entrusted with your care failed you. You suffered appalling physical and mental abuse, and endured horrific sexual crimes.

Today, we say we are sorry. Sorry that you were not protected, sorry that you were not listened to. We are sorry for refusing to trust the words of children, for not believing you.

It felt surreal to hear the crime of child sexual assault being spoken about in this way, in this place. A child being raped or sexually assaulted is a crime, which is not hard to understand. It was the Royal Commission investigating our stories that had finally tipped the scales and brought us to this point of being believed. It was a realisation that there would be no going back.

Our Reference Group had unanimously decided not to invite religious ministers to the apology, so they were neither present nor represented.

After Prime Minister Morrison's apology, the Leader of the Opposition, Bill Shorten, read his apology, touching on aspects the PM had not. Mr Shorten spoke of 'Indigenous Australians, who are over-represented as institutional abuse victims'. He gave mention to 'the people in the prison system, whose lives were shunted onto a track by the abuse they suffered as children', and to those people 'in the grip of addiction or poverty'.

Mr Shorten's speech was deep, and it hit me hard. I could see my Emma and Katie in his sentences. More tears had to be fought back because I sensed I was about to lose it. Anthony's image had come to me in those words. Years earlier, he'd said, 'When you see people living rough you never know what has happened to them but it's likely they have been abused.'

Mr Shorten continued: 'It was never your fault, not at all.' I could hear sobbing from the public gallery. 'Our nation let you down. We are sorry for every childhood stolen; every life lost. We are sorry for every betrayal of trust, every abuse of power. We are sorry it has taken so long to say these words.'

They were powerful words, the right words. My tears proved it. Children, through no fault of their own, had been tricked, bullied or threatened into rape, then worn chains of silence. Mr Shorten was breaking those chains. I was suddenly elated. He understood. Things would improve. We had come a long way since March 1996.

Afterwards, Parliament broke up. Many politicians came to members of the Reference Group with kind words. We then made a procession from the chamber to the Great Hall, where about 300 survivors who had won a balloted invitation (the only fair way to fill the limited seats) gathered to be addressed by Prime Minister Scott Morrison and Mr Shorten. When doors opened and the crowd saw Julia Gillard, there was thunderous cheering and applause. I was standing beside Julia and the sound was deafening. The whole room reverberated with love for the woman who had given us so much through establishing the Royal Commission. Never had so much attention and respect been given to victims, and here was the woman who had made it all happen standing with us. Julia was greeted with five years' worth of pent-up admiration and thanks. The joyous eruption continued for a long time.

Soon we were sitting down and I was the luckiest person in the room to be beside Julia. At one point, I leaned towards her, our heads lightly touching. Photographer Alex Ellinghausen captured this moment.

After the speeches, everybody mingled happily. There was some commotion when a man approached Julia in the crowd, got down on his hands and knees and kissed her feet. Julia was perturbed and helped him get back up. The man's name was Frank. He said he was a former student of St Patrick's College in Ballarat. 'I'm not a Labor person,' he told reporters. 'But I always said, "If I ever see Julia Gillard, I will drop to my knees and kiss her feet." She has done more to protect the safety and welfare of children into the future than all the other prime ministers combined.'

Nobody in the Great Hall was going to argue with him that Julia had done more for children than all her male counterparts.

After the formalities, we moved out of Parliament House and down to the front lawn where marquees and tables were set up for a long lunch. If you had not won the ballot for the limited number of seats in the Great Hall, you were welcome to the lunch. Katie, Corinne, Mum and I sat together and slowly got to see other friends. Manny Waks had flown in from Israel for the apology, giving us another chance to catch up. Senator Derryn Hinch, who'd sat on the Senate hearings into redress, shared our table for a little while. Katie enjoyed her time at the apology after-party. Her favourite singer, Daryl Braithwaite, gave a rendition of his timeless song 'The Horses'; she had her photo taken with him, as she had done about thirteen years earlier at another outdoor concert.

The National Apology had been an emotional but enjoyable event, a special day devoted to those who had suffered horrendous sexual assaults as children in institutions. It was a moment in time. A moment that was needed, deserved and treasured. Our job was done.

# Afterword

Life after the Royal Commission and National Apology is as hectic as ever.

My fury is still there, though partly extinguished by the extent of the truth exposed during our inquiries. That the priesthood's dirty linen have been exposed is of great solace. Their true souls have been recorded in the annals of the Victorian Parliamentary Inquiry and the Royal Commission. As far as I am concerned, the responsible members of the hierarchy should be in the court system fighting charges of corruption, child sexual slavery and racketeering.

As always, I have tried to keep a balance between being with my daughters and grandchildren, holding the Church accountable for its abuse and cover-ups, and travelling to see interesting parts of the world.

In late 2019 I double-booked a family holiday to Uluru and a lunch in Sydney. The lunch was, in fact, the Australian Human Rights Awards. Justice Peter McClellan, the Chief Commissioner from our Child Abuse Royal Commission, and I were joint finalists for the Human Rights Medal. My family and I flew to Central Australia. We loved being there, but in the middle of our trip I had to leave for the awards ceremony. In Sydney, I met Cathie, John and Monica, Dr Judy Courtin, Dr Viv Waller and Tonimbuk friends Andrew, Jan, Roz and Lindsay. Joan and Ian came down from Queensland, and Peter and Penny Fox and John and Nicky Ellis. It was another reunion of fellow advocates.

I waited as the president of the commission, Rosalind Croucher AM, opened the envelope and unfolded the paper. She announced that Peter McClellan and I were the joint winners. Our tables cheered. It was quite a shock. After being presented with our award and the Human Rights Medal I read a speech I had written (all finalists had been asked to write one just in case they won).

'Thank you to the best family and friends I could wish for,' I began. 'You were there for Anthony and me and now you are there for me – I thank you. I cannot thank the commissioners and extensive staff of the Child Abuse Royal Commission enough. They have changed our world.'

I turned and addressed Justice McClellan. 'Peter, you are a hero to so many of us. You were a strong, gentle and intelligent judge and we could not have asked for better.'

Now I spoke about my daughters and late husband. 'This award is for Emma, it is for Katie, it is for Aimee, it is for Anthony,' I said. 'It is for all children who have suffered this insidious crime and their families. It is recognition of our pain.'

Justice McClellan then made a moving speech about his time as Chief Commissioner to the Royal Commission.

The following day I returned to Uluru, one of the most magnificent places in the world. My family and I wished we could stay there in the shade of the ancient desert.

Back home, George Pell's fate was being determined by a jury. I received a text message from a friend saying he had been found guilty – unanimously – on all five counts of sexually assaulting two boys. News of the jury's guilty verdict had travelled fast, albeit not publicly. There was still no media coverage, although several major newspapers carried front-page statements that there was a story they could not publish.

When the guilty verdict was made public, the cardinal was remanded in custody awaiting sentencing. Circumstances and details of the court cases were analysed and debated throughout the media. Without the day-to-day reporting of the case there had been no time for the public to process and discuss case details, so when the sudden guilty verdict was announced it split the community into believers and non-believers.

Sentencing took place at the County Court on 13 March 2019. I was in Canberra attending a Healing Foundation seminar with the National Office for Child Safety. Pell got six years in prison with a minimum term of three years and eight months. In the first week of June 2019, he appeared before the Victorian Court of Appeal. I attended the two-day hearing. By a majority of two to one, the panel of three judges dismissed Pell's appeal against his convictions. He would remain a prisoner.

I was surprised by the decision. I had believed the cardinal would win his appeal because statistically about half of offenders convicted in child sex cases do.

On 7 April 2020, Pell's conviction of child sexual assault charges was quashed by the High Court of Australia.

Victorian Premier Daniel Andrews tweeted a consoling message: 'I make no comment about today's High Court decision. But I have a message for every single victim and survivor of child sex abuse: I see you. I hear you. I believe you.'

It is problematic to comment on Pell's case. So many people have had their say. My views concentrate on the legal system. In our law courts, the best and fairest method of deciding cases is to bring together juries comprising twelve men and women from the community, drawn at random, who have no connection to the case and who can bring into court their life experience, fair judgement and good sense. These were the sentiments expressed by Judge Kidd during the retrial. It was the jury's duty to determine what the truth was from the evidence presented to them in court by both the prosecution and the defence.

Whereas ordinary people from the community are chosen as jurors, seven High Court judges eventually decided Pell's case.

They ruled that there was a 'significant possibility' that an innocent man had been convicted and that there was sufficient doubt to demand an acquittal.

The reasons for the acquittal, as stated by the High Court, were certain parts of the case, which I attended, that had been fully examined in court by a jury – but they were not going to look at the trial transcript.

The High Court decision must have been crushing for the survivor and families involved. The sad fact is that the Victorian Law Reform Commission found that a maximum of 10 per cent of people who were sexually assaulted as children will ever report those crimes to the police. This means that for every 1 000 children sexually assaulted, about 100 will go to police, but of these, only about six will ever achieve a conviction against the offender. In research conducted by Dr Judy Courtin, about half of all convictions for child sexual abuse in Victoria are appealed, of which half will be successful.

Until 2020, the Royal Commission had redacted parts of its findings in reference to Pell. This was to allow him a fair passage through the legal system. After the acquittal, the commission released unredacted findings that will forever stain the reputation of the Catholic Church's most senior Australian official. The commission found, among other things, that Pell's evidence that he had been kept in the dark by Bishop Mulkearns at the time had been rejected as 'not tenable'.[216] Also, that by 1973 (when he was an assistant priest at Ballarat East), Pell had been aware of child abuse being committed.

'We are also satisfied,' the commission found, 'that by 1973 Cardinal Pell was not only conscious of child sexual abuse by clergy but that he also had considered measures of avoiding situations which might provoke gossip about it.'[217]

The Royal Commission found Pell had known why Fr Ridsdale was relocated within the diocese of Ballarat as early as 1982. In his evidence, Pell had said it was a 'sad story and it wasn't of much interest to me'. But the commission determined that in a 1982 meeting, Pell (as a member of the diocese's College of Consultors) had been explicitly told that Ridsdale's 'sexual transgressions' were the reason he was being moved from the parish at Mortlake in Victoria's south-west.

'We are satisfied Bishop Mulkearns gave reasons for it being necessary to move Ridsdale,' the commission said. 'We are satisfied that he referred to homosexuality at the meeting in the context of giving reasons for Ridsdale's move. However, we are not satisfied that Bishop Mulkearns left the explanation there. As Cardinal Pell said, there would have been a discussion. Cardinal Pell gave evidence that the bishop did not give the true reason for moving Ridsdale – namely, his sexual activity with children – and that the bishop lied in not giving the true reason to the consultors. We do not accept that Bishop Mulkearns lied to his consultors. We are satisfied that Bishop Mulkearns told the consultors that it was necessary to move Ridsdale from the Diocese and from parish work because of complaints that he had sexually abused children. A contrary position is not tenable.'

More findings came down against Pell in relation to his handling, as auxiliary bishop, of Fr Searson. 'It was a failure of management and a failure by the individual Church personnel to press that action be taken,' the commission said. 'Those individuals identified (Monsignor Connors, Monsignor Deakin, Monsignor Cudmore and Bishop Pell) should have advised Archbishop Little to act. Instead, they accepted the inaction of the Archbishop. We consider that this constitutes a series of individual failures by those priests to advise, urge or influence the Archbishop to take action.'[218]

There were other criticisms of Pell.

On the balance of evidence, the commission was satisfied that by the early 1970s, Pell had been told by some students and other priests about Christian Brother Ted Dowlan's offending and that he had not then told Bishop Mulkearns. 'Cardinal Pell told us that, with hindsight, he should have done more,' the commission said. The Royal Commission accepted the evidence of a student at St Patrick's College in Ballarat, who had approached Fr Pell at a swimming pool and told him, "We've got to do something about what's going on at St Pat's."'

The commission accepted that after the student said Br Dowlan was touching boys, Pell said words to the effect of 'Don't be ridiculous' and walked away.[219]

If George Pell had even remotely acted like a man of God, an archbishop, a Christian, a human being, to Anthony and me in our February 1997 meeting, we would never have pursued him for twenty-five years. His verbal assault on us, his rudeness, cruelty and ruthlessness told us that we and victims alike were of no worth at all. His attitude shouted to us that child victims, including our daughter, would be cast aside in a violent manner by him and his regime. Every fibre in my and Anthony's bodies told us we had to fight him for justice for all victims – we understood how defenceless and broken our daughter and all victims were.

George Pell minimised what he knew about the number of offending clergy and his knowledge of their crimes. He minimised the experience of victims. He minimised payouts. He did his best to silence victims and take away their rights. He was a bully and a liar hiding behind the word 'God'. He had a civilised persona for those he considered important and a cruel persona for victims. When it came to criminal offending by Catholic clergy, he trod on people he saw as a threat to the status quo. He did nothing to improve the lives of the people his colleagues had raped as innocent children; instead, he behaved unchristianly in order to evade responsibility and account-ability and to save the Church's reputation and protect its money. Such conduct was in stark contrast to Christian ethics, morals and his promises to help the poor and sick and hungry. There was no basic kindness, just legal responses and threats. The world and the Church will be a better place with him no longer a member of the Catholic hierarchy.


I will be stepping back from child abuse activism but will still follow the subject. I think too many years of my life have been consumed by it. All of my family's lives have been stolen in one way or another by the Church. I am continuing my role as an archivist. I cannot switch off from the child sexual abuse happening in churches around the world. For instance, as I was writing the final chapters of this book there was scandalous news from Germany, where large-scale sexual assaults against children were committed by Roman Catholic priests between 1946 and 2014. According to a leaked report, 1677 German clergymen committed sex attacks on 3677 boys and girls. I calculated that with 1677 clergy offenders, the number of victims would have been far greater than 3677 – 2.1 victims per offender was a low figure. The true number of victims would have been tens of thousands more.

In the USA, the Pennsylvania Attorney General gave a scathing speech against the Church after his state's grand jury revealed its findings: 'The church had covered up the abuse of more than 1000 children by about 300 priests over 70 years.'[220] More findings from other US states would follow.

The Netherlands also discovered the truth of clergy abuse. 'Twenty-nine of thirty-nine Dutch Cardinals, Archbishops and Auxiliaries covered up sexual abuse, allowing perpetrators to cause many more victims'[221] between 1945 and 2010.

France would join them. After a four-year investigation starting in 2018, it was revealed there had been 3200 paedophile priests and 216,000 child victims in the Catholic Church since the 1950s.[222] The figures were staggering.

Holy men? Celibate men?

In 2021, a report from Canada stated that the remains of 215 children, some as young as three, had been found in unmarked graves at the Kamloops Indigenous Residential School site in British Columbia (run by the Catholic Church from 1890 to 1978). Searchers using ground-penetrating radar found the remains. The school, one of many across Canada, was created to 'forcibly assimilate Indigenous children by removing them from their homes and communities',[223] the government report said, and had forbidden 'them from speaking their native languages. Physical, emotional and sexual abuse were rampant within these schools, as was forced labour.'

Four weeks later another 751 unmarked graves were discovered near the Marieval Indian Residential School site in Saskatchewan, operated by the Catholic Church from 1899 to 1997. The following week a third site was discovered with the remains of 182 children close to St Eugene's Mission School in British Columbia, which was operated by the Catholic Church from 1912 until the early 1970s. One chief, Jason Louie, interviewed by CBC radio said, 'Let's call this for what it is – a mass murder of Indigenous people.'[224]

Another focus for me post–Royal Commission is the treatment of Indigenous survivors here in Australia, who are over-represented in all statistics of institutional abuse.

As I had discovered from visiting New Norcia, there was an incredible number of sex offenders among the ranks of monks. Children were also subjected to beatings, hard labour, hunger and other acts of cruelty.

The Royal Commission found that Aboriginal and Torres Strait Islander people represented 14.9 per cent of survivors, a very high proportion considering they make up only 3.3 per cent of the population.

In 2019, I received a request to interview Wakka Wakka Wulli Wulli woman and author Tjanara Goreng Goreng about her book *A Long Way from No Go* at the Williamstown Literary Festival. She had worked as a public servant in Aboriginal affairs and provided counselling to remote communities. I read that in one tiny Western Australian community almost 1 000 kilometres north of Broome, Tjanara found that a Benedictine mission (the same order of Catholic monks who ran New Norcia) had started another monastery in the 'early years of the twentieth century'. 'In mid-2007,' Tjanara wrote, 'sixteen Aboriginal men, including community leaders, were charged with 103 sexual assault offences, such as molesting young children and exchanging cigarettes for sex with underage girls'.

After much counselling, a witness came forward from the community. 'An old white-haired man in a wheelchair had been among the first lot of children housed in the dormitories which the Benedictine mission built,' Tjanara wrote. 'He was among the first children sexually abused by the priests who found it all too easy to prey on them while their parents lived in rusty iron sheds out in the bush. After all the kids were snatched and herded into the dormitories, the priests tied up the fathers and beat them into submission.'

These atrocities committed by mercenary monks, priests and religious Brothers needed to be told. I interviewed Tjanara about her important memoir to a full audience, as was appropriate for such a courageous book.

My attempts to get the cap on redress changed were in vain, but before I gave up on it I took Anthony's place in roundtable discussions organised by the Federal Government. One of the meetings was on 30 November. The three-and-a-half-hour meeting in Sydney only frustrated me. It was a hopeless cause to try to get the government, which had already made up its mind and implemented the redress cap of $150,000, to change it back to $200,000 as recommended by the Royal Commission.

Towards the end of the meeting I spoke my mind: 'As far as I can see the two biggest offenders – the Catholic Church and the Federal Government – have got together in workshops and decided to alter the Royal Commission recommendations to save themselves money and screw the victims.'

A brief silence followed. Then another child protection advocate said, 'Again.'

Meaningful legal changes continue to flow from the work of the Royal Commission and Victorian inquiry. New South Wales followed Victoria in scrapping the Ellis Defence. This means that

Australia's two most populous states, Victoria and New South Wales, have abolished a major obstacle presented to victims who wanted to go through our independent legal system to seek compensation from their abusers.

The effect of the Victorian Government abolishing the Ellis Defence was beginning to be felt by the hierarchy. There were 'at least 800 new legal actions for child sexual abuse in the wake of landmark legislation allowing victims to sue the church and revisit unfair settlements made under in-house compensation schemes'.[225] Ballarat was the source of one such case, which led to a payout of up to $3 million.[226]

Belatedly, Victoria created a new law to break the seal of confession. The Church was furious, albeit unclear in its messaging. Archbishop Comensoli had previously said, 'I uphold the seal of confession but I uphold mandatory reporting as well.'[227] I wasn't sure how he was going to uphold both when the two opposed each other.

'Clearly they've learnt nothing from the Royal Commission and the lives they've destroyed,' Victorian Health Minister Jenny Mikakos said of the Church's position.[228]

I went into Parliament for a reading of the Children Legislation Amendment Bill 2019. I sat in the Lower House. With the exception of some other parliamentary business, from morning to late in the afternoon, every ten minutes a different politician, from various parties, stood up and delivered a heartfelt speech on protecting children and why the new law needed to be enacted. Throughout the day as politicians walked past the public gallery to exit the chamber, several said hello to me and some said, 'This must be a hard day for you.'

'No, it isn't; it's the best day,' I said. 'It is wonderful to hear such strong words.'

I felt the politicians had now taken up the burden that Anthony and I had placed on ourselves of protecting children from Catholic clergy and were making the necessary changes to enforce a safer future. Seeing and hearing our state leaders united and displaying their understanding, passion and power in our Parliament was something to behold. Politicians understood; they were acting. It was a huge relief and a joyful moment. A dream come true.

Jon Faine interviewed me that day outside Parliament. Other than praise the politicians, I explained the meaning of the word 'sacrosanct', a Church word familiar to many but perhaps one not fully understood. I said, 'Sacrosanct means something that is too important or valuable to be interfered with.' This is exactly what our children are – the bodies and lives of our children are sacrosanct. After the interview I asked Jon, who was interviewing Archbishop Comensoli later, to ask the archbishop if he had read my book yet. Jon obliged. Comensoli repeated his earlier response, saying he had read parts of it.

I am often asked whether the Church has changed its attitude towards survivors after the Victorian Parliamentary Inquiry and Royal Commission exposed clergy and put the hierarchy's actions under a microscope.

It is a good question. For the answer we should always look to the heart of the Catholic Church.

Pope Francis held a summit at the Vatican from 21 to 24 February 2019. He called it 'Meeting on the Protection of Minors in the Church'. The Pope summoned every president of the Catholic Bishops Conferences from around the world – 190 bishops – to discuss the prevention of child sexual abuse within the priesthood.

Expectations of the summit among Australian survivors and advocates were low. I didn't know one single Australian victim or supporter who intended to travel to Rome for it. I think we all considered it a waste of time.

SBS News interviewed me. I said I didn't expect much change because the Pope had recently blamed the devil for the Church's child sexual abuse crisis.[229] I added that the Pope had since announced that offender priests should hand themselves over to police.[230] If the Pope was serious, I said, a better idea would be for him to order all his bishops and archbishops throughout the world to hand over their Secret Archives on offender priests to police. A part of my interview was aired on the BBC to a European audience.

Three days later, the Pope spoke to pilgrims in Rome. I felt he was talking to me. 'One cannot live a whole life of accusing, accusing, accusing the Church,' he said. 'Those who spend their lives accusing, accusing, accusing are not the devil's children because the devil has none. [They are] friends, cousins and relatives of the devil.'[231]

People accuse, accuse, accuse the Church because they want to expose the truth of clergy child rape. This would not be necessary if the Church expelled paedophile clergy.

The clergy child sexual assault crisis first came to worldwide public attention in 1985 with the Fr Gauthe case in Louisiana, USA. Nobody could have dreamt of the magnitude of this crime among Catholic clergy, but the hierarchy knew the prevalence of the crime. Their Secret Archives were already full of complaints. It was now 2019, *forty-five years later*, and the Pope was holding his *first* conference of bishops to attempt to fix the problem.

If one Pope had taken meaningful action through leadership, victims and their advocates like me would not be condemned to a life of 'accusing, accusing, accusing'. It had taken forty-five years of accusing to arrive at this meeting. The priesthood, left to its own devices, would still be sexually assaulting children as it had done for centuries. If the Pope was a good leader, he would not have said such an insulting thing about those good, decent, blameless people seeking justice, accountability and a safe church for children.


I have watched closely matters of Church influence over our elected leaders in the Royal Commission's aftermath to see if anything has changed. School funding is an example.

Malcolm Turnbull's government, assisted by Education Minister Simon Birmingham, attempted to implement a ten-point plan for needs-based funding for all schools. This would inevitably result in a reduction of public money going to some independent and Catholic schools.

In 2017, the Church was worried about a funding cut to its schools; Catholic education leaders suggested the government's so-called Gonski 2.0 plan would force them to pay students' fees.[232] Victorian Liberal Party politicians began lobbying for change. Political pressure was growing.

This Catholic Church anxiety was short-lived. After the Liberal Party replaced Malcolm Turnbull with Scott Morrison as prime minister, Senator Simon Birmingham departed his Education Minister post and was replaced by Dan Tehan. Within three weeks, Morrison announced a funding 'fix' that would see Catholic schools receive an extra $4.1 billion over the next decade.[233] I could hardly believe what I was hearing.

Two years later, ousted PM Malcom Turnbull wrote in his memoir, *A Bigger Picture*, about the attitude of the Catholic hierarchy to Gonski funding plans. 'Over the years Catholic bishops, like George Pell, have always insisted the virtue of funding the Catholic schools in the one lump sum, as a system, was so that they could cross-substitute the poorer schools at the expense of those in the wealthier suburbs,'[234] Mr Turnbull said. 'And this claim seemed so plausible, given the Church's mission, that none of us gullible politicians questioned it. As it turned out, quite the reverse was the case.' Mr Turnbull went on to describe his disappointment. He said the school funding conversations he'd had with Sydney Archbishop Anthony Fisher were 'some of the most unedifying and disappointing I'd ever undertaken with a church leader'.

The former prime minister finished with some wise words. 'Fisher's objections to transparency and the accountability which came with it underlined the heart of the problem with so much of the Catholic hierarchy, tragically chronicled by the Royal Commission into Institutional Responses to Child Sexual Abuse. Like many Catholics, my relationship with the Church has been shaken by the shameful revelations of child sexual abuse and its cover-up by Church authorities.'[235]

Future politicians could learn from Turnbull's experience and his dealings with the Catholic Church hierarchy to understand that things are not always as they are portrayed to be. We need to learn from the past.

Of course, it was this strength of Church influence that allowed priests – employees of a foreign entity – to obtain money through the Federal Government's 2020 pandemic assistance program JobKeeper. After clergy not initially qualifying, the Federal Government then changed the rules to permit them payments. Investigations found one New South Wales bishop was going against the rules by writing to all his priests asking them to donate half their allowance back to Church coffers.[236]

Other influences persist. The Red Mass (a tradition in Paris since 1245 and in England since 1310) is an annual mass held by Catholic archbishops and bishops around Australia and the world where the hierarchy invites the local judiciary – judges, magistrates, tribunal members, judicial registrars, KCs, barristers, lawyers, court attendants and staff – to celebrate mass together to mark the beginning of the legal year. An invitation to the Melbourne Red Mass read: 'As this is Archbishop Comensoli's first Red Mass since becoming Archbishop of Melbourne, it is important for the legal community of Melbourne to welcome His Grace with as many members of the profession in attendance as possible.' This is the same archbishop who said he would defy child protection laws rather than report admissions of child sexual assault made in the confessional. When Victoria passed legislation removing clergy exemption from mandatory reporting of a reasonable belief that a child has been sexually abused, Comensoli said he would rather go to jail than obey the new law.

The invitation concluded: 'After Mass, the judiciary, members of the legal profession, staff and their families are invited to join Archbishop Comensoli for morning tea in the Cathedral Presbytery.'

I believed that our judiciary should not support Catholic clergy in this way after extensive revelations of criminal child sexual assault. I wrote an opinion piece on my thoughts of this union.[237]

On the day of the 2020 Melbourne Red Mass at St Patrick's Cathedral I attended a protest at the gates of the cathedral with a few friends and members of CLAN holding placards. I had my own placard. In response to the guilty verdict of Cardinal Pell of offences committed at the very cathedral we were standing outside, it read 'Crime Scene'. (At the time Pell was still in prison serving his sentence.)

At one stage, Comensoli came out to speak to the protesters. He was friendly, with protesters returning his greetings. I could see it was going to be a quick hello, so when he greeted me, I thought I would politely ask again, 'Have you read my book yet?' To my surprise he replied, 'Yes.' Pleased that he had, I then asked, 'Did it help you understand how victims and their families feel?', to which the archbishop said, 'I read it a year ago, I don't remember' as he kept walking. I was left standing there stunned, looking at the back of him as he walked away.

To recap the time line and responses of the archbishop being asked if he had read my book:

1. 30 August 2018. I asked at the Melbourne Press Club lunch. His reply: 'I've read parts of it.'
2. 14 August 2019. Jon Faine asked on his ABC radio program. His reply: 'I've read parts of it.'
3. 28 January 2020. I asked at the Red Mass. His reply: 'I read it a year ago.'

I have one last piece of evidence to share. It is a 16 September 1994 'MEMO' written on 'Office of the Archbishop' letterhead by a priest called BJ Fleming, the assistant to Archbishop Sir Frank Little. This document was part of Case Study 35: The Archdiocese of Melbourne, but as far as I know it was not publicly shown during the Royal Commission. I found it while examining the tender bundle of documents. It was about our daughters' abuser, Fr O'Donnell. It was clear from the language that O'Donnell's history of abuse, which had been known to the Church for decades, was about to become a big problem.

Fr Fleming had spoken to O'Donnell's lawyer and was reporting back that some of the priest's 'victims had spoken to lawyers about seeking "damages" from the Church through the legal courts but might consider a settlement from the Church'.

'$150,000 (possibly down to $100,000) each,' the letter said. 'The VG [vicar general] was thinking about this proposition, a possible good solution against the inevitable bad publicity of a court action, and one that would involve settlement by CCI (less our $25,000).'

Fleming stated: 'We badly need a round table conference of CCI, Corrs [Corrs Chambers Westgarth – the Church's legal firm], the VG, the Business Manager, and, if he thought fit, the Archbishop himself, to ensure that we all know what each is doing and that there is a single authority in charge of the whole procedure.'

Two years before Pell established his Melbourne Response scheme with a payment cap of $50,000 (with an average payout of $24,000), the Archdiocese was marshalling its legal and moneymen troops for the looming crisis – willing to pay $150,000 to 'each' (victim) to keep a lid on their corruption.

After reading this explosive letter, I returned to the first and second paragraphs. It seemed various lawyers had been speaking about O'Donnell, 'especially whether he had any evidence of official Church contact with him about his past relationships with his accusers'. They were worried about proof of a cover-up. When asked about this, Fr O'Donnell's lawyer replied, 'heaps of evidence; the Church has done a massive cover-up job'.[238]

To date, the hierarchy of the Catholic Church has not been held accountable for its knowledge and non-reporting of oral, anal and vaginal rape and other sex crimes against children; for its aiding and abetting paedophile clergy in committing further crimes; for the massive cover-up it directed and managed in order to protect clergy offenders and conceal sex crimes against the youngest in our communities; and, in the end, for premeditation because concealment became the norm, a chosen path, as shown by the decisions it took time and again. It was no accident, it was no coincidence. It was deliberate, calculated and clandestine. It was international.

In 2020, Father Bill Melican, the only Ballarat College of Consultors to admit that members knew Ridsdale was being moved for abusing children, stated, 'I wasn't interested [. . .] In those days abusing children wasn't the desperate thing that it is now [. . .] It wasn't a big deal.'[239] Similarly, in 2016, during evidence given to the Royal Commission hearing in Rome, Cardinal Pell stated of Ridsdale's offending, 'It's a sad story and it wasn't of much interest to me.'[240]

This priestly attitude, the culture – the shared morals of the clergy community – from the top down led to this: sixteen Catholic clergy paedophile rings operating in Victoria. In her doctorate research for the University of Queensland, Dr Sally Muytjens established this shocking revelation from data collected in both the Victorian Parliamentary Inquiry and the Child Abuse Royal Commission.

I call on a brave police department, lawyer or politician to take up the fight and take action against all high-ranking clergy who enabled and prolonged the sex crimes of adult holy men against the small bodies of children for an average of 2.2 years each child. Justice has not yet been served. How can our criminal law allow Church hierarchy to just walk away from what it heartlessly orchestrated for decades, for centuries?

# Postscript

What has the last twenty-six years done to my faith in God? It is a question I am often asked. That question has spent decades in the too-hard basket. It is unresolved.

In 1985, when I suffered from postnatal depression and un-diagnosed panic attacks gripped my life, I prayed a mother's prayer, a desperate plea for the protection of my children – it was a pure, honourable, heartfelt and desperate begging to protect my babies, my three little girls, all under three-and-a-half years of age. I could not, in my wildest dreams, have predicted the future crisis. My fear was that I only had two hands, yet I had three little hands to hold.

My entreaty resulted in me feeling peace – an answer – that I would protect my girls when they were with me, and God would protect them when I was not with them. Only two years later Fr O'Donnell, God's representative, was sexually assaulting Emma at school, the one place I was apart from her.

It was a stab into my heart and faith.

Anthony said what happened to us at the hands of priest and hierarchy proves there is no God and I tend to agree, unless . . . I was chosen to kick the priesthood's collective arse – that certainly rings true. And kick it I did.

It is a reality that as much as I was devoted, I am now equally undevoted. At the Melbourne Forum of the Melbourne Archdiocese in October 1996 my words were read out: 'All I can say now is, My God, My God, why have you forsaken me?' The destruction of our children, our family, were all with the compliments of the Catholic priesthood – men who claim to be another Christ. God and I are not speaking, although in a few of my darkest moments I have said a little prayer.

My experience has led me to *act* instead of praying for help. This is not what the priesthood hoped for. They wanted paralysed people on their knees who prayed – not acted – while they preyed.

Years earlier I experienced the force of acting for myself instead of waiting for rescue – it was a learning curve. At the depth of my post-natal depression, after visiting my doctor yet again for help, I came home without any answers. I was in despair for my future and my life. I got out of the car to open our heavy gate, thinking *nobody can help me*, when from deep inside a strong and powerful thought entered my head: 'I will do it myself.' It countered my distress and gave me hope and direction; it was the beginning of my long road to recovery.

So, on 26 March 1996 when Emma disclosed that O'Donnell had sexually assaulted her, I did not leave it to God to act. Knowing the devastating and life-threatening effects of ongoing sexual assault on children, I acted to expose priestly crimes, cover-ups and deception.

It would be nice if God and heaven existed, but I just don't know.

# Acknowledgements

**CHRISSIE FOSTER**

In 1997 Deborah Coddington wrote a book – *The Australian Paedophile and Sex Offender Index* – in which she listed a brief history of the hundreds of paedophiles, rapists and sex offenders convicted in courts around Australia. Considered outrageous at that time, it was not allowed to be displayed in bookstores; instead you had to know the few booksellers who stocked it, then know you had to ask for a copy because it was kept under the counter, out of sight, just like the worst pornographic magazines. When I requested a copy at my local bookshop, I received a most icy stare for some moments, but I was not deterred. Fr O'Donnell and many other Catholic priests and Brothers familiar to me were included in its pages, so, standing my ground, I waited patiently until the bookseller relented and produced a copy for me.

We have come a long way since then. There are many people to thank for this evolution, not least the journalists who have provided an avalanche of articles and investigations throughout Australia in recent years. Their reporting has transformed the public's understanding of the prevalence and gravity of this crime. But they would have nothing to report without brave people coming forward.

I would like to acknowledge and thank all those survivors who spoke out at the Victorian Parliamentary Inquiry into the Handling of Child Abuse by Religious and Other Non-Government Organisations, and the Royal Commission into Institutional Responses to Child Sexual Abuse. Your bravery has changed the future for children. Our governments have heard us and changed laws to help protect future children, which is why we broke our hearts again in retelling our stories. As many thousands of individuals, our humanity and care for others propelled us to speak because, out of compassion, we didn't want others to suffer as we had. Our collective voices have broken the chains of disbelief and have educated the nation.

My thanks go to Victoria's politicians who created and ran the Parliamentary Inquiry.

My gratitude to former prime minister Julia Gillard, who established the Child Abuse Royal Commission.

Also, my thanks to the Hon. Peter McClellan AM and all the other Royal Commissioners for directing Australia's truth-seeking and principled Royal Commission.

I would like to thank my daughters Katie and Aimee who elevate my life with their love and who are forever supportive. My dear grandchildren who provide light, love, smiles and hugs. My mum Dawn for always being on my side and for our endless conversations. My late dad for standing by us. My brothers Ray and Geoff and their wives Linda and Zoe for their loving support. My Auntie Cel and all my cousins who are always there with love and friendship.

I thank my late husband Anthony. Had he not been by my side for so many years, I would not have been brave enough to confront the men of the church, nor would I have found the fortitude to exercise our right to demand justice and accountability. Anthony taught me so much, I thank him for his kind and gentle nature, his strength, his honesty and for being his wonderful lovable self. Forever missed.

To my co-author – for a second time – Paul Kennedy, I say a huge thank you. As busy as you are, you made time to work with me again. For nearly twenty years, we have shared kindred words and opinions on this criminal issue and together we have created another exposé and a handbook for history. Once again, Paul, it was an honour and privilege to work with you.

I would like to thank my publisher Nikki Christer at Penguin Random House Australia who believed in me from the beginning. Your words of care and guidance encouraged me and revealed the way forward. Both my books have now been nurtured by you. I gratefully thank you.

Many thanks to our editor Clive Hebard, who after months of editing, helped make *Still Standing* the best it could be. Thank you for always being available to answer questions, give an opinion and provide gentle direction. It has been quite a journey and having you at the helm has made it an easier task.

To cover photographer Julian Kingma, a thankyou for your kindness and professionalism.

My thanks to Clare Forster, our agent at Curtis Brown whose help and assistance makes for an easier time in navigating the world of publishing.

Significantly, my very special thanks go to my dear friends in Oakleigh, especially those around the corner, where conversation and sparkling wine flows, as well as to friends further afield in Melbourne, country Victoria and interstate; without your caring love, Anthony and I and our children would have been depleted in energy and life. You helped make us brave in adversity.

The production of this book has been a group effort. I thank you all.

## PAUL KENNEDY

I was a young newspaperman when I met the Fosters. They told me they wanted to help protect children from sex abuse. After a long and tearful campaign, they succeeded. On behalf of my wife, Kim, three sons Jack, Gus and Leo, and all the other children who wake up every day in a safer world, I give thanks to amazing Chrissie and Anthony. Chrissie, we feel privileged to have a friend like you, and we dearly miss your brave husband.

I would also like to pay tribute to my parents, Michael and Joan. Mum worked for decades in child protection. I'm sure she would like me to mention that many of our nation's children are still vulnerable. Governments need to spend more time fixing stressed child protection services. There are young people out there right now, in the cities, suburbs and towns of Australia, waiting for you to do your job. You did yours, Mum.

My last word goes to Anthony Foster. He lived for others. He was, as Aimee said, a rare man. I miss him.

# Notes

1 Robertson KC, Geoffrey, *The Case of the Pope*, Penguin Books, 2010.
2 *Herald Sun*, 10 November 2010, 'Concealing sex abuse a grave evil'.
3 *Herald Sun*, 13 November 2010, 'The Catholic Church must give all victims a Christian response'.
4 *Irish Times*, 21 July 2011, 'Vatican relationship at new low'.
5 *Irish Examiner*, 21 July 2011, 'Dysfunction, disconnection, elitism and narcissism'.
6 *The Age*, 14 April 2012.
7 *7.30*, ABC TV, 20 April 2012.
8 *The Courier*, 18 April 2012.
9 *The Age*, 18 April 2012.
10 *Brisbane Times*, 17 April 2012.
11 *The Age*, 11 October 2012, 'Police slam Catholic Church'.
12 *The Age*, 12 October 2012.
13 *The Age*, 20 October 2012.
14 *Herald Sun*, 20 October 2012, 'Police damn Church silence on abuse'.
15 Ibid.
16 Newcastle *Herald*, 7 November 2012, 'Top cop attacks Catholic Church'.
17 *The Age*, 9 November 2012, 'Brothers "pack raped" boys'.
18 *The Times*, 27 March 2010, 'Verona deaf school ex-pupils tell Italian TV of sex abuse by priests'.
19 *The Age*, 12 November 2012, 'Pell urged to close order over abuses: Psychologist says order hid documents'.
20 *The Age*, 12 November 2012, 'List grows of abusers moved from parish to parish'.
21 *The Australian*, 12 November 2012, 'Investigate Church abuse, PM told: Government MPS, Independents push for Royal Commission into Catholic "Cancer"'.

22  *The Australian*, 12 November 2012, 'Pell shuns commission, saying apology was enough'.

23  *The Age*, 30 October 2010, 'Two of Us'.

24  *The Age*, 14 November 2012, 'Pell blames media "smear"'.

25  *Herald Sun*, 15 November 2012, 'Confess truth or run risk of jail, priests warned'.

26  *Sydney Morning Herald*, 14 November 2012, 'Pell defends confessional silence over sins of fathers'.

27  *The Age*, 14 November 2012, 'Pell blames media "smear"'.

28  *Herald Sun*, 15 November 2012, 'Court told God to blame'.

29  *Herald Sun*, 10 October 2013, 'Abuse rife at school'.

30  *The Age*, 17 November 2012.

31  *Sydney Morning Herald*, 16 November 2012.

32  *Sydney Morning Herald*, 15 November 2012.

33  *The Age*, 17 November 2012, 'Church holds sex dossiers on clergy'.

34  *Sydney Morning Herald*, 17 November 2012, 'Catholic Church's secret sex files'.

35  *The World Today*, ABC Radio, 14 November 2012, 'Pell an "embarrassment", says retired bishop'.

36  *Sydney Morning Herald*, 17 November 2012, 'Catholic Church's secret sex files'.

37  *The Age*, 17 November 2012, 'Church holds sex dossiers on clergy'.

38  *Sydney Morning Herald*, 17 November 2012, 'Church holds sex dossiers on clergy'.

39  *The Age*, 23 November 2012, 'Church's clinic shielded paedophiles – Encompass Program was a euphemism for "Contain & Conceal & then let them go again"'.

40  *Sydney Morning Herald*, 23 November 2012, 'Diagnosis was "smokescreen" to hide known paedophiles'.

41  Letter to Chrissie Foster from Vicar General Hart, 24 June 1997.

42  Letter to Chrissie Foster from Vicar General Hart, 16 October 1997.

43  *The Age*, 23 November 2012, 'Church's clinic shielded paedophiles'.

44  *Sydney Morning Herald*, 23 November 2012, 'Diagnosis was "smokescreen" to hide known paedophiles'.

45  *The Australian*, 28 November 2012, 'US victims of priest sent "for treatment" to appear'.

46  'The Church covered up for Father Paul Ryan for many years, but eventually he was jailed', Broken Rites Australia website, 6 May 2022; available at http://www.brokenrites.org.au/drupal/node/54.

47  *Sydney Morning Herald*, 2 December 2012, 'Spreading the rot of child sexual abuse'.

48  *The Age*, 3 December 2012, 'Sex accused flees Sri Lanka'.

49  *The Age*, 8 December 2012, '"Ballarat bishop" moved paedophile priest overseas'.

50  *The Age*, 13 December 2012, 'Catholic commission set up to advise on sex abuse'.

51  *The Australian*, 14 December 2012, 'Church abuse council branded a smoke-screen'.

52 *The Guardian*, 28 August 2013 '"Independent" church body for abuse inquiry controlled by bishops'.

53 Royal Commission into Institutional Responses to Child Sexual Abuse (hereafter Royal Commission), 'Formal opening of the inquiry at the County Court of Victoria on Wednesday, 3 April 2013 at 10.00 am', p. 2; available at https://www.childabuseroyalcommission.gov.au/sites/default/files/file-list/transcript-3-april-2013.pdf.

54 *Herald Sun*, 30 April 2013, 'Records destroyed: Offending priests were moved on'.

55 *The Age*, 30 April 2013, 'Catholic Church "facilitated" abuse'.

56 *The Australian*, 30 April 2013, 'Bishops admits "tragic mistake" over paedophile'.

57 *The Age*, 30 April 2013, 'Catholic response "unChristlike"'.

58 *The Australian*, 30 April 2013, 'Bishops admit "tragic mistake" over paedophile'.

59 Kieran Tapsell, 'Bishop Ronald Mulkearns: Blaming the foot soldier', *Pearls and Irritations: John Menadue's Public Policy Journal*, 7 April 2016, available at https://johnmenadue.com/kieran-tapsell-bishop-ronald-mulkearns-blaming-the-foot-soldier/.

60 *The Age*, 30 April 2013, 'Catholic Church "facilitated" abuse'.

61 Family and Community Development Committee: Inquiry into the Handling of Child Abuse by Religious and Other Non-Government Organisations (hereafter Victorian Parliamentary Inquiry), Melbourne, 30 April 2013, transcript, p. 4.

62 *The Age*, 1 May 2013, 'Abuse victim won $450,000 payout'.

63 *Sydney Morning Herald*, 7 May 2020, 'Pell knew in 1982 that Ridsdale was being moved to keep lid on scandal'.

64 *The Standard*, 27 May 2013, 'Pell tells abuse inquiry of Ridsdale support'.

65 *The Australian*, 3 May 2013, 'Four paedophiles in same parish an accident of history, Christian Brothers tell parliamentary inquiry'.

66 City of Casey *Journal*, 24 March 1997, 'Priest stood down'.

67 Minutes, meeting of Archbishop's Personnel Advisory Board held in the boardroom on Wednesday 8 January 1992 at 10 am.

68 Ibid.

69 *Herald Sun*, 7 May 2013, 'Police "mafia" hid church sex abuse'.

70 *Sydney Morning Herald*, 7 May 2013, 'Police colluded with priests, says detective'.

71 *Herald Sun*, 7 May 2013, 'Police "mafia" hid church sex abuse'.

72 AAP, 21 May 2013, 'Abuse was covered up: Melbourne archbishop'.

73 Victorian Parliamentary Inquiry, Melbourne, 27 May 2013, p. 50.

74 *The Age*, 28 May 2013, 'Church leadership still found wanting'.

75 *Herald Sun*, 28 May 2013, 'Sins, cover-up: Priests' ugly sins were covered up'.

76 *Herald Sun*, 28 May 2013, 'Shameful cover-up'.

77 *Herald Sun*, 2 June 2013, 'Domus Australia: Inside the $30m villa used by Cardinal George Pell'.

78  *Herald Sun*, 14 November 2013, 'Law to jail sex fiends'.

79  *The Age*, 14 November 2013, 'Nowhere to hide for Church sex offenders'.

80  *The Age*, 16 November, 'The unbearable lightness of seeing'.

81  *Sydney Morning Herald*, 26 July 2013, 'Priest's credibility challenged; Church sought to contain scandal'.

82  Ibid.

83  *Sydney Morning Herald*, 2 August 2013, 'Church should realise it's not above the law'.

84  *Newcastle Herald*, 2 August 2013, 'Priest admits rape of more children'.

85  *Newcastle Herald*, 23 June 2018, 'The Catholic Church turned its back on Father Glen Walsh, says his brother'.

86  *Newcastle Herald*, 11 October 2013, 'Church, police agreed on abuse reporting'.

87  *Newcastle Herald*, 3 October 2013, 'Church, police agreed on abuse reporting'.

88  Suzanne Smith, 'Analysis: Operation Protea is a welcome move by the NSW Police watchdog', ABC News, 3 October 2014.

89  *Canberra Times*, 22 June 2015, 'Former DPP Nicholas Cowdery accuses NSW Police of collusion with Catholic Church'.

90  Police Integrity Commission transcript, 13 October 2014, page 9.

91  Natasha Robinson, 'Child abuse royal commission: NSW Police back controversial blind-reporting of cases', ABC News, 20 April 2016.

92  *Herald Sun*, 8 December 2013, '"Keeper of secrets" Father Ronald Mulkearns has nothing more to say'.

93  Ibid.

94  Victorian Parliamentary Inquiry, Melbourne, 29 April 2013 transcript, p. 2.

95  'Cardinal Parolin: "A priest is always another Christ"', Opus Dei website, 5 September 2020.

96  Royal Commission: Public Hearing (Day 26), Wednesday 11 December 2013 at 10 am.

97  Royal Commission: Public Hearing (Day 26), 11 December 2013, p. 2751.

98  Royal Commission: Public Hearing (Day 26), 11 December 2013, p. 2749.

99  Royal Commission: Public Hearing (Day 26), 11 December 2013, p. 2704.

100 Royal Commission: Public Hearing (Day 26), 11 December 2013, p. 2752.

101 *The Age*, 11 October 2003, 'Priest and predator'.

102 Ibid.

103 *The Independent* (UK), 17 January 2014, 'Shocking figures reveal Pope Benedict defrocked child-molesting priests at a rate of more than one every two days during his last years in office'

104 *Insurance Journal*, 2005, 'Lawyers for Pope seek immunity in sex abuse lawsuit'

105 *Herald Sun*, 7 February 2014, 'Vatican caned by UN: "Hand over abusers"'

106 'Scathing UN report demands Vatican "immediately" act against child sexual abuse', ABC News, 6 February 2014.

107 ABC Radio, 'UN report blasts Catholic Church for policies allowing abuse of children', *AM*, 6 February 2014.

108 Royal Commission, 'Royal Commission releases findings on the Toowoomba case study' [media release], 12 February 2015.

109 Royal Commission: Public Hearing (Day Q1), 17 February 2014, p. Q105.

110 Royal Commission, *Report of Case Study No. 6: The Response of a Primary School and the Toowoomba Catholic Education Office to the Conduct of Gerard Byrnes*, January 2015.

111 *The Australian*, 3 May 2011, 'Vatican punishing crusader against school sex abuse'.

112 Royal Commission: Public Hearing, Case Study 8 (Day 55), Thursday 13 March 2014 at 10 am.

113 Royal Commission: Public Hearing, Case Study 8 (Day 57), 18 March 2014, p. 5945.

114 Royal Commission: Public Hearing, Case Study 8 (Day 60), 24 March 2014, p. 6346.

115 *The Australian*, 12 February 2014, 'Church got it wrong: bishop'.

116 Royal Commission: Public Hearing, Case Study 8 (Day 62), Wednesday 26 March 2014.

117 Royal Commission: Public Hearing, Case Study 11, 2014.

118 *The Australian*, 9 May 2014, 'No time limits for sex abuse claims'.

119 *The Australian*, 5–6 July 2014, 'Vatican rejects calls for abuse papers'.

120 Barbara Blaine, *National Catholic Reporter*, 28 June 2010, 'Outraged over police raid on Church offices? Wait for what it revealed'.

121 *Rolling Stone* 720, November 2011, 'The Catholic Church's secret sex-crime files: How a scandal in Philadelphia exposed the church's most guarded archive – documents that reveal a high-level conspiracy to cover up decades of sexual abuse by Catholic priests'.

122 *The Australian*, Barbara Blaine, 28 June 2010, 'Outraged over police raid on Church offices? Wait for what it revealed'; *The Australian*, 18 April 2012, 'Victim groups call on Catholic Church to lay bare its archives on child sex abuse'.

123 James A. Coriden, Thomas J. Green & Donald E. Heintschel (eds), *The Code of Canon Law: A Text and Commentary*, Paulist Press, Mahuah, NJ, 1985, p. 396.

124 Royal Commission: Public Hearing, Case Study 16 (Day C041), Melbourne, 21 August 2014, p. C4520.

125 Ibid., p. C4509.

126 Royal Commission: Report of Case Study 16, pp. 95, 96.

127 Ibid., p.14.

128 *Herald Sun*, 12 February 1997, 'The ascension of Pell'.

129 Royal Commission: Report of Case Study 35, Catholic Archdiocese of Melbourne, November 2017, p. 30.

130 Ibid., p. 27.

131 Royal Commission: Public Hearing, Case Study 35, Melbourne, 2 December 2015, p. C13974.

132 John Kevin O'Donnell's plea, Melbourne County Court, 4 August 1995.

133 John Kevin O'Donnell's sentence, Melbourne County Court, 4 August 1995.

134 Royal Commission: Statement of Professor Richard Ball, 12 August 2014.

135 *The Age*, 1 January 2018, 'Richard Ball 1928–2017: Pioneer in transgender health studies'.

136 *The Code of Canon Law*, p. 396.

137 *The Age*, 31 March 2015, 'Arson investigated at former church of paedophile priest'.

138 *The Age*, 2 April 2015, 'Church arson not a solution: Abuse victim'.

139 *Herald Sun*, 2 April 2015, 'Church fires abuse probe: links to paedophiles'.

140 *Herald Sun*, 9 May 2015, 'Spiders' playground: They were meant to nurture children in their care. Instead they preyed on them in the most evil way'.

141 *Herald Sun*, 9 May 2015, 'Return to the house of devils'.

142 *Herald Sun*, 28 May 2015, 'Church knew of Ridsdale in 1982'.

143 *The Age*, 29 May 2015, 'What is the connection between these senior Catholics?'.

144 CCI Catholic Church Insurances Limited Master Policy No.00111, issued to Australian Catholic Bishops Conference Special Issues Committee, c. 1992.

145 Desmond Cahill OAM's Submission to the Parliament of Victoria, Family and Community Development Committee, August 2012.

146 *The Age*, 17 September 2019, 'Revealed: How paedophile priests in Australia worked together to share victims'.

147 *Times of Acadiana*, 23 May 1985, 'The tragedy of Gilbert Gauthe pt 1'.

148 Royal Commission: Public Hearing, Case Study 35, County Court of Victoria, Melbourne, 3 December 2015.

149 Nine News, 20 May 2013, 'Abuse was covered up: Melbourne archbishop'.

150 Royal Commission: document no. CTJH.221.04013.0574_R, dated 14 October 1994.

151 Royal Commission: document no. CTJH.221.06059.0162, dated 16 June 1988.

152 Transcript of Victorian Parliamentary Inquiry, Melbourne, 30 April 2013.

153 *Sunday Age*, 6 December 2015, 'The $62m saving: How the Catholic Church short-changed abuse victims'.

154 Royal Commission: Public Hearing, Case Study 28, County Court of Victoria, Melbourne, 7 December 2015.

155 *Herald Sun*, 9 November 2015, 'Evil priest "protected": Top cop tells of "cover-up"'.

156 *Herald Sun*, 16 December 2015, 'Leading Catholic bishop Brian Finnigan accused of lying to Royal Commission'.

157 *Courier-Mail*, 27 December 2015, 'Calls for Bishop Brian Finnigan's sacking after royal commission into child sexual abuse'.

158 *The Courier*, 31 December 2015, 'Bishop Brian Finnigan retires'.

159 *The Sunday Mail*, 3 January 2016, 'Abuse victims "after money"'.

160 *The Age*, 17 December 2015, 'Priest accused of lying to commission to "save" Pell'.

161 *Sydney Morning Herald*, 23 December 2015, 'Priest John Walshe who defended George Pell accused of sexually abusing teen'.

162 *The Age*, 23 December 2015, 'Child sex crime detectives investigate abuse claims at Melbourne's St Patrick's Cathedral'.

163 *The Age*, 24 December 2015, 'St Patrick's centre of police inquiry'.

164 *The Age*, 12 January 2016, 'Children sexually abused at Eureka Stockade Pool in Ballarat in 1970s: Police'.

165 *Daily Mail Australia*, 10 May 2016, 'Heart condition improving then, George? Cardinal Pell pictured tucking into steak, chips and beer in a Roman piazza – weeks after claiming he was "too ill" to come home to face child sex abuse royal commission'.

166 *The Age*, 11 February 2016, 'Doctors offer to get Cardinal George Pell back to the royal commission safe and sound'.

167 *The Age*, 18 February 2016, 'Pell urged to come home and face the music'.

168 *Herald Sun*, 20 February 2016, 'Police Probe Pell: Top-Secret investigation into sex abuse claims against Cardinal'.

169 *The Age*, 21 August 2002, 'Sex-abuse allegations force Pell to stand aside'.

170 *The Age*, 15 October 2002, 'Both sides claim win as Pell cleared'.

171 Report of an inquiry into an allegation of sexual abuse against Archbishop George Pell, October 2002.

172 Royal Commission: Public Hearing, Case Study 28 (Day C150), Ballarat Magistrates' Court.

173 Royal Commission: Public Hearing, Case Study 28 (Day C153), Ballarat, 25 February 2016.

174 *Herald Sun*, 26 February 2016, 'I'm so sorry: Bishop admits failing children but "can't recall"'.

175 Lisa Millar, ABC News, 'Child abuse royal commission: George Pell's secretary asks colleagues in Rome to attend hearing for support', 25 February 2016.

176 *Il Tempo*, 1 March 2016, 'Gil Oscar puntano il dito contro I preti pedofili' [Oscar points the finger at paedophile priests].

177 Spotlight Investigation, 1 July 2002, 'Geoghan preferred preying on poor children'.

178 Royal Commission: Public Hearing, Case Studies 28 and 35 (Day 159), 29 February 2016.

179 *La Stampa*, 1 March 2016, 'Il Cardinal Pell alla fine ammette: "Sui nostri preti o sbagliato. Credevo a loro, non alle famiglie"' [Cardinal Pell finally admits: 'We were wrong about our priests. I believed them, not our families'].

180 Royal Commission: Public Hearing, Case Studies 28 and 35 (Day 159), 29 February 2016, p. 16186.

181 *The Guardian*, 29 February 2016, 'George Pell: Church had "predisposition not to believe" children who complained about priests'.

182 *The Age*, 2 March 2016, 'I have "the full backing" of Pope Francis: Pell'.

183 Royal Commission: Public Hearing, Case Studies 28 and 35 (Day 160), 1 March 2016.

184 *National Catholic Register*, 7 June 2021, 'Cardinal Pell represents the life of the Church in our age'.

185 *Who Weekly*, 4 April 2016, 'Our fight for justice'.

186 *Herald Sun*, 2 March 2016, 'See no evil, hear no evil, stop no evil'.

187 *The Guardian*, 1 March 2016, 'Cardinal Pell "wasn't much interested in stories of abuse by priests". Which was lucky for his career'.

188 Royal Commission: Public Hearing, Case Studies 28 and 35 (Day 161), 2 March 2016.

189 *Who Weekly*, 4 April 2016, 'Our fight for justice'.

190 Royal Commission: Public Hearing, Case Studies 28 and 35 (Day 163), 4 March 2016.

191 Ten Eyewitness News, 20 July 2015, 'George Brandis' secret meeting with George Pell'.

192 Royal Commission, Report of Case Study 44: The response of the Catholic Diocese of Armidale and Parramatta to allegations of child sex abuse against a priest, November 2017.

193 *The Australian*, 23 May 2018, 'Archbishop faces jail threat'.

194 *The Age*, 7 December 2018, 'Conviction for failing to report abuse overturned'.

195 *Sunday Age*, 9 October 2016, 'Pell associate banned in Ireland'.

196 *The Guardian*, 26 October 2016, 'Cardinal George Pell interviewed by Australian police in Rome over sexual abuse claims'.

197 *The Guardian*, 4 November 2016, 'Child sex abuse survivors may get up to $150,000 in national compensation scheme'.

198 *The Guardian*, 18 November 2016, 'Catholic Church doubles maximum compensation for Melbourne abuse victims to $150,000'.

199 Community Affairs Legislation Committee, Queensland Parliament Senate, 16 February 2018, p. 71.

200 *The Australian*, 2 December 2016, 'Catholics want law to protect confessional'.

201 Royal Commission: Public Hearing, Case Study 50 (Day 242), Sydney, 6 February 2017.

202 *Sydney Morning Herald*, 11 August 2009, 'Sex abuse victim told to "go to hell"'.

203 *The Age*, 17 July 2008, 'Don't be so cranky: Bishop's advice to sex abuse victims'.

204 *The Australian*, 17 March 2015, 'Archbishop Philip Wilson: "I didn't hide child sex"'.

205 Royal Commission: Data analysis of claims and substantiated complaints of child sexual abuse in relation to the Christian Brothers in Ballarat.

206 *The Australian*, 7 April 2017, 'Right to the very end, the Church wasn't listening'.

207 *Sunday Age*, 5 March 2017, 'Bones of babies at convent'.

208 Saskia Weber (director), *Ireland's Children of Shame* [documentary film], Sunset Presse, France, 2015.

209 Yuliya Talmazan, Adela Suliman & Helena Skinner, NBC News, '9,000 children died in Irish mother-and-baby homes, report finds', 13 January 2021.

210 *The Australian*, 18 August 2017, 'Evil hid behind handy seal of confession'; *The Sunday Age*, 17 June 2018, 'Break the silence for the children'; *The Australian*, 21 August 2019, 'Priesthood must own sins of the fathers'.

211 *The Age*, 12 February 2018, 'The Church, Inc.'.

212 Danny Tran & Matt Neal, ABC News, '"Ellis Defence" scrapped as Victorian law change opens Church up to abuse legal action', 25 May 2018.

213 Inquiry into the National Redress Scheme for Institutional Child Sexual Abuse (Commonwealth Powers) Bill 2018, Parliament House, Brisbane.

214 *The Advertiser*, 15 June 2018, 'SA to cut laws protecting religious leaders that kept silent on child abuse confessions'.

215 *Australian Financial Review*, 20 September 2022, 'Lawyers audition for Catholics work Corrs vacated'.

216 Royal Commission, *Report of Case Study 28: Catholic Church Authorities in Ballarat*, November 2017, p. 70.

217 Royal Commission, *Report of Case Study 28: Catholic Church Authorities in Ballarat*, November 2017, p. 56.

218 Joseph Dunstan et al., ABC News, 'George Pell "surprised" by Royal Commission finding he was told of Ridsdale abuse', 7 May 2020.

219 Ibid.

220 *Sydney Morning Herald*, 25 August 2018, 'Pennsylvania report reopens painful wounds for Australians'.

221 *The Guardian*, 16 September 2018, 'Dutch Catholic Church accused of widespread sexual abuse cover-up'.

222 Reuters, ABC News, 'Independent investigation finds about 3,000 paedophiles in French Catholic Church since 1950s', 4 October 2021; ABC News, 'Report finds 216,000 children have been sexually abused by French Catholic Church clergy since 1950', 5 October 2021.

223 *The Guardian*, 29 May 2021, 'Canada: Remains of 215 children found at Indigenous residential school site'.

224 AP, ABC News, 'Canadian Indigenous group says human remains found at former Catholic Church-run residential school', 1 July 2021.

225 *The Age*, 25 September 2019, 'Catholic Church swamped with hundreds of new sex abuse claims after legal change'.

226 *The Courier*, 28 September 2019, 'Landmark legal payout'.

227 *The Age*, 14 August 2019, 'Church digs in to defy abuse disclosure laws'.

228 *Herald Sun*, 15 August 2019, 'Priests set to defy new law'.

229 Philip Pullella, Reuters, 'Pope blames devil for Church divisions, scandals, seeks angel's help', 8 October 2018.

230 *New York Times*, 21 December 2018, 'Pope Francis calls on abusive priests to turn themselves in'.

231 Bridget Brennan, ABC News, 'Pope Francis's comments linking Church critics to the devil criticised by abuse victims', 22 February 2019.

232 *Catholic Leader*, 10 May 2017, 'Catholic schools are mobilising against new Gonski funding plan'; *The Age*, 30 October 2017, 'Catholics warn of more school closures in Victoria under Gonski 2.0'.

233 *Sydney Morning Herald*, 30 January 2019, 'Revealed: Catholic schools reap $4.1 billion windfall in Scott Morrison's funding "fix"'.

234 Malcolm Turnbull, *A Bigger Picture*, Hardie Grant, Richmond, Vic., 2020, p. 529.

235 Ibid., p. 531.

236 Pat McGrath & Alison McClymont, ABC News, 'Priests eligible for JobKeeper asked to donate the extra allowance to their Catholic diocese', 16 June 2020; ABC News, 'Priests eligible for JobKeeper following an amendment to the scheme's rules in May', 17 June 2020.

237 *The Australian*, 13 January 2020, 'Church, judges in unholy union'.

238 Memo of phone call from Office of Archbishop, Melbourne, re K. O'Donnell, 16 September 1994.

239 Niall Fulton & Sarah Ferguson (directors), *Revelation* [ABC documentary series], Sydney, 2020, episode 3, 'Goliath'.

240 Royal Commission: Public Hearing, Case Studies 28 and 35 (Day 160), 1 March 2016.

Chrissie Foster was born in Victoria and grew up in Black Rock, a beach-side suburb on Port Phillip Bay. She worked as a public servant for nine years. During 1976 and 1977 she took time off and travelled extensively around Europe, the US and Mexico. She married Anthony in 1980 and by 1985 they had three beautiful daughters, Emma, Katie and Aimee, whom they raised in suburban Melbourne with what they hoped were the right values. Chrissie could not have known that the stranger-danger she feared actually lurked in the presbytery attached to the girls' Catholic primary school, with both Emma and Katie victims of clergy sex abuse. Chrissie's heartbreaking account of her family's suffering – and of the Church's lies, silence, denials and threats – *Hell on the Way to Heaven*, was published in 2010. The Foster family's case was one of those that prompted the establishment of the Victorian Parliamentary Inquiry into the Handling of Child Abuse by Religious and Other Non-Government Organisations and the subsequent Royal Commission into Institutional Responses to Child Sexual Abuse. Chrissie has since continued to fight for justice and redress for victims and survivors of child sexual assault by Catholic clergy. In 2018 she jointly won the Australian Human Rights Medal with Chief Royal Commissioner Hon Peter McClellan AM. Then, in 2019, Chrissie was named in the Australian Honours List as a Member of the Order of Australia (AM) 'For significant service to children, particularly as an advocate for those who have suffered sexual abuse'. Her ongoing activism inspires others to challenge once-powerful male-dominated institutions.

Paul Kennedy is a journalist, television presenter, documentary maker and author. He is married with three sons and lives in Melbourne.